"This rich collection of essays contains some of the most original studies of the interaction between Islam and African cultures. In their specific focus on the centrality of the religion to the oral literature and indeed the entire range of expressive culture among the Yoruba people of Ilorin, the studies demonstrate the way in which Islam has functioned not as a constraining factor, as it has been widely presumed, but rather as a liberating force of the creative energies in Yoruba society."

–F. Abiola Irele,
Harvard University,
author of *The African Imagination:
Literature in Africa and the Black Diaspora*

"*African Discourse in Islam, Oral Traditions, and Performance* is the most important stylistic analysis of oral traditions published in the last twenty years. It is an original and groundbreaking study of the intertextual relations between tradition and modernity, Islam and the indigenous religions in Africa, oral poetry and popular music in Nigeria. Professor Abdul-Rasheed Na'Allah is exceptionally brilliant in his accounts of how Islam penetrated African oral traditions and music and filled them with Islamic verses and the names of Prophets from the Holy Quran . . . Na'Allah's analysis of the theories of translation, adaptation and change will also constitute an important contribution to comparative textual studies."

–Manthia Diawara,
Distinguished Professor of Comparative Literature and Film,
New York University,
author of *We Won't Budge: An Exile in the World*

African Discourse in Islam, Oral Traditions, and Performance

African Studies
History, Politics, Economics, and Culture
MOLEFI ASANTE, *General Editor*

Kwame Nkrumah's Contribution to Pan-Africanism
An Afrocentric Analysis
D. Zizwe Poe

Nyansapo (The Wisdom Knot)
Toward an African Philosophy of Education
Kwadwo A. Okrah

The Athens of West Africa
A History of International Education at Fourah Bay College, Freetown, Sierra Leone
Daniel J. Paracka, Jr.

The Yorùbá Traditional Healers of Nigeria
Mary Olufunmilayo Adekson

The 'Civil Society' Problematique
Deconstructing Civility and Southern Nigeria's Ethnic Radicalization
Adedayo Oluwakayode Adekson

Maat, the Moral Ideal in Ancient Egypt
A Study in Classical African Ethics
Maulana Karenga

Igbo Women and Economic Transformation in Southeastern Nigeria, 1900–1960
Gloria Chuku

Kwame Nkrumah's Politico-Cultural Thought and Policies
An African-Centered Paradigm for the Second Phase of the African Revolution
Kwame Botwe-Asamoah

Non-Traditional Occupations, Empowerment and Women
A Case of Togolese Women
Ayélé Léa Adubra

Contending Political Paradigms in Africa
Rationality and the Politics of Democratization in Kenya and Zambia
Shadrack Wanjala Nasong'o

Law, Morality and International Armed Intervention
The United Nations and ECOWAS in Liberia
Mourtada Déme

The Hidden Debate
The Truth Revealed about the Battle over Affirmative Action in South Africa and the United States
Akil Kokayi Khalfani

Britain, Leftist Nationalists and the Transfer of Power in Nigeria, 1945–1965
Hakeem Ibikunle Tijani

Western-Educated Elites in Kenya, 1900–1963
The African American Factor
Jim C. Harper, II

Africa and IMF Conditionality
The Unevenness of Compliance, 1983-2000
Kwame Akonor

African Cultural Values
Igbo Political Leadership in Colonial Nigeria, 1900-1966
Raphael Chijioke Njoku

A Roadmap for Understanding African Politics
Leadership and Political Integration in Nigeria
Victor Oguejiofor Okafor

Doing Justice Without the State
The Afikpo (Ehugbo) Nigeria Model
O. Oko Elechi

Student Power in Africa's Higher Education
A Case of Makerere University
Frederick Kamuhanda Byaruhanga

The NGO Factor in Africa
The Case of Arrested Development in Kenya
Maurice Nyamanga Amutabi

Social Movements and Democracy in Africa
The Impact of Women's Struggle for Equal Rights in Botswana
Agnes Ngoma Leslie

Nefer
The Aesthetic Ideal in Classical Egypt
Willie Cannon-Brown

The Experience of Economic Redistribution
The Growth, Employment and Redistribution Strategy in South Africa
Clarence Tshitereke

The Role of the Press and Communication Technology in Democratization
The Nigerian Story
Aje-Ori Agbese

The Politics of Ethnic Nationalism
Afrikaner Unity, the National Party, and the Radical Right in Stellenbosch, 1934–1948
Joanne L. Duffy

Mobutu's Totalitarian Political System
An Afrocentric Analysis
Peta Ikambana

Indigenous Medicine and Knowledge in African Society
Kwasi Konadu

Africa in the 21st Century
Toward a New Future
Edited by Ama Mazama

Missions, States, and European Expansion in Africa
Edited by Chima J. Korieh and Raphael Chijioke Njoku

The Human Cost of African Migrations
Edited by Toyin Falola and Niyi Afolabi

Trans-Atlantic Migration
The Paradoxes of Exile
Edited by Toyin Falola and Niyi Afolabi

African Minorities in the New World
Edited by Toyin Falola and Niyi Afolabi

The Ancient Egyptian Family
Kinship and Social Structure
Troy D. Allen

The African Origins of Rhetoric
Cecil Blake

Balancing Written History with Oral Tradition
The Legacy of the Songhoy People
Hassimi Oumarou Maïga

African Discourse in Islam, Oral Traditions, and Performance
Abdul-Rasheed Na'Allah

African Discourse in Islam, Oral Traditions, and Performance

Abdul-Rasheed Na'Allah

Taylor & Francis Group

NEW YORK AND LONDON

First published 2010
by Routledge
605 Third Avenue, New York, NY 10017
4 Park Square, Milton Park, Abingdon, Oxon OX14 4RN

Routledge is an imprint of the Taylor & Francis Group, an informa business

© 2010 Abdul-Rasheed Na'Allah

All rights reserved. No part of this book may be reprinted or reproduced or utilised in any form or by any electronic, mechanical, or other means, now known or hereafter invented, including photocopying and recording, or in any information storage or retrieval system, without permission in writing from the publishers.

Trademark Notice: Product or corporate names may be trademarks or registered trademarks, and are used only for identification and explanation without intent to infringe.

Library of Congress Cataloging in Publication Data
Na'allah, Abdul Rasheed.
　African discourse in Islam, oral traditions, and performance / Abdul-Rasheed Na'Allah.
　　p. cm.—(African studies history, politics, economics, and culture)
　Includes bibliographical references and index.
　1. Folk literature, Yoruba—History and criticism. 2. Folk literature, Hausa—History and criticism. 3. Yoruba language—Discourse analysis. 4. Hausa language—Discourse analysis. 5. Folklore—Nigeria—Performance. 6. Islam and culture—Nigeria. 7. Islam—Nigeria—Influence. I. Title.
　GR351.32Y56N33 2009
　398.20966.—dc22
　　　　　　　　　　　　　　　　　　　　　2009024127

ISBN13: 978-0-415-65348-0 (pbk)
ISBN13: 978-0-415-80592-6 (hbk)
ISBN13: 978-0-203-86358-9 (ebk)

*For Ilorin oral poets,
and
For Bayo Alayande and Yemi Zubair,
both of Radio Kwara, Ilorin*

Contents

Acknowledgments		xiii
1	Ẹ̀làlọ̀rọ̀: A Yorùbá Indigenous Discourse on Criticism and Interpretation	1
2	Ẹ̀làlọ̀rọ̀ and Translation	17
3	Some Thoughts on Traditional Hausa Aesthetics and Arabic Influence on Yorùbá and Hausa Written Traditions in Nigeria	28
4	*Horses of Memory* and *The Word is an Egg*: Osundare's Poetic Voices	55
5	Cultural Poetics, African Diaspora, and the Global World: Tanure Ojaide's *I Want to Dance and Other Poems*	73
6	African Cultural Revival as an Important Message in *Death and the King's Horseman* and *The Lion and the Jewel*	84
7	Language and Culture in an African Adaptation of Sophocles' *Oedipus Rex*	98
8	Yorùbá Egungun: Some Critical Thoughts	128
9	Traditional Oral Genre in a Muslim Ilorin: Survival Challenges	136
10	Mamman Shata Katsina and Omoekee Amao Ilorin: Islam, Performance, and Orality	148
Appendices		165
Notes		167
Bibliography		175
Index		181

Acknowledgments

First, I will like to acknowledge African oral poets and other community oral resources used in this book. As communities to which I am a member, I acknowledge the value in communal ownership of the materials and affirm the role of every generation in keeping traditional culture alive. I also acknowledge, with thanks, the permissions granted me to use materials from the following published materials:

Dandatti AbdulKadir, "The role of an oral singer in Hausa-Fulani society: a case study of Mamman Shatta." Ph.D. Thesis, University of Indiana. 1975.

Abdul-Rasheed Na'Allah's review of *I Want to Dance and Other Poems*, by Tanure Ojaide, (African Heritage Press, 2003), *The International Journal of African Historical Studies* 39.3 (2006): 531–3.

Abdul-Rasheed Na'Allah, "Oral traditions, Islamic Culture and Topicality in the Songs of Mamman Shata Katsina and Omoekee Amao Ilorin." *Canadian Journal of African Studies*. 28.3 (1994): 500–15.

Abdul-Rasheed Na'Allah, "Dadakúàdà: The Crisis of a Traditional Oral Genre in a Modern Islamic Setting." *Journal of Religion in Africa*. 22.4 (1992): 318–330. Courtesy of Koninklijke Brill N.V.

Tanure Ojaide, *I Want to Dance and Other Poems* (Lagos, Nigeria: African Heritage Press), 2003.

Niyi Osundare, *The Word is an Egg* (Ibadan: Kraft Book Limited), 2000.

Niyi Osundare, *Horses of Memory* (Ibadan: Heinemann Educational Books (Nigeria) Plc, 1998.

My gratitude goes to the Almighty Allah, *Rabbu 'L Harsh*, and to my family, nucleus and extended. Also to friends, students, and colleagues who have continued to be strong sources of inspiration to me.

It is my hope that this book would contribute to critical discussions of African and global cultures and strengthen many scholars' aspirations to explore African tradition globally.

Finally, some of the issues discussed here I have had occasions to present in different versions and at different forums, and I am glad that I am finally able to gather my thoughts into a book.

Abdul-Rasheed Na'Allah
Macomb, Illinois

1 Èlàlọ̀rọ̀
A Yorùbá Indigenous Discourse on Criticism and Interpretation

Aféfẹ́ lẹ́lẹ́ máa gbóhùn mi r'òkun
Èfúùfù lẹ̀lẹ̀ máa gbóhùn mi r'ọ̀sà

Softly blowing wind, take my voice to the ocean,
Tenderly moving wind, take my voice to the sea!

This chapter introduces a Yorùbá discourse on criticism called Èlàlọ̀rọ̀. Èlàlọ̀rọ̀ is a concept for discourse analysis and interpretation rooted in ethnic, historic, linguistic, and community rhetoric in native wisdom and local analytical pattern. By community, here I mean the local Yorùbá community. Èlàlọ̀rọ̀'s conceptual application could include any community or communities by using their rhetorical tool and discourse patterns in understanding cultural materials indigenous to them. The use of Èlàlọ̀rọ̀ introduces an indigenous African discourse strategy to cross-cultural critical practice.

In short, an invocation of Èlàlọ̀rọ̀ is also a call for a closer and more critical examination and understanding of a performance or cultural material, for example, a speech, poetic or ordinary, through the use of cultural paradigms of casting, recasting, representation, or rephrasing in simpler but equally rich words to arrive at cultural interpretation and meanings in which both the process and results of interpretation are equally important and desirable. To put it in another way, Èlàlọ̀rọ̀ asks for a "surgical" operation using community wisdom, which resides in proverbs, adages, and metaphors. Abiola Irele (1981, 2001), while representing what he calls the three levels of orality, also makes a case for what I now call Èlàlọ̀rọ̀ when he readily asserts that "manifestations of the imagination in our traditional societies . . . rely primarily on an oral mode of realization" and also acknowledges their "implications for our conception of literature and our values of interpretation" (9). Here is how Irele recalls his three levels theory:

> With regard to the oral literature of Africa, I recall the scheme of three levels of orality that I have proposed elsewhere (Irele 1981, 1990). There is, first, the level of ordinary communication with a purely denotative use of language, as in simple factual statements and commands. At a second level, we have the forms of orality associated with the rhetorical uses of language, forms that are not necessarily reserved for special situations but are ever-present in traditional African discourse through the use of proverbs and aphorisms, which regularly channel communication in African cultures and therefore provide what one

might call a "formulaic" framework for speech acts, discursive modes, and indeed the structure of thought. As the Yorùbá metaproverb puts it: *Owe l'esin oro* (Proverbs are the horses of discourse). Finally, we have the strictly literary level, which is concerned with and reserved for the purely imaginative uses of language. (9)

Irele's three levels, which he says exist as a continuum, can be collapsed into one in Èlàlòrò. His above statement strongly affirms the importance of African indigenous discourse traditions and sets the tone for my present introductory discussion.

Thus, this chapter only attempts to present some thoughts from an Èlàlòrò paradigm and to challenge contemporary African scholars—or any critic or interpreter of African material—to explore traditional African discourse strategy in their scholarly interpretation of culture, art, science, and other life features and performances. This book will use simple language to present what is sometimes complex interpretative method in its attempt to be true to an African traditional interpretative tradition of making art, artistic meanings, and cultural aesthetics accessible to the ordinary. My aim here is not to insist on an Èlàlòrò ideal for any scholar but to continue the push that many great scholars initiated when they promoted the urgent necessity for indigenous theorizing in the postcolony—especially in our global century.[1]

First, let me announce a disclaimer. Although I may be partly responsible for the popularization of the term Èlàlòrò, I am not its originator or first user. Yet, while the use of Èlàlòrò as a theoretical terminology and concept is mine, the process, the strategy in critical discourse, and the characteristics of discourse content are indigenous to Yorùbá and many African oral traditions and are nothing new! In short, this will not be the first public proclamation of the process that Èlàlòrò has championed. In addition to local forums, such as community meetings, traditional professional sessions, or informal moments among the Yorùbá, Hausa, Tiv, Akan, Ewe, Zulu, and other indigenous African communities, for decades now this process has also been adapted to the electronic media such as radio and television programs in Africa. Since the inception of radio stations in Nigeria starting from the western region, for example, an opportunity has presented itself that extended local family plus community forums and centers to the radio stations, as every radio station introduces programs where the traditional art of critical performance, evaluation, and reevaluation through community wisdom in proverbs, adages, allusions, anecdotes, and other indigenous rhetorical tools are regularly featured in the local African languages.

I remember several such programs that I listened to in Hausa on Rima Radio in Sokoto and on Radio Nigeria in Kaduna. I listened in Yorùbá on Radio O-Y-O (booming to Ilorin from Ibadan) and on Radio Kwara stationed in Ilorin city. Adebayo Alayande and Yemi Zubair were exponents of such programs on Radio Kwara. Every day they brought in guests who, through critical performance and individualized interpretation of daily life affairs, enabled the beauty of traditional Yorùbá discourse on radio to come to life. No moment or situation passes without Yemi Zubair invoking Èlàlòrò. He takes every opportunity to invite Yorùbá traditional experts to perform critical explications on air. The power of the moment for all listeners (and for me in particular) was always in the process, in the strategy employed, and in the interpretations of community and world issues provided. As the electronic media created an extension to traditional forums, local oral poets, storytellers, family, and community elders, never ceased playing their own roles as cultural critics and interpreters in their own homes, in community centers, on streets, and in family compounds.

The first part of the term, Èlà, is another name for Ifá (Olokun n.d., 5). Ifá, in Yorùbá religion, is believed to possess the power to see the past, the present, and the future and is consulted through the Babaláwo or Ifá priest by adherents who want to inquire about matters that are confusing to them (see Abimbola 1977). Irele, while describing the Ifá corpus of the Yorùbá as a distinctive African canon, also comments about its unique performance by the Babalawo whom he calls "guardians of the word."[2] Also, from her personal experiences and the impressions she gathered researching Yorùbá gods, Judith Gleason (1971) describes Ifá as an "embodiment of knowledge" (3). It may be said, therefore, that Èlàlòrò has both critical and spiritual significance. Thus, the critic cannot be afraid to be critically assertive (though not necessarily harsh), imaginative, and innovative.

Èlàlòrò terminology can also be derived from a Yorùbá sentence, Ohun tá à ń là ni òrò (what we [do] break [into pieces] is a word/speech). It is rooted in what the Yorùbá calls Àlàyé, a Yorùbá semantic poetics, "what is broken or cut into pieces, or what is explained, in order for it to be clearer." The Yorùbá may say, là á yé mi, literally break (or cut) the issue or word into pieces so as to make me understand it. The asker here is a recipient of understanding rather than an active interpreter of meaning. It is the critical performer in a position of knowledge who thus breaks the speech into pieces for other people's understanding. Là is a Yorùbá verb for break or cut. In Àlàyé, therefore, the emphasis is on both là and yé (break-into-pieces and understand, appreciate, respectively). Iyè (brain), also called làákàyè (làákàyì) (ability to understand), is perhaps a word formed from the root yè (survive) [or live]. Yet yé, with a change of tone, means understand. Yorùbá language has a morphological process of nominalization of verbs through prefixation: lo (go), ilo (the art of going) jà (fight), ìjà (the art of fighting), bì (throw up or vomit), èébì, (the substance thrown up or the art of throwing up), mò, (know), ìmò, (knowledge), kà (recount), èka (the act of recounting), san (pay), and èsan (result or consequences). Thus, the name or term Èlàlòrò is formed by simply following the Yorùbá word formation strategy by prefixing "e" to Là, Èlà (the cutting [nominal]), and completing it with the phrase, ni òrò, (li òrò) (is speech or word)! Èlàlòrò is linked to the process of discourse or knowledge-seeking among the

Yorùbá. Whether through consultation of the Ifá priest, dialogue among Ìjálá poets in the forest, interpretation of ritual dance among traditional festival audience, during an audience-performer dialogue in Dadakúàdà poetry, or as part of any community dialogue activity in ọ̀dẹ̀dẹ̀ (inner house), agbo ilé (compound), ìta gbangba / ojúde (ojú òde)—(outside), Ẹ̀làlọ̀rọ̀ performances are rooted in the process of interpretation, criticism, knowledge-giving, receiving, and understanding.

Ọ̀rọ̀ in Ẹ̀làlọ̀rọ̀ may be compared to a person taken to an operating theater, not because that person is unwell or because the doctor wants to destroy parts of his or her anatomy, but because the surgeon wants to learn from and further appreciate the person's physiology and wants to help other people understand it by critically analyzing his makeup. The traditional Yorùbá idea of là, operating or cutting, in Yorùbá rhetoric, is very central to the critical process. There is also a Yorùbá sentence, ọ̀nà là, the route/way is clear, giving là another meaning—clear, ó là kedere, it is crystal clear, and ojú ọjọ́ là kedere, the day is very clear (today)! Therefore, when a Yorùbá person says ọ̀rọ̀ là, he is asking that a word or speech be made clear to him, or, if the person says ọ̀nà là, he or she is asking that the road to take, the choice to be made, or some unclear issue be clear to him or her!

The Yorùbá interpreter, critic, or rhetoricist is also interested in the beauty of performance. The speaker or performer seizes every opportunity to be rhetorical, as we shall come to appreciate better later. The uncompressed rendition of the invocation of Ẹ̀làlọ̀rọ̀ will be Ẹ̀là ni ọ̀rọ̀; however, it is commonly pronounced with the play on the lateral /l/ sound, often used in Yorùbá as a substitute for /n/, thus 'Ẹ̀làlọ̀rọ̀'. For believers of Ifá, Ẹ̀là (in this term) can be said to be an invocation of the power of the Yorùbá god to make clearer to a person or people what has become unclear to them.

Without necessarily asking for repetitions, tropes, or reversions as a means of explaining and understanding literary creativity and revision,[3] Ẹ̀làlọ̀rọ̀ as a discourse strategy approaches critical imagination and appreciation with values rooted in aspirations for societal growth and development. It aspires for the betterment of the critical and appreciative mind. Readers can therefore learn to invoke the concept of Ẹ̀làlọ̀rọ̀ as a discourse tool or to understand the rhetoric and critical framework in any contemporary writing that derives its heritage from Yorùbá oral tradition. It can also be used as a strategy for critical discourse world over. It should be possible—in my view—for scholars looking for an indigenous critical heritage from Africa to explore Ẹ̀làlọ̀rọ̀ tradition as they "read for the social"[4] as a way of giving their critical approaches a genuine touch of traditional African theoretical course. One interesting example of how an Ẹ̀làlọ̀rọ̀ performance can be accomplished in an oral community is shown next.

Whenever Yorùbá critical minds—either elderly or young—gather around their art, whether for deliberating important community issues or just passing the time using humor, riddles, or jokes, they invoke Yorùbá critical strategies, calling for textual performances and explications of intricate utterances according to indigenous rhetorical principles. The following sample performance by Asabi and Onikepe shows one of the ways the Yorùbá invoke this critical tool:

Asabi: *Béẹ bá jẹ́ n wí ẹ ó gbọ́rọ̀ ẹnu mi, àìjẹ́ n wí ma f'ẹ̀dọ̀ mi l'órí òróòro*
Onikepe: *Saáwòó!*
Asabi: *Ẹni táa fẹ́ l'amọ̀ a ò m'ẹni t'ófẹ́ni dé'nú. Ẹni a ní ó f'ẹni l'ójú t'ó fi ata s'ẹ́nu*
Onikepe: *Kàyéfì!*
Asabi: *T'ó bá r'ájá tó ru iná l'órí, àwọn ará ilé rẹ̀ s'àgbákò*
Onikepe: *Ẹ̀làlọ̀rọ̀.; ọ̀rọ̀ kìí le kokoko k'á yọ̀bẹ tì í*
Asabi: If you allow me to speak, you'll hear words from my mouth, if you refuse to let me speak I'll let my liver [continue to] rest on my pancreas.
Onikepe: Speak, let's 'see' [hear, examine] it!
Asabi: We only know the person whom we love, not the one who truly loves us his or her heart. The person that we requested to fan our eyes had put pepper in his mouth!
Onikepe: Awe!
Asabi: If you see a dog carrying fire on its head, [know that] its household is in real trouble.
Onikepe: *Ẹ̀làlọ̀rọ̀*! A word [speech] does not become so difficult for us to bring a knife upon it.

In the above performance, Onikepe invokes Ẹ̀làlọ̀rọ̀. She asks the narrator (Asabi) to break her parable into pieces. But Onikepe, as a co-conversant, might have invited an outsider or passerby to do the job, or she herself might have invoked Ẹ̀làlọ̀rọ̀ and engaged in a reexamination or critical rephrasing of the narrative for a better understanding. An outsider to the conversation—a passer-by who stopped to be a part of the discourse—might have declared Ẹ̀làlọ̀rọ̀ and went on to examine the wordings, characteristics, and message of the literary performance, or the narrator herself might have deplored Ẹ̀làlọ̀rọ̀ to show that she intended to break her heavily idiomatic text into clearer pieces.

WHAT Ẹ̀LÀLỌ̀RỌ̀ IS NOT

Reading Niyi Osundare's (1994) "How Post-Colonial is Africans Literature?", I thought the Yorùbá rhetorician in him became stronger when he summarized his disappointment in Joseph Conrad's contemporary Western critics:

> I was expecting poststructuralist open surgery on Conrad's *Heart of Darkness*, but what I got is a complex series of evasions, open-eyed

blindness, willful forgetfulness, or simply, intellectual and racial connivance with the European novelist. (210) (bold emphasis is mine)

Although Osundare might not have intended it, if one omits "poststructuralist" and replaces "open surgery" with the word Èlàlòrò, what remains is its striking definition, and its expectations of critical processes, through what they are not: not evasions; not open-eyed blindness; not willful forgetfulness; and not intellectual, ethnic, or racial connivance with the author of the written text, the oral singer, the dancer, or the performer of the original recorded speech. I will address the issue of "race" later.

One of the most important questions is whether the Èlàlòrò critic (the open-ended everyman or everywoman deployer of the Yorùbá Èlàlòrò paradigm) can be biased in favor of a writer from his race or sociopolitical or economic group. In short, does the Èlàlòrò concept ask for a de-personalized, unbiased, or "detached"[5] criticism, unlike what Osundare (1994, 209-16) read from Rose Murfin, Adena Rosemarin, and Brook Thomas's criticisms of Joseph Conrad's *Heart of Darkness* (1994?)

The Yorùbá often say that òrò kì í lé kokoko ká yo òbe tì ì. Ẹnu náà láá fí sọ ó, meaning that "a speech cannot be so hard to make us bring a knife upon it, we use the mouth to explain it." The reference to knife in this particular dictum refers to conflict or disagreement between two or more parties and espouse the idea that dialogue, rather than violence, is the most viable way to resolve such conflict. Further, in Yorùbá rhetoric, it is said that ẹní t'ó bá bèèrè òrò l'ó fẹ́ ìdí ẹ̀ gbọ́, meaning, "Whoever asks a question (about anything) desires to hear about the essence or root of the issue." In other words, a critic is required (and sometimes the narrator may put this burden upon him- or herself) to present "the root of the issue" to the questioner. The Yorùbá believe that criticism can be positive or negative and can be said either harshly or diplomatically. The Òyọ́ Yorùbá are counted among the most diplomatic groups in the Yorùbá world.[6] In other words, in Yorùbá rhetoric, there is a theory that òrò níí yọ obì l'ápò; òrò níí yó ọfà nínú apó . . . , meaning, "Speech may be uttered such that it either draws a kolanut from the pocket, or a bow and arrow from the case . . ." (notice the play on the word, apó and àpò).

THE DYNAMICS OF AN APPROACH

Why do I consider the Èlàlòrò paradigm as very dynamic and as very helpful in presenting, understanding, and interpreting ideas within their authentic contexts? Every culture has its own angle through which it sees the world, and although nothing stops scholars from borrowing from their cultural parameters for measuring other people's views, whenever that is done, a full disclosure of the foreign paradigm should be made, including a humble acceptance of its limitation. It is important, like a Yorùbá adage indicates, to start from a position that affirms the truth that for every local tradition or way of life, there is a different one abroad. *Bí ọmọdé ò b'a d'e oko ẹlòmíràn r'i, y'o sọ wí pé kò sí oko tí ó tó ti baba òun*, meaning, "if a child has never visited another person's farm, he or she would declare that no farm in the world is as big as his or her father's."

WHY I THINK ẸLÀLỌ̀RỌ̀ IS DYNAMIC?:

Here, my thoughts on why *Ẹlàlọ̀rọ̀* is dynamic, and why I consider it useful for critical interpretation and understanding:

1. *Ẹlàlọ̀rọ̀* is concerned not only with the cultural, ideological, or contextual aspects of a work, it is also interested in the nature and aspects of the "language" of composition.
2. The *Ẹlàlọ̀rọ̀* critical approach, in analyzing issues and views, also examines the type of language employed and can call for a reexamination or recast of every notable word, concept, or movement in "simpler" forms. However, it would also recognize the strength and originality of the source renditions and accord every interpreter the primacy of their art.
3. *Ẹlàlọ̀rọ̀* often considers both the metaphysical implication of discourse and the "language" of discourse. *Ẹlàlọ̀rọ̀* emanates not only from the semantics of cut or surgery, but also from the metaphysics of *Ẹlà*. The *Ẹlàlọ̀rọ̀* paradigm is often concerned (as believed by Yorùbá followers of *Ẹlà*), with the spiritual or metaphysical essence of cultural material.
4. "Beautiful" language explains "beautiful" concepts and cultural materials—the use of rich proverbs, anecdotes, folktales, and other metaphorical elements—form parts of linguistic and cultural elements of interpretations and criticism.
5. The uses of local or native sources in the interpretation of cultural materials are important, and every performance interpretation requires the indigenous context for an *Ẹlàlọ̀rọ̀* understanding, even when areas considered include mental and psychological analyses.
6. Although *Ẹlàlọ̀rọ̀* emphasizes native, ethnic, and other indigenous resources in decoding every material, it does not accept ethnic or native biases or solidarity in reaching judgments or providing interpretations of a material.

Let us consider for a moment an *Ẹlàlọ̀rọ̀* understanding of Ben Okri's *The Famished Road*. I have read some very interesting and rich discussions[7] that suggest that Okri subverts African oral tradition by creating a story, characters, and scenes that contradict the natural milieu of traditional oral narrative. Yet, we are reminded that nothing in traditional culture is homogenizing,[8] even folktales and folk performances! Quayson (1995) warns us that when reviewing literary writings by African authors such as "Tutuola and Okri and even Soyinka and Achebe," we are not to inquire "how true a reflection of culture a literary text is but *what* purposes the cultural concepts and categories are serving within the literary universe (102)" However, in asserting that Okri subverts the African tradition, Quayson is passing a judgment that Okri does not truly reflect the course of natural patterns of African traditions in his literary text.

Well, one can easily agree with Quayson's (1995) submissions about how a serious mistake it is for any scholar of African modernity to regard traditional African discourse as simplistic. Yet, I found that on this issue, the uncooked meat has not left the critic's chewing mouth and we cannot conclude so quickly about how sweet or bitter the meat is. It does seem right to me to declare an "error of ignorance" of African traditions to anyone who condemns African oral traditions as unscientific, especially when a such person accords the philosophy of Western literacy a proprietorship of freedom of discussion, hypothetical verification, or challenge and of historical processes. What is more historical or freedom oriented in performance processes than oral traditions!

One can never over emphasize the fact that African orality is relevant to contemporary sociopolitical life in Africa in the global century. This orality encompasses an African rhetoric of economic and scientific traditions for the majority of Africans in the marketplace and in the healing sanatoriums. It is still true today as it was yesterday that African orality records and recalls our history. It ensures that we appreciate our lineage identity through knowledge and performance.

Ben Okri is not a Yorùbá, but for the purpose of this discussion, we will explore his work, invoking important commonalities between Urhobo culture (his indigenous culture) and Yorùbá traditions. After all, there is a Urhobo traditional myth that traces Urhobo origin to Yorùbá sources. The Yorùbá have a causal adage that states as follows:

> *Ká ṣe é bí wọn tií s ṣe é*
> *Kó lè báà rí bíí tií rí*
> We must do things as they are done
> So they can result in what they often result

This adage perhaps shows us much better that if there is a problem with the transition of Azaro, the Abiku character in *The Famished Road*, it was because his parents did not observe the course of tradition, which would have ensured that the child's decision to live was cemented. We must at least remember that Azaro decided to stay in the real world in order to make his parents happy. Unfortunately, the parents "slept off" their responsibility despite the unceasing cry of their child: *Abiyamọ kì í gbẹ́kún ọmọ rẹ̀ kó sùn* (A good parent would not go back to sleep hearing her/his child crying).

It is clear, as Quayson (1995) says, that Azaro's staying behind causes a "continuous intercourse . . . between the real world and that of the spirit" (109), and the first èri-jẹ́-mi-nsó (evidence) of this is the fact that Azaro continues to see the spirits. The second is that the spirit companions of Azaro continue to entice him to return to the spirit world. The third is, the "spirit-figures come to the reality-plane to transport Azaro to the spirit-realm" (109). This is too much trouble to expose a child to. Even an Àbíkú who is trying to please his parents! Yet, it must be understood that as far as the Yorùbá tradition is concerned, these are not in any way arbitrary stories told about an Àbíkú. It is a major battle once the Àbíkú decided to stay in the real world. Necessary rituals must be performed to enhance the Àbíkú's decision. An Àbíkú's decision to stay forever looks like eye of fish to his parents, but it is the application of heat and ingredients that cook the fish before it might be found delicious.

The *báatiíse/bíítiírí* adage clearly clarified that Ben Okri commits no subversion of African oral narratives at all in his story, characters, or scenes in *The Famished Road*, and he does not contradict any "natural milieu of traditional oral narrative." Here's Quayson (1995) again, "In Yorùbáland, as in much of traditional Africa, the spirit world of the ancestors and the gods is accessed through special rituals. There seems to be a clear danger inherent in crossing into the spirit world without proper preparation through ritual" (105). It is very important to understand that the Yorùbá Àbíkú is not necessarily expected to remain in the real world due solely to his personal will to do so, and even if this is so, the parents and relatives also have their clear cut duties, prescribed for them by tradition, to enhance an Àbíkú's will to live. Thus, Àbíkú's "acts of volition" or "acts of rituals self-preparation" are often not the complete course necessary to keep Àbíkú permanently severed from the spirit-realm. If in the Azaro's case, there is a merger of the spirit-realm and the real-realm, it is because certain normal processes were not followed, and we must expect tension to continue to occur from Azuro's act of remaining in the real. The Yorùbá oral narrative would clearly and normally present this tension.

Yes, in the case of Yorùbá Àbíkú traditions, there is an expectation of a continued demarcation between "the real and the esoteric realms" for a peaceful resolution. It is not surprising that the lack of demarcation in the two worlds resulted in worst types of grotesque elements continuing to torment Azaro. The degree of bizarreness would only grow. In other words, the idea of an upheaval in traditional realms is already predicted once the required or normal course of actions is neglected as was done in the Azaro's case. My èri-jẹ́-mi-nsó (supportive materials) here is that for a parent (a father who shares Sàngó's qualities), such neglect is a terrible failure indeed. The parents should have performed rituals as their stamp for the efforts of Azaro. Incisions—permanent marks on the *ìpénpéj'u* (eyelids), offerings, invocations, or any other performance in *báatiíse*—would have done much to ensure the *bíítiírí*, the permanent separation of the two realms and, thus, ensured a permanent severance of Azaro from the Àbíkú world. Is it possible that the parent's preoccupation with misery made them unable to perform the ritual to keep Àbíkú safe in the real world?

THE PERFORMER, THE WRITER, THE CARVER, THE DANCER, THE CRITIC, THE AUDIENCE, OR THE INTERPRETER

Here again are some thoughts. They are not intended to be prescriptive. They are intended to enhance the understanding of Èlàlòrò paradigms:

1. The Èlàlòrò critic has an important responsibility to cultural discourse and to the society, and, thus, he or she must be committed to social issues, traditions, and community patterns and be dedicated to native identity and community meaning. The critic must be honest to their profession, must aspire for a synthesis of *iwà* and *ewà* (character and/or existence), and beauty in his or her own role. Yorùbá conceptual images are strongly rooted in oral traditions, and the effective artist or critic must aspire to be an expert of the people's traditional culture, orality, and social lives.
2. The writer, artist, or oral performer should also aspire to be personable—there is no fault if he or she doesn't achieve it. For example, the myth that the writer, dancer, or poet must have a flaw is not acceptable.
3. Critical concepts must be rooted in contexts; no beating around the bush— "*sojú abẹ níkòó* —"
4. Diplomacy and politeness are important in Èlàlòrò discourse:
Ọ̀rọ̀ níí yọ obì l'ápò
Ọ̀rọ̀ níí yọ ọfa nínú apó
Speech does draw kolanuts from the pocket,
Speech does draw bow and arrow from the case
5. Critical efforts should focused on constructing, reconstructing, and affirming society's values, not on destroying or displacing them. Derrida's double reading of the text—to show lack of synthesis within it—is not acceptable in Èlàlòrò. A "double reading" in order to prove that what the text stands to affirm—some elements within it actually disaffirms—does not reflect a critical tradition favorable in Èlàlòrò. "Deconstructing" the text, relativism, and pessimism as ways of promoting cultural pluralism do not reflect Èlàlòrò principles. While a basic post-modern precept that all traditions "have some validity" (Jencks 1989, 7) find acceptance in the Èlàlòrò cultural paradigm, Èlàlòrò would reject the idea of cultural pluralism as a thrust of hybridity. This is because Èlàlòrò rejects the postmodern *ersatz*, which relates to (mass) culture as

fake, artificial, imitative, and even bogus (Jencks 7). It is also because Èlàlòrò affirms society's ideas of truth, family lineage, identity, and cultural originality.

Èlàlòrò's cultural pluralism is people centered[9] and affirms the veracity of cultural originality and people's cultural identity within the scope of pluralism or multiculturalism. Human commonalty (or unity) is neither antithetical to Èlàlòrò's paradigm or to human plurality, and plurality does not make impossible individual cultural identity and authenticity. The Yorùbá cultural plurality, for example, is affirmed in the common belief by worshipers of Yorùbá religion in *Olódùmarè*. Among the Yorùbá, family, profession, and ancestry's cultural and religious calling sometime reflect deities of Ògún, Oya, Sàngó, Obàtálá, and others. For non-Yorùbá deity worshipers, cultural identities manifest in Islam or Christianity if they profess such faiths. For example, orthodoxy in the Èlàlòrò cultural perspective is not opposed to pluralism, and pluralism does not negate valuing a "fundamental" cultural principle or identity.

Èlàlòrò would most probably accept Arnold Toynbee's assertion about the decline of individualism in terms of the inference that western culture is the sole yardstick of civilization and sophistication as wrongly projected in colonialist criticism. Èlàlòrò pluralism defines "global village" in terms of how every element of the village has its own authentic voice. All people are capable of projecting their cultural and identity principles. Unlike Toynbee's postmodernism (Jencks 1989, 8) however, Èlàlòrò is not skeptical to truth and values, and it does not consider hybridity a replacement of cultural authenticity.

6. Èlàlòrò affirms what in Hausa (and perhaps many African cultures) can be described as a principle of "*Wanda bai ji bari ba, ya ji oho*" (the person who would not hear "stop it", would hear "serves you right")![10] The Yorùbá will say "*Ilé táa bá f'itó mo, ìrì ni yó wó o*" (a house constructed of saliva, will be bulldozed by dew). In essence, there's a cause and effect in society in relation to people's actions or lack thereof. Critical discourses must always be for the sake of life, for affirming society's rights, and for challenging its wrongs. This is the same principle that informs the strong didactic essence of African folk narratives.

One question I have heard asked, and which will be constantly thrown on our table, is how to define a community in terms of the constantly changing society. People now talk about the community of cyber users and the community of video gamers, not just family, township, or village-ship. In fact, we now hear such new terminologies as cyber village and cyber country. However, any development, change, or enhancement in terms of making a society better or more comfortable to live in only affirms the best human values and desires and does not contradict Èlàlòrò principles. When the Yorùbá metaphysical performer chants, "Afẹ́fẹ́ lẹ́lẹ́ máa gbóhùn mi r'òkun; èfúùfù lẹ̀lẹ̀ máa gbóhùn mi r'ọ̀sà," meaning, "softly softly wind, take my voice to the ocean, tenderly tenderly wind, carry my voice to the sea," he definitely demonstrates his or her ability to enhance performance by commandeering air and using the speed in natural phenomenon to cause some positive effects.

However, the way postmodern discourse presents the city (urban or cosmopolitan spaces) as a greater sign of pluralism and freedom would be unacceptable to Èlàlòrò. A person's "cultural looseness" (if that term may be used here) or the size of the space he or she occupies is not necessarily an indication of his or her happiness. It does not symbolize his or her freedom or attitude to self or society development. Whether as an African villager, a Hamlet dweller, or an American or European Cosmopolite, a person may have the human tendency to "character changes" and or personal ambitions. Thus, as Jaigbade Alao, an Ilorin oral singer, once sang, society itself does not necessarily change, it is people who force changes on society. It is "nature" which responds to the mistreatment of the environment by human society, not "society." Here is Jaigbade's Èlàlòrò:

> Nnkan mẹta n' bọ̀ wálé ayé, mẹ́ta ó tẹ̀ lé e
> Ìgbà tí ayé ò bá níláárírí mọ́, mẹ́ta ò padà séyìn
> Owó n' bọ̀ wálé ayé, iyì ló tẹ̀ lé e
> Ìgbà tí ayé ò bá níláárírí mọ́, iyì padà séyìn
> Ọba n' bọ̀ wálé ayé, àṣẹ pẹlu ikọ̀ lo tẹ̀ lé e
> Ìgbà tí ayé ò bá níláárírí mọ́, àṣẹ padà ó sì k'ọba.
> Ọ̀rẹ́ n' bọ̀ wálé ayé, òótọ́ inú tẹ̀ lé e
> Ìgbà tí ayé ò bá níláárírí mọ́, ọ̀rẹ́ la rí kò sóòótọ́.
> Ọ̀dàlẹ̀ àtèké ní n' j'ọ́rẹ̀ẹ́ lónìí.
> Ẹẹ̀rí i b'átibọ̀tan ayé ti rí!
> Awítàìwí wọ́n l'áyé ní n' yí.
> Ayé ò yí lọ ibì kankan,
> Ibi ọjọ́ n' yọ ni n' ti n' yọ
> Ibi òòrùn wọ̀ ni n' ti n' wọ̀
> Ilé ayé ò yí lọ ibì kankan
> Àwọn èniyàn inú ẹ̀ ni n' pà'wàdà!

When three things were coming to the world, three things followed.
When the world spoiled, three things would go back [disappear]!
Money was coming to the world, value followed it
When the world spoiled, value disappeared leaving money.
The King was coming to the world, authority followed.
When the world spoiled, authority disappeared leaving King.
Friendship was coming to the world, trust followed it
When the world spoiled, only friends without trust [remained]!

Cheats and hypocrites are the friends of today.
Can't you see what is becoming of our world?
Whenever we complain, they insist that the world is changing.
The world is not changing at all,
The Sun rises from the direction it rises from,
The Sun sets where it sets.
This world is not changing at all,
It is the people the occupants [of the world] who are changing their behaviors!

(Alao 1987)

Jaigbade's Èlàlòrò should be easy for us to comprehend. His metaphors make clear how he sees societal changes and development[,] and the human responsibility [to/for] enhancing them.

7. In Èlàlòrò perspective, a text is only contradictory when it goes against the norm of society's overall goodness. When the poet ceases to be his or her brother's and sister's keeper, and sings for their destabilization, it is not contradictory simply for being critical of their failings, nor the writer contradictory for performing his or her responsibility as society's keeper. The writer can only be working against Èlàlòrò principle because he wants to create turmoil through the exercise of his poetic talent:

Ẹni a ní ó fẹ́'ni lójú
Ata ló fi sẹ́'nu
Ẹni a ní ó kí'ni lẹ́'hìn
Ẹ̀gún ló fi s'ọwọ́

The person asked to help remove particles
irritating one's eyes
Puts hot pepper in his/her mouth
The person asked to rub one's back
Equips his/her hands with thorns!

CHINUA ACHEBE'S AND NIYI OSUNDARE'S CRITICISM OF JOSEPH CONRAD'S HEART OF DARKNESS

Chinua Achebe's (1989) positions on Conrad and his *Heart of Darkness* are very well known (1-20), but I will cite it here to make an Èlàlòrò point. Achebe does not mince words in casting *Heart of Darkness*'s author as a racist and his work as a racist novel: "The point of my observations should be quite clear by now namely that Joseph Conrad was a thoroughgoing racist" (11).

However, in this chapter, I will concentrate on Achebe's (1989) reactions to Conrad scholars who have seen nothing wrong in Conrad's work. Achebe continues:

> That this simple truth is glossed over in criticisms of his work is due to the fact that white racism against Africa is such a normal way of thinking that its manifestations go completely unremarked... The real question is the dehumanization of Africa and Africans which this age-long attitude has fostered and continues to foster in the world. And the question is whether a novel which celebrates this dehumanization, which depersonalizes a portion of the human race, can be called a great work of art. (12)

What yardstick does a critic use when describing an art, painting, or sculpture as great art, or a story as superb literature? Achebe insists that despite Conrad being "one of the great stylists of modern fiction and a good story-teller into the bargain," the *Heart of Darkness* is not "a great work of art." He was responding to a Conrad scholar who categorized the book as "among the half-dozen greatest short novels in the English language" (quoted in Achebe 1989, 3).

Similarly, as we have already referenced in this chapter, Niyi Osundare (1994), African scholar and poet, drives home Achebe's contention with some Western Conrad's scholars when he suggests that they have used a "dubious" approach, "a race card"—a "white defends white card"—in their appraisal of Conrad. In his criticism of one of such critical work, *Heart of Darkness: A Case of Study in Contemporary Criticism,* Osundare expresses complete disappointment over what he read in the book:

> I grabbed this book with effusive enthusiasm, eager to see Conrad's archetypal silence and ambivalences unraveled, the gaps in the tale filled in, the old parable interrogated with a revolutionary critical weapon in this last quarter of the twentieth century. I was anxious to see which theoretical practice could be able to engage the story, enter the text, initiate a humane dialogue with Conrad, ask him why there are no African human beings in a "yarn" whose setting is Africa. I was expecting poststructuralist open surgery on Conrad's *Heart of Darkness,* but what I got is a complete series of evasions, open-eyed blindness, willful forgetfulness, or simply, intellectual and racial connivance with the European novelist. (210)

I suggested at the beginning of this chapter that Osundare actually expected an Èlàlòrò on *Heart of Darkness*. Èlàlòrò qualifies, in my opinion, as the "humane dialogue" with the objective "to engage the story, enter the text." However, Achebe's (1989) and Osundare's (1994) submissions on Conrad critics bring forward the issue that Osundare calls "racial connivance" (210) in the critical process. There are two types of racial connivance—connivance against a race, and connivance in support of a race, and according to Achebe and Osundare, several white Conrad scholars have committed both—against the African race and in favor of the White race. A leading African scholar obviously has difference views on *Heart of Darkness* from that of white Conrad's scholars. Abiola Irele (2001) categorizes novels such as *Heart of Darkness* (he included Graham Greene's *The Heart of the Matter* as another example) as "literature of exoticism" (14) in which Europeans only try to play out their fantasies. In such novels, says Irele, "Africa itself is never an immediate reference, and the African is never envisaged as anything more than an element in a landscape to which the writer has ascribed a pre-determined meaning. . . . its peoples are also excluded as living figures . . ." (14).

As previously explained, Èlàlòrò as a critical tool has no room for "racial connivance" in the process of interpretation or critical judgment. Although historical and cultural context are crucial in Èlàlòrò discourse processes, they are elements for critical debate and assessment, for establishing society's values and its needs for the survival of culture and cultural identity survival, regardless of what ethnic or racial group that society represents.[11] Èlàlòrò's requirements of an honest and personable critic requires someone who will take the moral high ground by resisting racist connivance as an underlying tone of a critical discourse. In Yorùbá philosophy (informed by Yorùbá religion), the deity of creation determines people's physical traits, and, thus, it would be committing sins against the god to be biased against a person because of his or her color or physical traits. However, Èlàlòrò promotes identification by and in celebration of one's family, ethnic and cultural history, and traditions. They are all points of identity and reference, like ethnic marks, lineage names, and ethnic rites and rituals, which represent a mark of pride and solidarity among relatives.

ADOPTING ÈLÀLÒRÒ IN CRITICAL DISCOURSE

Although there is nothing radically new in its emphasis on contextual criticism, Èlàlòrò tries to expand critical discourse beyond most past and contemporary critical tools, such as formalism, structuralism, new criticism, postmodernism, poststructuralism, or postcolonialism. In some cases, Èlàlòrò sharply departs from these critical frameworks or concept like the "death of the author" in postmodern and new criticism theories. In other cases, Èlàlòrò opens up more areas for critical dialogue. (For example, the importance Èlàlòrò places on language even as it emphasizes history and culture/sentence fragment.)

In the ways it encourages the use of community wisdom expressed through adages and proverbs, Èlàlòrò as a critical tool demands that the critic explore the oral traditions of his or her culture and practice criticism with the aim of challenging issues in ways that uphold cherished community values and traditions.

CONCLUSION

While I have only presented a short introductory analysis of how Èlàlòrò can be explored in critical discourse, I am not unmindful of queries, which many readers may have. There is, for example, an old argument that proverbs cannot effectively represent people's wisdom. Some have again raised similar argument to Owomoyela (1996), asking whether proverbs can be reliable "in reconstructing the past?" They also indicate that African proverbs are gender biased and thus unsuitable for modern discourse. Owomoyela (1996) already presents very strong refutation of these arguments (see 155), but what I would like to add is that the idea of using proverbs is not to simply reconstruct the past, but to target the present, ensure cultural and historical relevance for people's understanding of life and traditions, and to be sensitive to their deeply rooted beliefs and world views.

Proverbs are expressions of community wisdom because they represent truths, lore, and traditions as seen by the community. They are created and owned not by an individual but by the entire community, who, jealously guard them, constantly recall them (almost every minute when one consider the use of proverbs in African communities) and then pass them on from generation to generation through community elders. Yet, the same community is happy to point out an *àsìpa òwe*, constantly challenges the currency of proverbs, their wrongly applications, and even raising proffering humor in ways of criticizing proverbs. *Àsìpa òwe* can be announced as a speaker wants to show a need to look for a proverb that suit a new development in human lives. Quoting Okediji (1990) about the deep-rooted approach needed for understanding Yorùbá carvings and images, Taye (1996) writes,

> their images are often loaded and saturated with metaphorical lyrics, which must be carefully deciphered in order to enjoy the messages . . . the images are not to be arrested only on their surface levels, because they are growth from a Yorùbá tradition, thriving on parables, symbols and allusions. (145)

Those who continue to derogate the employment of African oral proverbs in modern critical discourse are no doubt favorable to the view that literacy is superior to orality.[12] Some of such scholars, their writings have shown, are often apologetic for coming from an orality culture. Yet, proverbs are only one of the cultural elements that can be explored in Èlàlòrò discourse. Anecdotes, riddles, and important life metaphors of the day would be as strongly helpful as proverbs are in cultural criticism.

2   *Èlàlọ̀rọ̀* and Translation

Èlàlọ̀rọ̀, as an indigenous African discourse methodology, presents important frameworks for translation and critical interpretation. In this chapter, I will examine aspects of *Èlàlọ̀rọ̀* that show a translator's responsibility to their culture and to other important expectations for meaning, originality, and aesthetic initiatives. The chapter will also compare *Èlàlọ̀rọ̀* expectations with certain contemporary theoretical paradigms such as polysystem and postmodern approaches.

Let us begin with a few interesting propositions by two non-Africanist scholars who have important implications for how Western scholars might treat translation work. Even-Zohar's (1990) polysystem approach regards every translation to be at the same level as the original text, considering the translation as a work independent from the original and identifying many important formats through which the translator can show his or her originality (Dimic 1996).

While quoting Samuel Johnson's (1973) warning (to translators) against destroying a written work's purpose of "pleasing the reader," Maynard Mack's (1987) essay titled "A Note on Translation," ended with one of Johnson's sharpest defenses of literature: "To a thousand cavils, one answer is sufficient; the purpose of a writer is to read, and the criticism which would destroy the power of pleasing must be blown aside" (2657). This shows, in part, the importance for the translator of retaining the writer's original purpose. Mack was quick to point out early in his paper that no one of those who has attempted to translate Andromache's words, *daimonie, phthisei se to son menos*, to her husband, Hector, "knows exactly what shade of meaning daimónie had for Homer" (bold emphasis mine).

My intention while comparing the theoretical views of translation, will be to show how the *Èlàlọ̀rọ̀* paradigm, with evidence from Yorùbá oral traditions, defines the translator's job in ways that suits cross-cultural translation purposes.

TRANSLATION, INTERPRETATION, AND YORÙBÁ CULTURAL PRACTICE

It may not be far-fetched to assume that translation is as old as the oldest human community on earth and that it is made relevant not only when people translate from one language to another—a process I call *Intertranslation* (or *Extertranslation*) such as from Yorùbá to Hausa—but also when "translation" takes place within the same language—a process I call Intratranslation,[1] (such as from plain language to literary language, from a parable to plain language, or from eighteenth century spoken Yorùbá language to a modern or contemporary Yorùbá language of the twenty-first century.

How does a traditional Yorùbá practice of translation work? We will consider several examples as we explain the terminology and its concepts. Translation in the Yorùbá language is called *ìtumọ̀*, which, morphologically, speaking comes from two root words *ìtú* and *ìmọ̀*. "Knowledge" and "know-how" are commonly understood denotations of *ìmo*. *Ìtú* acquires additional meanings depending on where the tone is placed[2]. *Ìtú* (note tone marks) means wonder, as in *ìtú méje yààyà méfà* (seven magic, six wonders). And while *idán* is the Yorùbá term that most clearly means 'magic,' *ìtú* may also be extended to mean the same thing as *idán*, allowing both terms to function as indicators of something beyond a person's imagination— the extraordinary. The terms *ìtú* and *idán* are clearly interchangeable in this context. *Àrà* is another Yorùbá word whose denotative connection to "anything novel" imbues it with connotation links to magic and wonder—thus the phrase *ó dárà* could also be properly understood as "he or she performed magic/wonders/something novel."

Let us digress a little bit to a lesson in Yorùbá semantics and morphology and if, in the process, we learn one or two things about Yorùbá words, the digression might be a good "comic relief." While our aim in this chapter remains basically to discuss translation, this digression might be useful in showing some processes taken and choices made by Yorùbá speaker in translating one concept to another or in translating an "intention" to words within the same language. For example, the Yorùbá speaker may have used *yààyà* in my earlier example above only to help his intention of adding beauty to language (*ẹwà èdè*), and because *yààyà* also helps him to reemphasize the *ìtú* in the meaning he is conveying to his listeners. Another realization of *ìtú* may be when the [i] carries a lower or falling tone, *ìtú*, in that case there are two elements that carry meanings. The two morphemes in this word are [*ì*] "that which," and [*tú*]" is unwrap(ped)." *Ó tú u*, he/she unwrapped it. *Má se tú u o (má tú u)*, "don't unwrap it." It is rare for many Yorùbá native speakers to say "*ìtú u*," to mean that which is poured out from the mouth (rather, *nǹkan tí a tu dànù*, that which we spit out). However, *ìtú* can be used for, that which is used to unwrap something. *Ìtú idérí igò*, that which is used to open or loosen the cover of the bottle. The best realization of *tú u* pour from something (mouth, bottle, etc.) or spit out[3] will be *ó tú u*, he/she poured it out of the mouth, or *nǹkan tí ó tu láti ẹnu*, that which he/spits out from the mouth.

The two meanings of *àrà* and *tú* discussed here are very relevant to how the traditional Yorùbá people practice translation. Although translation can be said to be like performing magic because of the amazement that the skills of decoding parables generate, the art is not just magical, it is linked solidly to the knowledge of the translator and the knowledge wrapped up in the composition. Therefore, *ìmọ̀* is as strong as *ìtú* in *ìtumọ̀*. *Ìtumọ̀* (*ìtú ìmọ̀*) literally means the unwrapping of (encoded) knowledge.

Translation is a daily activity among the Yorùbá. Every speaker is expected to master at least Intratranslation in order to convey meaning and carry out cultural events in their community: *Bí òwe bí òwe là ń lù'lù àgìdìgbó, ọlọgbọ́n n ló ń gbọ́ o, ọ̀mọ̀ràn ló ń mọ̀ mọ́*, (the *àgìdìgbó* drum is beaten/drummed in proverbs, the clever ones hear it; the intelligent ones understand it). The elder person speaks often in parables, idioms, and proverbs. The young person has to listen closely. He or she must be smart enough to keep pace with the communication line. At different levels of the Yorùbá community, different people are entrusted with messages (and bear responsibility for delivering these messages) from person to person and community to community. *Ìránṣẹ́ Ọba*, identifies the messenger of the King, *Alárinà* is the go-between for the bride's family and the groom's family. Any mistake in translating (not just in transmitting) speeches and conveying their proper meanings may result in serious cultural consequences. The drum, the gong, and fire making in the bush or forest, are all examples of traditional vehicles for conveying messages.

Translation activities features even at higher levels of the Yorùbá community[4]: supernatural and spiritual levels. *Egungun* (ancestor) worship is an important aspect of Yorùbá religion. *Egúngún* are called *Ará ọ̀run* (ones from the ancestral world, who come as ancestors to the earth.[5] Whenever *Egúngún* speaks, a translator is at hand to convey the meaning of the speech to the people. Appointed members of the *Atọ́kùn*, an *Egúngún*'s messenger, accompany *Egungun* to translate whatever *Egungun* says to the audience. *Egúngún*, as a supernatural being, hears what everyone says to him, while he himself needs no translation. As a popular deity with many followers, the translator of the speech given by *Egúngún* to the people plays an important religious role of translating *Egúngún*'s message to adherents. This is a spiritual, metaphysical, and social role: sometimes giving good news of childbirth to the barren who believe the *Egúngún* can help them to have children of their own or simply conveying ancestral invocations on the worshipers.

In Chapter 8, I discuss why I believe the *Egúngún* tradition was originally foreign to the Yorùbá, that *Egúngún* spoke a foreign language which was translated by one of its followers and that this *Egúngún* translation tradition has been carried across generations to the present day by Yorùbá *Egúngún* followers.[6]

Another translation tradition rooted in Yorùbá culture is the translation of *Ọsanyìn*'s speech. *Ọsanyìn* is the Yorùbá deity of herbal medicine. The *Ọsanyìn* priest is the translator, and he translates *Ọsanyìn*'s speech to the client in ways the client would understand. The *Ọsanyìn* [oracle] is consulted for cure, and he speaks in voice that only his translator understands. The translator conveys the message to the client in ordinary or plain language. Neither the *Egúngún* translator nor the *Ọsanyìn* translator is forbidden to speak in parables during translation. When translating their deity's messages however, their responsibility is to convey the meaning intended by their deity in the clearest way possible to the receiver.

In the two instances explained above, source languages (if we may call them that) are not actual mother tongues as far as contemporary Yorùbá people are concerned; but they are not regarded as foreign languages either. For our purpose here, we may call them *Ohùn òrìṣà*, the voices of the deities, or the languages of the gods (let us forget temporarily that I will be challenging this assertion for one of these voices in Chapter 8). The most important thing here is the dedication of the translator to translate the voices of the gods to the worshipers or clients. How does the translator do this? Does he or she choose to convey implied information, implicit information, inadequate information, inadequate meaning, or inconclusive information? Or does he or she give a conclusive translation with adequate information and meaning? Does the translator consider the state of mind of the client before conveying bad news to the client? If he or she decides to highjack the process, who does he or she answer to? And what happens to the community who trusts the translator and relies on the information he conveys from their deity? What is the relationship between trust and translation?

Intratranslation is a process the Yorùbá expects every person (both children and adults, although less stringent on much younger children) to demonstrate. Each person must be capable of an explanation that his or her every action makes sense to the community and not just expect the community to accept such action. "Explanation" or "sense" here means translation, to make sense is to be able to explain one's actions meaningfully, to translate those actions in ways that demonstrate observance of the community's logic, values, and expectations. *Kí ni itumọ̀ ohun t'ó ṣe?* This sentence literally translates as "what is the translation (or meaning) of what you have done?" or "what is the logic of your action?" (translation) here means "meaning," "logic," and "sense." Everyday performances can be explained partly, as translations of community values and logic into actions.

In other words, the Yorùbá cultural understanding of translation is not only a thought-for-thought rendition from a source language to a target language or from proverbs or riddles into plain language, but it means a logical justification of actions in words. This is not a word-for-word narrative of action. This may also be the implication to the following query: *Ìwọ náà wò ó, kí ni itumọ̀ ohun t'ó wí/ t'ó sọ/t'ó ṣe nísisìnyí?!* (What is the logic of your utterance/action?) *kí ni itumọ̀ ìwà tó hù lónìí?* (What is the meaning of your character today?) meaning simply, "can you defend your behavior today?"

ÈLÀLỌ̀RỌ̀ AND THE THEORY OF TRANSLATABILITY

Èlàlọ̀rọ̀ is rooted in the art of performance discourse, interpretation, and explanation of society's meanings and values. *Èlàlọ̀rọ̀* is rooted in the all-round relationships that the human being has formed with society, with the environment and all its members, and with the spiritual and metaphysical aspects of life. Èlàlòrò treats the process of speech-(-word)making (i.e., òrò-síso) as a social, spiritual, metaphysical process. The Èlàlòrò aesthetics affirms the "good" of the society and challenges its "evil." Similar to our discussion in the last chapter, the writer, dancer, carver, or oral performer who uses òrò (words) synthesizes ewà and iwà (beauty and behavior [or existence]). The interpreter should not "deconstruct" society simply to cause disarray or to challenge the idea of society's truths.

The concept of translatability is intrinsically rooted in the idea that *ilé làá wò ká tó s'omo l'órúko* (it is the house we look at before we name a [newborn] baby). Two things can be noted from this adage: first, the importance of the child's cultural and community identity in formulating his or her name, and second, the consideration of the contextual reality of a person in defining him or her throughout life. His or her identity is as important as his or her sociopolitical reality, economic reality, and spiritual reality. This is because all of these realities will be evident from the child's home. In other words, the translation of who the child is, what he or she brings to the world, what she or he aspires to be in the future, and the meaning of his or her life must flow from the reality of that child's home.

At a different level of discourse, another Yorùbá adage proclaims *Òrò sùnnùkùn, ojú sùnnùkùn la fií wò ó* (When a speech is complex, we must use a complex eye to examine it). The idea of using a complex eye here reiterates Èlàlòrò's metaphor of "breaking" the speech into simpler levels: *Ká là á sí wéwé* or *Ká fó o si wéwé kó baà lè yé wa* (see the discussion of "àlàyé" in Chapter 1), meaning to "cut" or "break" the speech into simpler or smaller pieces for clarity, yet to ensure that we recognize the intrinsic formation of the complex speech as we embark on a dialogue over it. History, culture, and identity always form the basis of every speech. A speech is like a human being, basically because speech has the same life as its speaker, it's the voice aspect of every individual. What is most important to Èlàlòrò in translation, therefore, is how the identity of speech is preserved. Translatability of word, speech, or action is not subject to question. Yet, questions are often raised about whether the translation retains its native or source identity or whether it has been subsumed under a different guise.

Translation should not result into losing or replacing the source voice and identity even in Intertranslation when translating from one language to another. This issue of identify loss is not often a problem in Intratranslation because the translator works from the same premises as the source material. Any imposition may be easily exposed. However, the translator in Intertranslation may easily forget that he or she has limitations. He or she may also operate from the perspective that the source material is not available to the reader of his or her work for verification.

There is a clear difference between translation and adaptation. Ola Rotimi's (1971) *The Gods Are Not to Blame* is an adapted work from Sophocles's *Oedipus Rex* (discussed in Chapter 7). In adaptation, concept[s] and basic source material tenets can change from one rendition of the material to another rendition. In an Èlàlọ̀rọ̀ paradigm, a translator must aim at an adequate representation of the original idea. The important aim is to retain the identity of the source text and not to impose extraneous concepts on it.[7]

Any argument that the translator must be free to be original and, therefore, to explore his or her skills and abilities in making the source text come to life in translation will not be justified when the original concept in the source text is compromised. Skills and originality in translation may be measured by how well the translator uses the target language to retain source concepts. To sustain diversity, the choice should be to retain world's plurality and not subsume one identity under another. Many translators have used loan words in order to retain source concepts. Some have used borrowing by directly translating "the meaning parts of the source word to equivalent meaning parts of the target language" (see wysiwyg://39/http://user.chollian.net/~h92002/glossary/glossl.htm).

This is a system of translation that retains the source's voice.

The translator, similar to the Egúngún or Òsanyìn medium, has the responsibility to convey messages of life and death, and the ethic of an Èlàlọ̀rọ̀ translation is to be loyal to the source, even while being creative and innovative with language.

STANDARD VERSUS NON-STANDARD LANGUAGE IN TRANSLATION

One of the issues most important to Èlàlọ̀rọ̀ discourse is that the village voice always be retained. It must not be subsumed under the city's voice or under the urban or the cosmopoli voice. The cosmopoli must not assert or present itself as the main symbol of freedom, and civilization nor the writer or critic show the village or the small town as archaic or outdated, and therefore unfit for cultural recognition or any other type of recognition.

Èlàlọ̀rọ̀ does not reject the idea of social or cultural hierarchy portrayed in works of art as it is rooted in traditional African cosmology such as the Yorùbá's. The hierarchy must not be in terms of which one is more important, and it must not be about which one is less important than the other. Hierarchy can be in terms of function, utility, and experience. It can be about age and its responsibility and functionality. ẹnu àgbà lobìí gbó (kolanut attains maturity in the mouth of the elder) emphasizes experience and wisdom conferred on a person by hold age. An Èlàlọ̀rọ̀ hierarchy is not based on simply asserting that one material is a canon and the other is a non-canon—a type of discourse that eventually creates independent and dependent categories. The dependent one eventually loses its own culture and identity and may end up being kicked out of existence. The Yorùbá seems to put so much emphasis on their traditional adages that Ọmọde gbọ́n, àgbà gbọ́n la fi dá ilẹ̀ Ifẹ̀, "we have used the wisdom of the young person and the wisdom of the elderly person combined to create Ifẹ̀."

Yorùbá mythology regards Ifẹ̀ as the cradle of civilization, where humanity started. A second proverb is perhaps equally important here: B'ọ́wọ́ ọmọdé ò tó pẹpẹ, t'àgbàlagbà o wọ akèrègbè (If a child's hand cannot reach the roof, the elderly person's hand can [also] not enter the gourd). In other words, each person needs help from the other.

Èlàlọ̀rọ̀ does not recognize status or variations of language termed standard and/or non-standard dialect in terms of literary creation or the translatability of source material. Every expression, even when there are many forms of it in a single ethnic or language group as occurs with the Yorùbá, ought to represent itself and retain its own identity.[8] Once a creative piece losses its identity, such as the so-called standardization of dialects, the literary work is no longer original. From this principle, language variation does not determine the greatness of a text.

Among the many reasons for Èlàlọ̀rọ̀'s stand on language standardization is that originality and identity are lost in literary creativity whenever one dialect is sacrificed for another. Some might present an argument that standardization is often used for purposes of maintaining linguistic unity of the written texts in a given ethnic group. Èlàlọ̀rọ̀, however, recognizes and seeks to retain plurality, even in a single ethnic group where every speaker speaks in his or her village or city dialect and where the singer sings in his or her native people's language variation. Among the Yorùbá people, the *orin ọpa* genre is performed in Bunnu dialect of the Yorùbá, *Dadakúàdà* genre, in the Ilorin dialect, and *sákára* genre in the Egba dialect. Èlàlọ̀rọ̀ does not raise the status of the written at the expense of the spoken.

Although the following cultural and community expressions are generally used among the Yorùbá people, there may be variations in dialect of expressions and in community performance. While not trying to translate them into a non-Yorùbá language, I am still interested in asking what meaning would a Yorùbá speaker—other than an Ilorin, an Ibadan, or an Oyo—where the following native variant is common render them? This is perhaps an assignment for readers to seek help from speakers of Yorùbá.

1. "Ọ̀rọ̀ sùnnùkùn, ojú sùnnùkùn la fií wò ó,"
2. "Ohun tí a bá wí f'ógbó l'ogbóọ́ gbó, ohun tá a bá fi f'ógbà l'ogbàá gbà, k'óṣẹ k'óṣẹ ni tìlákòṣẹ,"
3. "Gbohùn lẹ́nuù mi k'óo sọ ọ́ d'orin,"
4. "Akì í síwájú ẹlẹ́ẹ̀ẹ́dẹ́ pèẹ́dẹ́"
5. "Báa ránni níṣẹ́ ẹrú a fi t'ọmọ jẹ́ ẹ,"
7. "Báa lá m'ónìí ọ̀la làá mú,"
8. "Iṣuú p'aradà ó diyán, èlùbọ́ p'aradà ó dàmàlà, àgbàdo paradà ó d'èkọọ yangan,"
9. "Àyínìke, àyínìpadà," (Bó o bá m'àyínìke o ò lè m'àyínìpadà; Ẹni t'ó màyínìke kò lè m'àyínìpadà)
10. "Ìbàdàn lo mọ̀, o ò mọ Lálúpọn,"
11. "Táa bá gúnyán sínú ewé táa bu ọbẹ sèèpo èpa, ẹni máa yó á yó."

TRANSLATION AND THE GLOBAL MARKET

Translation serves the purpose of transporting materials across the globe to both the nearer communities and the far-away communities of the world. Intratranslation is a single activity that would further energize an active world's multiculturalism, where everyone is presented with an opportunity to share in the thoughts and concepts of everyone else without necessarily being physically present in those person's communities. The English would deal with the original concepts of the Yorùbá, the India of the Papua New Guinea and the Japanese would engage with concepts from the Congo. The purpose of translation, therefore, must be to preserve the source's identity in the target language. In other words, in an Èlàlòrò translation, deception and counterfeiting or compromising in any way an original meaning for a commercial reason or to create a stereotypical situation or satisfy a so-called aesthetic purpose is unacceptable.

An Èlàlòrò justification for translation is the introduction of one culture to another. It is the presentation of one thought in dialogue with another thought. It is to allow one social context opportunity to enter into another. However, surrendering a concept or identity of one culture to another culture because a publishing house or a journal demands so is unacceptable. It is unacceptable to surrender a culture in order to satisfy the biases of a target audience. Èlàlòrò principle for translation will not support rendering a culture as a commodity for sale to the highest bidder.

It is often common that writers are forced to give up their cultural idiosyncrasies as a condition for publishing their works or for accepting them into a scholarly forum. In my opinion, the Global Village metaphor of the electronic age is not meant to indicate a place where people suppress unique voices and differing identities. Rather, it is a place to show those voices. It is a place to show how nearer and closer they are to us. Electronic technology has compressed the world and reduced the distance between one corner of our world from another. It has created a village of instant information dissemination rather than a village where all cultures must be compressed into one single culture. Unfortunately, scholarly and critical practices in the West, even when they are done in lines with the so-called postmodernist's pessimism and relativism, are always eager to impose western yardsticks as a one-way critical traffic.

ÈLÀLÒRÒ AND COMPARATIVE PERSPECTIVES

It is interesting looking at where Èlàlòrò agrees or stands at odds with other translation paradigms that already circulate through western scholarship. I will discuss only a few areas where Èlàlòrò agrees or disagrees with translation concepts with which many translation scholars are more conversant.

Perhaps the first important point to make here is that whereas translation theories are important, the translator must not lose sight of the primary responsibility to cultural authenticity or the dignity of the source material. Translation done because of the rush to satisfy a global appetite for what might be called "diversity with one voice" cannot be justified in an Èlàlòrò. For Èlàlòrò, multiculturalism means every culture component has a life and is visible. Thus, translation done for a postmodern "mass culture" basically in order to prove that "minor cultures" have lost their originality into it (a larger conglomeration called "mass culture") is unacceptable to Èlàlòrò.

Emily Apter (2001) in "On Translation in a Global Market" discusses the "problems that arise from the question of a global market in cultural and aesthetic forms" (1). They include an imposition of an internationalized aesthetics, the rush to globalize canons, the identification of some literature as "national literature," and the politics of publishing houses that try to impose their "in-house styles" and socioeconomic publishing standards. Apter thinks that these various issues that confront translation bring about the "questions of cultural commoditization and, thus, ideology" (2). What are the works commonly translated? Who are the authors? Why are they the usual selected authors for translation? Why are some often selected as non-western texts for courses such as global literature? Apter probes: "The most obvious explanation—that these and other writers among the 'happy few' are selected because they are universally acclaimed, excellent writers—obviously fails to fully account for their predominance" (3).

The reason for selecting works for translation ought not be for creating canons of national literature, global literature, or for globalization of ideas. Èlàlòrò translation is more concerned with cross-cultural dialogue intended to introduce people to ideas that are either similar or foreign to their own indigenous concepts. In other words, globalization in Èlàlòrò's perspective is the affirmation and retention of diversified global perspectives.

Many contemporary and older translation theories have useful perspectives that continue to enrich translation traditions and to guide translators. The Frankfurt School, the Prague School, the Geneva School, and the Porter Institute all have introduced excellent translation ideas. Since these ideas are generally similar and because the Porter Institute's contributions are the most recent, I intend to identity a few places where Èlàlòrò translation strategies differ from the Porter's Systemic theory's target-oriented approach to translation (Weissbrod 1998).

Milan Dimic and Marguerite Garstin introduce polysystem theory as follows:

> The polysystem theory was developed initially by Itamar Even-Zohar in the late 1960s and later expanded by Gideon Toury, Zohar Shavit, Shelly Yahalom, and other colleagues and disciples of the Porter institute for Poetics and Semiotics at Tel Aviv University, on the basis of previous

work by the Russian Formalists, including Juri, Tynjanov, Boris M. Ejxenbaum, and Roman Jakobson (Dimic & Garstin 178).

Basically, even though the polysystem theory was developed in the Middle East, it is rooted in European formalist paradigm, with some very important departures.

Weissbrod (1998) insists that the polysystem theory on translation focuses on real world phenomena. She says, "the concepts and distinctions described combine to form a theory and translation, whose main justification is in that it does not force itself on reality" (4).

Thus, perhaps the greatest similarity between Èlàlòrò and the polysystem approach is in the the claim that latter allows different cultures their unique voices, and it recognizes that translation cannot be a one-way traffic jacket. Here again is Weissbrod:

> The assumption underlying them is that translation is conceived differently in different cultures and in different periods. Thus it is not impossible that what is considered a "good translation" under certain circumstances would not be considered good, or even a translation at all, under other circumstances in a different culture or at a different time (4-5).

Another similarity Èlàlòrò shares with the polysystem approach is in their provision that source languages need to be given preference by the target languages. As intriguing as these similarities are, Èlàlòrò translation principles disagree with areas of the polysystemic approach that contradict its "differences" principle.

The polysystem theory has been described as "the model of the system" (Dimic & Garstin 179). Every work is a part of "a network of relations that obtain between texts . . . they both 'belong to' and 'constitute' one whole, usually labeled 'literature'" (Even-Zohar 1986, 463, as quoted in Dimic & Garstin 180). Weissbrod explains further that Even-Zohar (1990) views literature as a system of systems "which can be described by a series of oppositions: between the <u>center</u> (which dictates norms and models to the entire polysystem) and the <u>periphery</u>, between the <u>canonized</u> system (which usually occupies the center of the polysystem) and the <u>non-canonized</u>, between the systems of adult's and children's literature, between translated and non-translated literature" (3).

The polysystem, therefore, emphasizes independent versus dependent traditions, even while it claims that every component of the system is linked. By classifying one literature as canon or center and others as peripheral—even if doing so is intended to attract attention to the periphery (Dimic & Garstin 184)—it has not given the so-called periphery any genuine independence. Èlàlòrò principles do not favor a hierarchical set up that shows one aspect (e.g., genre, category, author) of literature as central and the other one as dependent. The polysystemic theory favors the standard versus non-standard literary classification, even as it tries to give voice to the periphery.

Here are other areas where the polysystem approach is at odds with Èlàlọrọ̀:

- Polysystem's provisions of norms (otherwise "do"s and "don't"s), which "dictate" the selection of texts to be translated
- Norms that allows "adjusting the translated text to the system receiving it" (Weis 4)
- Translations are based on the so-called canon languages—then, the idea of a "global" is "dangerous" and meaningless to the smaller communities who all deserve recognition.
- The creation of a number of heuristic constructs such as mode, repertoire, canonized and non-canonized texts, primary and secondary systems, periphery, and center (Dimic & Garstin 180). Even where hierarchy may not be the problem, the meaning given to each part of the system is problematic.
- The connotation that a translation can be "alien" (Dimic & Garstin 183); this terminology does not promote mutual respect for the source materials.

Èlàlọrọ̀, as this chapter discusses, favors the retention of the identity of the source material in every process, because its basic objective for translation is for multicultural or cross-cultural interaction. Contemporary globalization forces must not be allowed to suppress small town or village voices under the city's voices and mass culture tradition must not be allowed to commoditize translation.

Èlàlọrọ̀'s translation principle reiterates the need to involve indigenous or source culture in theorizing about translation. Every translator, therefore, should look to use community values and ideas from their original materials' native sources. If followed with clarify, translation can be used in the New World societies, such as the Americas, for greater diversity and multicultural purposes.

3 Some Thoughts on Traditional Hausa Aesthetics and Arabic Influence on Yorùbá and Hausa Written Traditions in Nigeria

It will be exciting to briefly discuss how some Hausa writers explore traditional Hausa oral aesthetics in their written poetry. *Rubutaciyar waka* is the Hausa name for written poetry. The book *Wakokin Hikima* (Yahaya 1979) is a very interesting collection of 20 Hausa poems. With the exception of Adamu Jingau and Alhaji Kabir Inuwa Magoga, born in Sakkwato and Benue-Plateau areas respectively, all of the other poets who contributed to this book are indigenes of Kano, an ancient Muslim city in Nigeria. The writers are all Muslims and are writing both from their perspectives as Muslims and from their backgrounds in communities where traditional oral performances take active place in cultural and educational expressions. From the book's title, meaning "Songs of Wisdom," the poets assume the name of "wisdom poets," discussing what they consider their own and their community's ethics with their readers and performers. It is often the folktales that teach moral lessons, and within the folktales, songs and drama performances reinforce community expectations for good behavior. These Hausa poets have explored the oral literary aesthetics in their written poems for their people.

Although this is an anthology of written poetry that definitely imitates some Western and Eastern traditions (having been written in the Roman script and adopted some Arabic poetry styles, especially in the use of rhyming in their poems), the poets prefer to call their poetry "songs" in agreement with the traditional African characteristic of poetry. African oral poetry is not composed in verse or lines but according to breaths, and a sentence or utterance can be as long as the oral poet can hold his or her breath. This will almost always be longer than what usually occupies a single line in European poetry. *Wakokin Hikima* (Yahaya 1979) definitely shows some of these characteristics. Often times, it seems to be a struggle for the poets to cast their songs in lines, as they demonstrate their skills of writing in the Roman script. These poets received colonial *boko* education in addition to their Islamic traditional upbringing, and their writing in the Roman script instead of the Arabic script, demonstrates the success of colonial education in Northern Nigeria. The majority of those who constitute the audience of this type of writing are mainly young children in colonial schools (i.e., primary and post-primary institutions sponsored by colonial government, later inherited after Nigerian Independence from Britain by local, state, and federal governments of Nigeria). The *boko* or the Roman script writing has thus continued its significance among the Hausa populace as these young children become adults and began work in local administration or continue their education at post-secondary levels.

The one thing they do not have to struggle to show is the traditional aesthetic of wisdom-teaching, as they may prefer to call it. In analyzing some of these poems, it is crucial to further explain elements of Hausa poetics that reveal creativity. Hausa rhetorical and literary corpuses involve a process of cultural arrangement that makes every composer conscious of two important requirements: (1) an affirmation of societal truth even when vigorously reexamining it and (2) an avowal of the consequence for deviance from it. Although the poetics is a community-wide cultural perspective, every composer, critic, and consumer of art often consciously involve these binary yardsticks for ensuring that the society continues to project acceptable ethics, truths, and other forms of community morality. In other words, literature is a platform for creative talent, community survival, and cultural strength. Obviously, postmodern literary ideologues with pessimistic society values who often reject any idea of an affirmed truth would have a problem understanding the Hausa composer's eagerness to satisfy his community poetics. The following is how the Hausa state an important oral theory:

> Wanda bai ji bari ba
>   Ya ji oho

> Whoever wouldn't hear "stop it"
>   Would hear "serves you right"

There is obviously some problem in rendering the Hausa cultural theory into English. "Stop it," (or cease doing it) and "serves you right" do not totally translate "bari" and "oho," respectively. The two words are like cause and effect in Hausa rhetorical expressions. The critics of Hausa literature need to understand this dual framework to interpret Hausa literary compositions.

To explain what Hausa poetics is not, perhaps readers should remember the structuralist and post-structuralist Derida. While interpreting and criticizing a text, he often adopts a strategy of a "double mode of reading," trying to show a lack of synthesis between a text and the philosophy it claims to represent. Jonathan Culler (1979) puts this better when he says that Derida is always as follows:

> Attentive to the ways in which texts implicitly criticize and undermine the philosophies in which they are implicated, he carries on a double

mode of reading, showing the text to be woven from different strands which can never result in a synthesis but continually displace one another. (*Structuralism and Since* 155)

While analyzing language and structure of a text, Derida concentrates strongly on the text's internal effect. As he discusses Edmund Husserl's views about the origin of geometry in his *L'Origine de la gãometrie* (1962), Derida says that language and writing, which Husserl claims will make geometry an ideal subject, contain within them problems they are meant to be solved (157). Furthermore, In *Of Grammatology*, Derida says that speech also possesses characteristics of writing, and he discusses the possibility of "inverting the hierarchy" and "orienting a theory of language not on speech but on a generalized writing" (158). Derida's constant effort at deconstructing the text would not play well in the Hausa "Bari" and "Oho" traditions, not because there may be no paradox or contradictions inherent in the life of a composer or even in his or her text, but because the exercise of "deconstruction" must not be seen as jeopardizing community ethics, its layers of truth, its aspirations, and other cultural orientations. There are challenges all the time to community values and sometimes paradigms are cast and recast to accommodate new views or developments. However, "good literature" is that which creates a good person and enhances a useful community. It is not necessarily a literature that shifts the community or its people from the base of its values of goodness and cultural harmony. Perhaps this view is captured better by Jaigbade Alao[1] in an Ilorin oral song:

Awi talaiwi won ni ile aye nyi
Ile aye o yi sibikankan
Ibi ojo n yo ni tin yo
Ibi orun ti n wo ni tin wo
Ile aye o yi sibi kankan
Awon enia inure ninpawada

We had only spoken a little when they interrupted
    saying that the world is changing
The world isn't changing to anywhere/anything
The day rises where it rises
The sun sets where it sets
The world isn't changing to anywhere/anything
Only people occupants are changing their behaviors!

Among other things, Alao insists that "good" and "bad" have recognizable yardsticks, and no one needs another person to remind him or her that the two categories happen because of his or her actions. The song also reinforces the society's belief that truth is constant and that while human beings continue to change to satisfy their selfish interests, nothing would change about what is humane or charitable and what is inhumane or uncharitable behaviors.

The poetics of "Bari" and "Oho," while not asking for Derida's "double mode of reading," allows both the poet and his or her critics to protect the society from "uncultural" and "unethical" behaviors. The Hausa writer is like the oral performer who is a custodian of the humane cultural behavior and who constantly defines the society from the rhetoric of inclusion and wisdom of community and individual responsibility. Spider (called *Gizo*), trickster character in Hausa folktales, did not farm; Spider stole from other's farms, Spider was punished, condemned to remain naked forever. However, in instances where Spider escapes punishment, the oral singer or writer searches the cultural upheavals and locates the failure from the context of societal reality. *Bari* includes affirmation of value preoccupations of society; cultural norms; and challenges of its abuses, miscalculations, or mismanagement as they may occur. "Wanda bai ji bari ba" also includes those who the Blindman in "Makaho Mai Fitila"[2] claims to have no eyes. Eyes not just for seeing paths to trek on, but for seeing what is beautiful and what is ugly, the *kyau* and *marakyau* of life. Constantly, the poetics of "society must survive," and society is a platform for growth. To identify with the "Bari" and "Oho" of society is to defend society's laws, protect its sanity, and uphold its pride. With every new concept, theory, and life challenges are prod into and graded according to society's need for growth, peace, and survival. Basically, this agrees with the Èlàlòrò critical discourse theory (Na'Allah 2000), which provides that literary dialectics, abstract or concrete, must meet the test of the ever important society. The *Bari* concept also implies that the writer or artist has a responsibility to warn the society against destructive tendencies, to relieve people of their fears, to educate them, to entertain them, and to engage them in fruitful processes of society's regeneration and rebirth. "Bari" and "oho" go together; the writer's work constantly shows the repercussion of abandoning the path of good, the ways of society's socio-cultural growth.

Basically, all the Hikima poets are "bari" and "oho" poets. Alhaji Rabi'u Ahmed (1986), in his "Satura Ita Ce Mutum" (meaning human beings are cloths) discusses what he calls "son zuciya," love of one's self (or of one's heart), and writes:

Bayan haka nan ina yin kira
Ga 'ya 'yan musulmi ina so su lura
Su dinga tunani a kan bin nasara
Irin sa tufafinsu du ku bura,
    Ku watsad da shi du ga baki daya (*Wakokin Hikima*, 38)[3]

Now, I'm appealing
To all Muslims, I want them to pay attention
To be careful chasing after success

(It's) Like putting on their cloths only to blow them off
    And spreading them all at once

It is not uncommon for people of Kano, a community of nearly 100% Muslim population, to refer to anything meant for the populace as things meant for Muslims. The cloth mentioned above is a metaphor for success, and if you spread it out, and show excessive love for big gowns simply because you have the money to purchase it, you can have the cloths tripping you or impeding your movement. In other words, love of *zuciya* (chasing after your own heart) may result in a person making senseless and inordinate choices. In other lines of the poem, Ahmed (1986) says,

Kun sanya wando wai na jan kasa,
Fadin sama ya fi ai kalmasa,
Riga a kirji tana can bisa,
Ba ta da girman da za ta isa,
    Ta kare mutuncin jiki bai daya. (38)

You put on trousers, the type that drag all dirt from the ground
Sky is wider than to attempt reaching all its sides
Heading for the top to find their cloths
No height to reach there,
    It ends human value, not one (value) left!

The metaphor of trousers, of its oversize measures, "Sky is wider than to attempt to reach all its sides," and of the recklessness of surpassing all society's moderation as represented in this poem, are very striking. Yet, another stanza of the poem states:

Ya jama'a kar mu yarda mu bi su,
A Kan ra'ayinsu na son zuciyarsu,
Sai dai mu yo addu'a bisa kansu,
Allah ya shirye su dukkaninsu,
    Ya sa su dawo biyar shiriya. (Ahmed 1986, 39)

All you people, we musn't let ourselves imitate them,
Their attitude of their love for their personal hearts,
We must pray for them,
God, help all of them,
    He should lead them to return to moderation!

The poet is mobilizing for a solution in which every member of the community would participate in achieving a solution for any crisis, "We must pray for them," he says. There is no questioning the fact that this poet has been influenced by the Islamic religion in the manner in which he is sermonizing.

However, throughout the lengthy poem, the philosopy of "Bari" and "Oho" reveals his preocupation, as he is eager to protect the societal values of decency amd moderation and to make every member of the community his or her brother's and sister's keeper. The poem, however, has two parts, and the second part is addressed to women, having used the first part for male metaphor. He calls the second part, "siket" a word borrowed from the English "skirt." Continuing on the topic of "love of heart" or selfishness, the poet portrays "skirt" as an expensive foreign taste, yet incapable of covering the entire woman's body. Ahmed (1986) says to the woman in Skirt:

Kin fita tsarin mutum na kirki,
    Dukkan kazanta tana wajenki.

Kai ya fi kyau ma ki dau karanki,
    Ki bar gari don mu bar ganinki.

Domin mutuncinmu ya fi naki,
    Sa satura yai daban da naki.

Kin yi daban je ki naki aiki,
    Kar ki dawo gummu ba mu sonki.

Kunya dai tai min tsarin ganinki,
    Jakar birnin kama da doki.

Du mace mai gaskiya da aiki,
    Babu ruwanta da yin kamarki.

Matan Kirki suna ga daki,
    Babu ruwanta da yin kamarki. (42)

You have opted out of a decent personality,
    All dirts are now garthered around you.

It is better surely for you,
    Leave town, so we stop seeing you.

Because our respect for values are greater than yours,
    We use our cloths different from yours.

You've done worse, and go ahead with your own work
    Don't return to us becuase we don't really want you.

Shame, indeed, is so little with you,
    See a woman looking as if she's a doll.

All women truthful to their work,
>Would never aspire to be like you.

Decent women at home,
>Would never aspire to be like you.

This second part is rather harsh on the "westernized woman." Ahmed (1986) seems to want to banish her from the community, and seems to be saying, "Please leave; don't pollute other women." Ahmed does not work as hard for the woman's cultural rehabilitation as he does for the man, and he almost wants to throw away the baby with the bath water. He's more concerned with other women not taking after "the westernized woman" as we see in the following stanza,

Du mace mai gaskiya da aiki
>Babu ruwanta da yin kamarki. (42)

All women who are honest at work,
>Would never aspire to be like you.

Once towards the end of the poem, Ahmed (1986) asks the westernized woman to "roki Allah ya taimake ki" (ask God to help you)!

We can see in the way that each line of the Hausa poem ends that the poet is also interested in the beauty of the lines such as what a rhyme scheme may present. Most of the lines in the first part end with the vowel /a/ as in la, ya, ra, na, sa, ka, etc, whereas every line in the second part ends in /i/, and in the word "ki," The poet is no doubt conscious of gender pronoun in Hausa and has reflected them in ending lines of the relevant part. The Hausa "Ka" is a masculine pronoun (sometime possessive marker), and "Ki" is feminine.

Most line arrangements resemble the arrangements prevalent in many *Ajami* poems, and perhaps they are imitation of Arabic or Islamic poems. Ahmed offers Islamic prayers at the beginning of his poem. He ends his poem with his signature, "Sunan Mawaki a tambayarki,/ Rabi'u AMSA kawai in ba ki." This reads, "The poet's name if anyone asks you/ Rabi'u TAKE IT let me offer you" (1986, 42)

Another poem I like to discuss is titled, "Wakar kishi" (the songs about jealousy) by Rukayyatu Sabuwa Nasir Adakawa (1986). The poet's starting and ending formulas are similar to Rabi'u's. She discusses the evils of jealousy and mobilizes her people, especially women, against jealousy. Adakawa says in one of the stanzas:

'Ya 'uwana kun ga kishi,
Bai da amfani a bar shi,
Shin ko kun san ma'anarshi?

Hada ma son kai da kyashi,
    Da rashin bin gaskiya. (61)

My mother's children, take note of jealousy,
It has no use whatsoever,
Do you actually know its meaning?
Add for the Selfish a deep sadness,
    And the refusal to follow truth.

"My mother's children" is like saying "folks," and this is often used to show deep personal involvement on the issue being addressed. Adakawa (1986) seems to be saying that jealousy blinds one's eyes from being truthful about the other person, and it also causes tension. In another stanza,

To dukkan ko tarayya,
In ana so gaskiya,
Sai a nisanta kiyayya,
A cikinta a daura niyya,
    Tattalin bin gaskiya. (62)

Now to all people,
If we want to stick to truth,
We must abandaon jealousy,
We must bring intention,
    To follow truth always.

At one point, Adakawa (1986) addresses women directly on the issue of jealousy in a polygamous home. Polygamy is common among Muslims in Nigeria and also has strong presence among traditional African religion followers. The poet says:

Ya 'yan 'uwana mata
A aje kishi a huta,
Kun ga sa kai ya fi bauta,
Wahala zakkar jiki ta,
Wohoho dajageniya!

Lokaci ya yi garemu,
Da za mu lura da kammu,
Don mu nemi abin fa kammu,
Mu bar bata lokacimmu,
    Ai ga kishin kishiya.

Shi fa kishi wahala ne,
Kuma kullum fargaba ne,

Kuma koma baya ne,
'Yan 'uwa da za a gane,
   'Yar'uwa ce kishiya. (63)

All you my mother's children, women,
We should put down jealousy and have a peace of mind
You know to put one's head forward is better than to bow one's head
Suffering put on one's body,
   Wohoho dajageniya!

The time is here with us,
To take good care of ourselves,
So that we can search to better ourselves,
We should stop wasting our time,
   jealous of the co-wife.

Jealousy is definitely suffering,
And every day it is tension,
And it is backwardness,
My mother's children if you'll understand,
   The co-wife is also your mother's child.

Clearly, Adakawa (1986) is asking everyone, especially women, to avoid jealousy. The most interesting aspect of the poem is the poet's solution to jealousy in polygamy households. She calls it suffering, tension, and backwardness, and she would want women to choose peace and harmony instead of tension. Perhaps, she'll want them to consider their choices before going into polygamy. The poet carefully chooses what sound ends her lines. Stanzas present similarly ending lines, with very minor deviation in a few of the last lines of some stanzas. *Wohoho Dajageniya*, is an exclamation which is perhaps like saying "You'll find yourself in real trouble!"

I cannot discuss all the poems in *Wakokin Hikima* in this type of paper. However, they all address sociopolitical, cultural, and religious issues and show poetry not only as a form to express poetic beauty, but also as a form to discuss community issues and mobilize people for socio-cultural causes. Other poems in the book include "The changing times" by Alhaji Isa Hashim, "The Hunting Gun of Talla," by Muahammadu Zayyanu, and "War with Ignorance" by Hauwa Gwaram Umaru. At the back cover of *Wakokin Hikima* is a short translation of a promotion blurb, the only English piece in the entire book, originally written in Hausa on the same cover:

> *Wakokin Hikima* contains twenty outstanding poems by members if the Hikima kulob, Kano. The poems which cover a wide range of metres, rhyme schemes and topics, are representative of the best contemporary poetry being written in Hausa. (Ahmed 1986, back cover)

Traditional Hausa Aesthetics and Arabic Influence 37

It is interesting that the poets here all belong to a poetry club. This reflects popular community activities among the Kano people: the farmer's club, the traders club, the tailor's club, etc. More interesting, however, is another fact that is not stated in the blurb but included in the editor's Opening Notes, "Bayani Daga Edita:"

> Baya haka, masu sauranron shirye-shiryen gidan rediyon N.B.C. na Kano sun sha jin wakokin wandansu mutane wadsnda Allah ya yi wa baiwa da ilmin wallafar wakoki a filin da aka ba kungiyar mawakan nan mai suna Hikima Kulob. (Ahmed 1986, 3)

After this, those who listen to N.B.C. Kano Radio programs must have heard poems by those people whom God has talented with skills of the creative art, in the time alloted to the poetry club called the Hikima Klob.

It is very significant that these Hausa poets place emphasis on oral rendition of their written poetry by carrying their poems to the people through frequent radio performances. The electronic media helps to ensure that African writers may continue to reach their people by transmitting their contemporary written work into the oral form.

HAUSA WRITTEN TRADITIONS IN NIGERIA

Writing experience in Africa, especially in what is now called Nigeria, preceded Western colonization and education. Indeed, it preceded any contact with Europe or the Americas by Nigerians. There is a Yorùbá saying, *N kan to wa lehin efa o ju eje lo*, literally, "beyond the count of six there is more than just the count of seven." This philosophy is the bedrock of humility among many cultural Yorùbá. It made many Yorùbá people open minded whenever they had contact with other Africans and with European missionaries and colonialists in the 19th century. This philosophy encourages persistent curiosity, which, for example, led to the embracing of foreigners whenever they entered Africa, in an effort to get to know them better, thus becoming what might be termed a knowledge of those numbers that come after their own number six. The question about writing system can be explained with this metaphor: for every number six, there is a number seven and more! Even though a five is less than a six, the five comes before the six and thus is older than the six, just as a few other numbers also come before, and are older than five.

Many indigenous African cultures have writing systems that are much older than the Roman script. However, most African scripts are not put into the kind of extensive uses of today's Roman script. Maulana Kurenga (1993) perhaps summarizes well this idea when he says:

[T]here were many scripts in Africa, including the three scripts of ancient Egypt—hieroglyphic, hieratic, and demotic; the Meroitic and Coptic scripts of Nubia; the Amharic, Sabean and G'eez scripts of Ethiopia; the Berber and Carthaginian scripts of North Africa; the Arabic script of North, Northeastern and Western Africa; the Swahili Perso-Arabic script of East Coast of Africa; the Nsibidi script of Nigeria; the Mende script of Mali; the Toma and Vai script of Liberia; and the Mum script of Cameroun. . . . This long list clearly exceeds the two main scripts of Europe, Greek and Roman. However, these scripts do not always have abundant historical literatures of either a given people or larger areas of the continent. (75)

Albert Gérard (1990) refers to the denial often made by European primitivists whenever issues of indigenous African writing systems are raised as the White man's "peerless pretentiousness." He adds:

In historical fact, important segments of sub-Saharan Africa had been introduced to writing and to written literature long before the first white man—whether exploiter or philanthropist—reached her shores. In fact, one part at least of the continent had produced written works in its own languages even before the earliest literatures appeared in the Celtic and Germanic languages of Western Europe. This was Ethiopia, which was invaded, at the beginning of the Christian era, by Semitic tribes from Southern Arabia. They took their own script with them, which was gradually adapted for the transcription of the local, Ethiopic, tongue. This is known as Ge'ez, and for several centuries it remained the sole medium for religious thought, culture, and literary writing. Indeed, this sacred language is still used by conservative writers, mainly for the composition of hymns, theological treatises, and other devotional works. The whole of Ge'ez literature has always been essentially religious and didactic in inspiration. (47)

Whereas the debate about the true nature of the connection between Southern Arabia and Ethiopia might be better handled in another paper, it is pertinent to reiterate here that available evidence continues to clearly establish that writing systems developed in Africa much earlier than it did in Western Europe.

The use of the Arabic script in Nigeria, especially among the Hausa and Yorùbá language groups (the script is called *Ajami*), preceded the use of Roman writing in Nigeria by about ten centuries. For many Hausa and Yorùbá communities, the Arab, the Berbers, and the Malians (mainly Muslims) brought Arabic as an already established "standardized" system of writing. They taught the local indigenous population how to advance this writing system in their own languages. In this chapter, I shall be discussing how Hausa and Yorùbá people use the Arabic script in their languages and why such a system is still the most viable to those people who still use it in Nigeria. I will also discuss the involvement of the oral form in writing traditions of Ilorin, a multilingual, multiethnic community in Nigeria. Furthermore, I shall examine some Hausa written poems within the paradigm of Hausa traditional literary discourse.

BRITISH COLONIAL REGIME AND ITS INFLUENCE ON INDIGENOUS WRITING SYSTEM IN NIGERIA

The British colonial administration forced Northern Nigerian institutions to abandon the Arabic system in favor of the Roman/English writing system. It vigorously pursued inaugurating the Roman writing system by embarking on massive campaign throughout Northern Nigeria through establishing Roman script publication bureaus, instituting creative writing contests, and setting up roman script newspapers. Yet, up until the 21st century, the Arabic writing system has not lost its viability in Nigeria. Books, journals, and newspapers are still being published in Arabic script called the *Ajami*. Personal letters are still being written among many Nigerians who use the Arabic script. Anytime the Nigerian state and federal governments embark on grassroots campaigns or mobilization for elections, immunization, etc., especially in northern part of the country, they use the Arabic writing system in order to reach most parts of Northern Nigeria. Furthermore, the Nigerian national currency still contains *Ajami* writing to indicate the denomination of each currency in the Hausa language.

THE INDIGENOUS WRITING IN HAUSA AND YORÙBÁ

We have to discuss further the issue of indigenous writing traditions in Nigerian. Two writing systems, Roman and Arabic, always come to mind whenever people discuss languages in Africa. The impression has always been that Africans, especially in sub-Sahara Africa, had no conception of writing until their contact with Western and Arabic cultures. Apart from the Egyptian hieroglyphs, an ancient writing system that predated the Roman writing system, and the other ones already named above by Karenga (1993), there is more history to tell about indigenous writing in Africa. Before the introduction of Arabic script, writing among the Hausa and the Yorùbá was widely practiced in the form of indigenous symbols for counting (i.e., numbers and patterns on domestic utensils and buildings). Some traditional games like the Yorùbá *Ayo* involve some writing in the form of strokes or lines used to keep record of plays, winnings, and losses. Perhaps major areas where writing is adopted in sub-Saharan African indigenous communities are in healing and religious circles. The herbalist or medicinal people make strokes on covering leaves, or calabashes, to indicate doses. The *boka*, traditional healers among the Hausa, would make some strikes to remind their clients about how many times some herbs must be taken and how much of the contents are to be consumed at a particular time. Although this is not an intensive use, it clearly indicates that the people already have a concept of writing and do minimally explore it for communication.

Perhaps *Ifá* is the most notable religious tradition among the Yorùbá to which writing is central. The *Ifá* priest has the *Opele* and makes some vertical strikes on the divination sand, interpreting the relevant message to the client. Wande Abimbola, in *Ifá Divination Poetry* (1977), describes the writing processes of the *Ifá* priest thus:

> The sacred powder of divination is kept inside a carved *Ifá* tray and placed in front of the diviner who keeps the sixteen palm-nuts inside one of his palms and tries to take them all at a single stroke with his other palm. If the two palm-nuts remain in his palm, he makes one vertical mark on the powder of divination. If one palm-nut remains, he makes two marks below the first mark. But if he succeeds in taking all the palm-nuts at once so that none remain in his palm, he will make no marks at all. In the same way, if more than two palm-nuts remain inside his palm, he will not make any marks on the powder of divination. The *Ifá* priest must make such marks four times on the right and four times on the left. The result will give him the signature of an *Odu* (chapter or category of *Ifá* literary corpus). (5)

A client well-informed about Ifá divination may be able to read these symbols him or herself. The *Ifá* written symbols, called *odu*, are the representation of *Ifá*'s speech. Idowu Olokun (n.d.) explains in his pamphlet, *Imole-Aye*:

> Odu Ifá ni amin isoro *Ifá*, ti o ba awon irumole kookan sokale lati wa da ile aye, olukaluku lo ni oruko tire, oruko won si yato sira won gege bi amin won ti se ri sira won. Bi mo ti so saaju Ejiogbe lo se etutu fun awon agba ati omo awo lode orun. Oun naa lo si koko dode aye. (8)

> Odu *Ifá* is the representation of *Ifá*'s speech, that descended with each deity to create the universe. Each of these symbols has its own name, different from one another just as the symbols themselves contain elements of differences. As I said before, Ejiogbe performed some rituals for both old and young of the deity at the heaven, and it is he [Ejiogbe] that first arrived here on earth. (English translation mine)

Olokun (n.d.) indicates that the original *Ifá* speech is oral, and that it is represented by the written form in the *Odu Ifá* symbols. There are altogether 256 patterns of these written symbols, and each has 600 poems attached to it (Abimbola 1977, 6). Although these symbols, are quite uncomplicated,

Traditional Hausa Aesthetics and Arabic Influence 41

as we can see below, they show that writing was not a foreign concept to the Yorùbá. This writing has some spiritual significance to it and, thus, commands some reverence. As is evidenced in Olokun's (n.d.) reproduction of *Odù Ifá*, the symbols are sometimes in the form of round marks or semi-circles which represent the palm nuts. Sometime, it can also be vertical (Abimbola 1977, 5–6). The number and distribution of each [o] symbol determines the name, meaning, and message encoded in each passage:

·Odi Meji	·Oturupon Meji	Owoarin Meji	Okanran Meji
·o·······o	o····o······o····o	o···o······o···o	o···o······o···o
oo·····oo	o····o······o····o	o···o······o···o	o···o······o···o
oo·····oo	o·············o	·o············o	o···o······o···o
·o·······o	o····o······o····o	·o············o	···o············o
Obara Meji	·Otura Meji	Ejiogbe	·Ogunda Meji
···o·············o	···o············o	o·········o	·o············o
o···o······o····o	o····o······o····o	·o············o	·o············o
o···o······o····o	···o············o	··o············o	·o············o
o···o······o····o	···o············o	··o············o	o··o·····o···o·
Oyekun Meji	·····Osa Meji	····Iweri Meji	Ose Meji
o····o······o····o	o····o······o····o	o····o······o····o	o·············o
o····o······o····o	···o············o	···o············o	o···o······o···o
o····o······o····o	···o············o	···o············o	···o············o
o····o······o····o	···o············o	o····o·······o····o·	o···o······o···o
			··
'Eka Meji	·Ofun Meji	Irete Meji	Irosun Meji
o····o······o····o	o····o······o····o	···o········o	···o············o
···o············o	···o············o	····o	···o············o
o····o······o····o	···o············o	o····o······o····o	o···o······o····o
o····o······o····o	···o············o	····o········o	o···o······o····o

Awon Amin Akoko Fun Imole Aye (The first 16 symbols in Yorùbá cosmology) (copied from *Imole-Aye*, [Olokun n.d.,.15])

The Opele divinatory chain used by Babalawo (*Ifá* priest) during divination has symbols [o] around it signifying half-nuts. According to Abimbola (1977), "If the chain is made of metal, the half-nuts are also made of metal in such a way that they look like the Opele half-nuts" (Olokun n.d., 6). The [o] symbol is an imitation of the shape of palmnuts. Abimbola (1977) explains that the palmnut is highly sacred to the *Ifá* (4–5). The following is how they appear as vertical written symbols:

Odi Meji	Oturupon Meji	Owoarin Meji	Okanran Meji
·|·················|	|···|········|····|	|····|········|···|	|····|········|····|
|···|················|···|	|···|········|····|	|····|········|···|	|····|········|····|
|···|················|···|	···|················|	··|················|·	|····|········|····|
··|····················|	|···|········|····|	··|················|·	···|··············|

The Babalawo prints these marks on the divination powder called *Ìyèrè Òsùn*. Abimbola (1977) states that "Since both the divining chain and the printed marks are read from right to left, like Arabic, the patterns on the right-hand side are considered basic and it is upon them that the 16 generic names are based" (16). Once again, the concept of writing is not new to the Yorùbá culture.

I strongly feel Walter Ong's (1982) definition of a primary oral culture must be revisited and recast in a way that truly represents the realities of people who live there. While defining what he calls primary oral culture, Ong says:

> Fully literate persons can only with great difficulty imagine what a primary oral culture is like, that is, a culture with no knowledge whatsoever of writing or even of the possibility of writing. Try to imagine a culture where no one has ever 'looked up' anything. In a primary oral culture, the expression 'to look up something' is an empty phrase: it would have no conceivable meaning. (31)

Among the Yorùbá oral communities, the expression to 'look up something' is not empty, for the *Ifá* priest always 'looks up' his scripted *odu Ifá* for answers to the questions asked by his clients, just as 'literate persons' would check the dictionary for meaning of words and concepts.

Still, it would not be out of place to call this kind of Yorùbá community an oral culture because of the limitations of writing. I prefer to call it an active oral society, as opposed to the passive oral society of the contemporary western world (Na'Allah 1999, 12–4). I have also argued that despite colonial and post-colonial influences on contemporary Yorùbá, including the possibility that some *Ifá* priests probably speak English and acquire the ability to write in the Roman script, the original writing culture of the *Ifá* divination has been retained.

ARABIC EDUCATION AND SCHOLARSHIPS IN NIGERIA

Writing about Arabic literary tradition in Nigeria, John Hunwick (1977) has the following to say:

> The use of Arabic as a literary and scholarly language has a historical depth of over five centuries and shows no sign of diminishing. The ratio of Muslims to non-Muslims in Nigeria continues to increase and hence education in Arabic and Arabic writing skills are likely to expand. While the old genres of Islamic writing (fiqh, tawhid, hadith, tasawwuf, etc.) will not disappear, there is likely to be more writing that is discursive in nature rather than bound to texts of the past. (219)

Hunwick is differentiating between Arabic literary tradition and the actual use of Arabic letters for writing local languages in Nigeria. From all indications, the latter is older than the huge literary tradition that has now taken firm root in Nigeria, which, surprisingly, is hardly mentioned when contemporary Nigerian education system is discussed. Nigerian writers of the English language are equally guilty because it was only in 1993 before the Association of Nigerian Authors brought its annual meeting to Ilorin,[4] and adopted as conference theme Arabic Writing in Nigeria. Until this time, Arabic literature or any topic related to it was never chosen as a theme of the association's annual meetings. The fact is that both the Arabic writing system and indigenous literature in Arabic language are about seven centuries older than the Roman writing system or literature written in English in Nigeria.

The early development of the Arabic script for Nigerian languages shows that people were more anxious about getting their languages into extensive writing forms than they were about learning to write in a new language. The history of writing in Arabic letters, according to Hunwick (1997), "extends over a period close to 800 years in the Nigerian region," starting from the North Eastern part of Nigeria, called the Kanem Borno. Abu Ishaq Ibrahim al-Kanemi was noted as a pioneer writer of grammar and poetry in Borno (210). In the 15th century, in many other regions of the present day Northern Nigeria (especially Katsina, Kano, and later in areas around Ilorin), merchants and teachers from Mali settled and introduced Arabic education and scholarship (210; Na'Allah 1985). According to Hunwick, a "revolution in Arabic-Islamic writing" in Nigeria came about the late 18th century and early 19th century, championed by Uthman Dan Fodio. Between Dan Fodio, his son, and his brother, "they produced over 300 works in prose and verse as well as dozens of occasional poems" (212) in Fulfude, Hausa, and Arabic. Some of the works are then translated from one language to the other (212), and translation became as important to the writer as original writings. Writers of Arabic script confronted all sorts of issues relating to translation and made choices similar to those often discussed today by translators. By the 19th and 20th centuries, Arabic writing culture had spread throughout the major areas of the present day Northern and Southwestern Nigeria. Again, Hunwick (1977) puts this better:

> Zaria emerged as a teaching center with an important school led by 'Umar Al-Wali and his descendants. Teaching institutions were established in Bauchi and Bida as well as Lokoja on the confluence of Niger and Benue. Each of these has produced a number of minor scholar-authors. Scholars of Nupe origin have tended to move on to bigger centers, either northwards to Zaria or Kano, or southwards to Ilorin, a city established as the most southerly emirate of the Sokoto Caliphate in the 1830s. (212)

Scholars have not done sufficient research on the use of Arabic script in Nigeria or on how Arabic and Islamic writings and culture have impacted the development of indigenous language writing and modern African literature. Often, people have dismissed this rich area as insignificant. Perhaps *The Companion to African Literature* (2000) sums up this issue more clearly:

> Islam has been a significant factor in the African imagination but there has been a temptation to sideline its impact on anglophone literature which may derive from the fact that writers from Islamic areas have written more in Arabic and their indigenous languages than in English. Shehu Usman bn. Fodio, the architect of the *Jihad* in Nigeria, for example, is reputed to have composed about 480 poems in Arabic, Fulfude, and Hausa, in addition to writing several books in Arabic. (249)

Razaq D. Abubakre and Stefan Reichmuth (1977), in their comprehensive and fine historico-cultural analyses of the nature and state of Arabic writings in Southwestern Nigeria, "Arabic Writing Between Global and Local Culture: Scholars and Poets in Yorùbáland (Southwestern Nigeria)," review issues they referred to as "cultural diversity" and "religious plurality" among the Yorùbá. They touch on how Christianity and missionary education contributed to "the flourishing of anglophone literature in southern Nigeria" (184). They discuss the development of Arabic writing in Southwestern Nigeria and refer to it as the "senior partner in this coexistence in Yorùbá nation" (185). In other words, even among the Yorùbá of Nigeria, Arabic writing was at least a century older than the Roman script. Abubakre and Reichmuth (1997) states that:

> Although the spread if Islam into the Yorùbá kingdoms can be dated back at least to the sixteenth century, the growth of Arabic literature was closely related to the *jihad* movement of the early nineteenth century and to the emergence of an Islamic Emirate in Ilorin in northern Yorùbáland which finally became part of the Sokoto Empire. Arabic writing developed first within the cosmopolitan community of Islamic scholars in Ilorin, which apart from the Yorùbá included Fulani, Hausa, Nupe, Kanuri, Dendi/Songhai, and even Arabs. Scholars of Yorùbá origin were soon to increase within that community, in a process of gradual Yorùbánization that subsequently pervaded the whole society of the town. (185)

According to Abubakre and Reichmuth (1997), Ilorin became "the cultural center for the Yorùbá Muslims, as Islamic communities were also growing in many places in the south." Perhaps what is most interesting in their paper is the statement that Arabic actually "became for a long time a medium of diplomatic correspondence, used by several Yorùbá rulers and Islamic communities in their communications with Ilorin and among each other" (185).

This statement is very significant. In northern Nigerian, Arabic actually became an official language, and became a language of diplomacy in the south. Moreover, there is a minority ethnic group in Borno, northern part of Nigeria, called the *Shuwa Arab*, and they are said to speak an Arabic dialect or a language that has similar characteristics with Arabic language. As usual in a country of about 400 languages and several religions, even the issue of Arabic script has been policised.[5] There was a statement early in 1999 on an Internet-based discussion network[6] credited to Wole Soyinka. He was protesting the use of what he called the "Arabic language" on the Nigerian national currency.[7] The colonial efforts discouraging the use of *Ajami* has definitely resulted into a surprisingly high level of ignorance among some Nigerians about the existence of *Ajami* writing system in many Nigerian communities. In Kano, Zaria, Sokoto, and Katsina, many Nigerian language newspapers are still written in the Arabic script. Government campaign publications in Hausa are sometimes written in Arabic script in many northern states. Many Nigerians continue to write letters and literary works in the Arabic script. Among many Hausa and Yorùbá, the Arabic script, called *'ajami* in Hausa, is the only script they respect and in which they always write and teach their children to write. They think that the Roman script, called *Boko* in Hausa, has no chance of becoming their written script. Ayodele Awobuluyi once observed that the English language did not qualify to be Nigeria's national language because Nigerians had neither allegiance nor feelings of emotional attachment to it.[8] Perhaps some Nigerians are also declaring their lack of allegiance to the Roman script.

In Nigeria, Arabic script has been used for all kinds of subjects, whether in local languages or in Arabic. Most of such writings are on religious topics such as acts of worship. Others would include praise poetry for the prophet of Islam, Muhammad. Occasionally, poetry is also composed for local leaders and scholars in *Ajami*. There are *Ajami* poetry books on how to govern and on responsibilities of the governed. Other topics covered are individual people's behaviors, and topics in medicine and health care, especially on areas that Hunwick (1997) has categorized as cognitive sciences, logic, and history (217). Hunwick says that:

> In the sciences, while there has been a little writing on mathematical calculation, especially as it relates to the horology (*'ilm al mawaqit*), and a few works of astronomy or astrology, there has been more interest in, and knowledge about medicine. The earliest work in this category is a small work on the treatment of hemorrhoids by Al-Tahir b. Ibrahim al-Fallati of Bornu (fl. 1745), a medical problem also discussed by Muhammad Bellow, who wrote as well on the treatment of intestinal worms and on the use of senna as a purgative. He also wrote a treatise on diseases of the eye, *Masugh al-lujayn*, and two works on Prophetic medicine (*al-tibb al-nabawi*), in which field al-Hasan, another son of Shaykh 'Uthman, as well as a grandson, 'Umar

b. Muhammad al-Bukhari (d. c. 1883), and a great-grandson, Hayat al-Din b. Sa'id (d. 1898), also wrote (on these scholars, see *ALA* 2: 152, 157, 181). (217–8)

Some Arabic writers have written plays and poetry on many sociopolitical events in Nigeria dating back to the Nigerian independence from Britain and continuing to the present moment. For example, Adam Abdullahi al-Iluri has written many plays, among which are those that address the 1967 Biafra war. Abubakre and Reichmuth (1997) have this to say about al-Iluri's play:

> The play by which he expressed his support for the Federal Government in its struggle against Biafra, and which was staged for a large audience including diplomats from Arab countries, was couched in strong Islamic terms: it treated the first victorious battle of the Muslims at Badr where the Meccan army was defeated. The script of this play, which vividly portrayed the mood of the Muslims within the national struggle of the time, has not been found. (199)

Shaykh Abu Bakr Agbarigidoma wrote poems about the Biafran war and compared the war to the secession politics in Ilorin in the fifties (Abubakre and Reichmuth 1997, 203). Also, Zakariyau I. Oseni (from Auchi, Southern Nigeria) wrote a play, *Al-'Amid al-mubajjal* "The Honorable Dean" (200), reflecting on the corruption in the Nigerian society of the 1990s and strongly depicting the filthy circumstances in many Nigerian universities of the Babangida-Abacha eras.

Writing styles vary from classical Arabic poetry patterns to local styles of oral praise poetry in the community. Some examples of Arabic writings from Ilorin will show how interesting these writings are. First, from Shehu Alimi's poem, "Khudh", written in the early 19th century. Here is how Abubakre and Reichmuth (1997) analyzed it:

The title of the poem, *Khudh* ("Take!"), hints to the first line, which expresses his admonition:

> Keep to the word of the scholars, my brother, those who know the *sunna* and act according to it, not out of hypocrisy.

'Uthman b. Fodiye himself is described as the "light of time," as the leading scholar, saint, and renewer of faith (*mujaddid*). The poem thus enshrines the religious and ideological foundations of the Islamic state both in Sokoto and in Ilorin itself and affirms the position of the religious scholars. (188)

An early 20th century Ilorin poet, Ahmad Yanma, also made the following impression on Abubakre and Reichmuth (1997) in a poem he wrote in 1915 to welcome a new Ilorin community head appointed to replace another one that passed away that same year. Yanma's poem reflected the sociopolitical situation of Ilorin, then under British colonial rule. Abubakre and Reichmuth review it as follows:

> The sense of loss in a novel situation comes out even more in a poem that was written in the same year in praise of the new emir of Ilorin, Shu'ayb Bawa (1915–19). It begins with a lamentation about the evils of the time, especially about the colonial rulers and their highhanded behavior in the town, ranging from the imposition of forced labor to the introduction of a *jizya* tax on the poor Muslim population. He was by this alluding to measures which two years earlier had led to demonstrations and riots in which the religious scholars and preachers had played a very significant role and had even wrested some important concessions from the administration. (189)

Abubakre and Reichmuth (1997) named many Arabic writers in Ilorin and in many areas of the southwestern Nigeria who have attained some level of literary and scholarly achievements among their readers. Among those they mentioned are Habib B. Al-Hasan (1830s), Muhammad Belgore (1831–1913), Muhammad al-Takunti (d. around 1900), Ahmad b. Abi Bakr omo Ikokoro (d. 1936), Abd al-Rauf b. Muhammad al-Busiri b. Harun (around 1946), Harun Matanmi (d. 1935), Muhammad al-Sanusi (around 1910), Abd al-Salam Alkinla (d. 1960), Muhammad al-Labib (also called Taj al-Adab) (1885–1923), Bunyamin b. Motala, Isaac Ogunbiyi, Mashud Mahmud Jimba, Uthman b. Abi Bakr b. Yusuf Eleyinla, Isa Alabi, Shaykh Adam Abdullahi Al-Iluri, Zakariyau I. Oseni, Abd al-Salam Okekoto, and Shaykh Abu Bakr Agbarigidoma (188–203). A comprehensive list of the Arabic writers who are Yorùbá will be too large to provide in this chapter. More and more writers are springing up daily around the country, and very exciting developments are taking place in Nigerian academia. Yorùbá folktales and proverbs are being translated into Arabic. Wole Soyinka's play, *The Trail of Brother Jero*, is being translated into Arabic by an Ilorin writer, Mashud Jimba. Jimba is also completing an Arabic translation of D.O. Fagunwa's Yorùbá novel, *Ogboju Ode Ninu Igbo Irunmole (A Brave Hunter in the Forest of A thousand Demons)*.[9]

Quranic schools are on almost every street or household, and many modern Arabic and Islamic schools are in most cities. In northern and southwestern states in Nigeria, most of these schools are affiliated to universities in Arab countries. Many Nigerian universities also offer undergraduate and graduate programs in Arabic and Islamic studies. A few have combined honor programs in Islamic and Common law, and a few more universities have programs solely in Islamic Law. Most graduates of these programs work in Sharia Courts of Appeal in northern Nigeria, dealing with Islamic law. Many Arabic books are published through commercial presses such as Kewulere Press in Ilorin and Shebiotimo Press in Ijebu-Ode.

USING ARABIC SCRIPT IN HAUSA AND YORÙBÁ WRITING IN NIGERIA

The Arabic script, called *Ajami*, is popular among majority Muslim population in Nigeria, especially at the grassroots. Oftentimes, they use *Ajami* script for writing personal letters and keeping very intimate records of family events in personal diaries. People in Ilorin, for example, frequently use *Ajami* to write letters to give their daughters away in marriage to the grooms. AbdulRazaq Abdullahi (1989) has a good enumeration of the uses of Ajami:

> Many letters were written in Yorùbá in Arabic scripts. These letters include, friendly letters, business letters, letters relating to social matters (like giving out one's daughter in marriage), writing down a Will and so many others. Among the features of such letters is that, in commencing a good letter, one must write:
>
>> In the name of Allah, the Mighty,
>> Praise be to Allah, the all-knowing,
>> Blessings and peace be upon the Holy
>> Prophet Muhammad (S.A.W.) (85)

The kind of uses enumerated above are so personal and intimate that they serve as evidence to show why the script is so dear to those who write in it.

Sana Camara (1997) once describes the consideration of "African literature only in terms of that which is written in European languages" as a "troubling tendency," and criticizes "the publishing houses with offices overseas" for helping to reinforce this phenomenon by only "marketing books written in those languages" (163). What kind of irony was one to call the situation in which many centuries of pre-colonial *Ajami* writing in Nigeria do not seem important to the official Nigerian education system.

Nigeria was not all about Missionary and colonial education! Sokoto caliphate was not about how Jihad "forced people to convert to Islam," or, in the case of Ilorin, how "the Fulanis were sent from Sokoto to kill Afonja and forced the people to convert to Islam." Such were the grave distortions that colonial education imparted to students. It programmed them to turn a blind eye to common practices such as *Ajami* among their own people. Camara's (1997) article shows that *Ajami* literature is as popular in Senegal as it is in northern and Muslim areas of southwestern Nigeria. Camara gave example of Wolof language *Ajami* "which has existed since the seventeenth century" (164). Camara says:

> As the most widely spoken language in Senegal, Wolof is used not only in the regions of Bawol, Kajoor, Jolof, Waalo, Njambur, and Saalum, but is also employed by an important segment of the Senegal of the

Gambian population. . . . The translation of the Bible laid the foundations for a Wolof literature written in the Latin alphabet. But if this literature continues to be practiced, it holds very little interest among the Senegalese, who, as Muslims, turn for their edification to Wolof literature in the Arabic alphabet—a literature whose inspiration is above all religious. (164)

Camara (1997) identified poetry as the most widely practiced of *Ajami* literature in Senegal and named some of the important poets to include Mbay Jaxate, Momar Kayre, Samba Jaara Mbay, Masamba Njaay, Baay Maalik Mbay, El Adji Abdoulaye Thiaw, El Adji Sakhir Gay, Mamadou Laye Ndir, Assane Sylla, and Sëriñ Muusaa Ka. Camara discussed in detail the poetry of Sëriñ Muusaa Ka, showing its artistic patterns, and themes as well as explaining the historico-cultural and linguistic significances of the poet's works.

I find many issues that Camara (1997) discussed about Wolof *Ajami* literature to be quite relevant to the important issues of *Ajami* in Hausa and Yorùbá languages in Nigeria. Almost all users of *Ajami* writing in Nigeria are Muslims. However, both Hausa and Yorùbá languages are also spoken outside the borders of Nigeria, and the *Ajami* practice in them, therefore, goes beyond the Nigerian border. For example, Hausa is also spoken in Niger, Ghana, Sudan, Cameroon, Burkina Fasso, Sierra Leone, Guinea, Liberia, Mali, Togo, Gabon, Senegal, Chad, and Ivory Coast.[10] Yorùbá is spoken in Benin and Togo, Nigerian neighboring countries. Whereas most of the Hausa people in all the named countries above are Muslim and will probably use *Ajami*, it is not certain what percentage of the Benin and Togo Yorùbás are Muslims or whether they will use the *Ajami* as is popularly the case in Nigeria. My contention here is that any discussion of *Ajami* among the Hausa and Yorùbá Muslims in Nigeria may have implications for similar groups beyond the Nigerian border.

According to Abdul Razaq Abdullahi (1989) in his "The Various Uses of Ajami Writing Among Muslims in Nigeria: Hausa and Yorùbá as a Case Study," the word *Ajami*[11] *is derived from an Arabic proto word, 'ajama,* meaning "to try," or "to test" (1). Abdullahi uses some examples in Arabic and I will transcribe them as follows: ['*ajuumu*]—"he chewed it for the purpose of eating or [for] a trial"—['] at the word initial here represents a voiced glottalized fricative in the sense that some minimum friction is caused in the pharyngeal during the flow of air when the phoneme /a/ is pronounced. More examples include *maa 'aynii mundha kadha,* meaning, "my eye has not seen thee since such a time" (1). Abdullahi claims that other words such as *'ajamtu* mean "he had impotence, or an impediment, or a difficulty, in his speech or utterance" (1), and that *'ajam* "denotes 'Foreigners,' as meaning others than Arabs" (1), and that *'ajami* is its plural and "signifies one who is of the race of the *'ajam*" (1–2). He says that 'ajmiit will mean "a speech, or language, foreign to the Arabs" (1–2). In other words, '*ajami* is a very appropriate name for adopting the Arabic script for non-Arabic languages.

In using the Arabic script for Hausa and Yorùbá languages some diacritics are introduced to the original Arabic letters in order to create new letters that will properly represent local sounds that are not available in Arabic language, or to which there are no existing Arabic letter equivalents. Although there is still no standardized *Ajami* writing in Nigeria, especially among the Yorùbá Ajami writers, in terms of what may be recognized in formal or official settings as the standardized orthography of *Ajami*, there seems to be a general informal consensus among many people as to what letter is used for what sound, with only a very few deviations. Perhaps the printing press is where consensus is easily obtainable, as newspaper and book publishers would not want to create confusion of what letter represent what among their readers. However, very little of such a consensus exists among Muslims who use *Ajami* for private communications. Local scholars attempted to standardize *Ajami* orthography during and after colonization. According to Abdullahi (1989), as recently as 1985, the first official step was taken to standardize *Ajami*:

> The first step for the standardization of ᶜAjami of Hausa, according to Mallam ᶜUmar Ibrahim, was made in 1985. The suggestion was moved by the United Nations Educational Scientific, and Cultural Organization (UNESCO). The UNESCO moved for the standardization of ᶜAjami writing system, when they realised that many languages of the world, particularly, most of West African countries where Muslims form the majority of the population are using Arabic script in the writing of their mother tongues. This suggestion of UNESCO led to the formation of a special committee which was empowered to undertake the work. This committee comprises, Mallam Sani Ibrahim of Bayero University, Kano, Professor Haliru Binji of Uthman Dan-Fodio University, Sokoto, Mallam Naibi Sulaiman Wali, Dr. Gidado Bello, the National Director of Mass Education, Dr. AbdulHamid Abubakar, Deputy Vice-Chancellor, University of Maiduguri, Mallam ᶜUmar Bello, Head, Department of Islamic Studies, Uthman Dan Fodio University, Sokoto, with ᶜUmar Makorshi as it Chairman. (14–15)

Part of the challenges placed before this committee was the need to make *Ajami* writing easier for users. I strongly believe this committee would be able to develop a standardized *Ajami* writing and introduce *Ajami* to contemporary Internet usage, as Arabic language is already quite advanced on computer keyboard.

The first example of *Ajami* text in Hausa that I like to discuss[12] is a story that I myself read many times in the Boko[13] script as a young elementary school pupil in Sokoto.¹⁴ It is a story about a blind man carrying a lamp in the night. A boy who came across him stopped stupefied, and asked him why he was carrying the lamp since he was blind. The blind man replied that it was to ensure that people like the young boy who "truly had no eyes" would not step on him.

Regarding the characteristics of this *Ajami* text, anyone familiar with standard Arabic letters should have no difficulty recognizing most of the letters or even reading the entire text. However, some letters have additional diacritics in order to realize the correct Hausa words. The word /ʃe/ is realized with a regular Arabic letter for /ʃ/ and an addition of one dot below. For /tʃ/, to which there is no equivalent phoneme in Arabic, the writer uses one of the three dotted Arabic sounds [th], and adds a vowel, fat-ha or kasra, to it in order to produce what is then pronounced as /tʃa/ or /tʃI/ respectively. It is important to note that Hausa language does not have the Arabic sound /th/, or word [tha] voiceless inter-dental fricatives /T/. A new diacritic is added below the Arabic /th/ sound symbol to realize the Hausa word /tʃe/. There are other interesting examples easily recognizable by any person who has minimum knowledge of the Arabic script. I have provided in the Appendix 1 a copy of the *Ajami* script, a Roman script transcription of the essay in Hausa language, and an English translation. A comparison of these materials may be quite interesting.

The next example we shall consider is a Yorùbá language letter written in *Ajami*.¹⁵ This letter was written in Ilorin, by one Mallam Abubakar Yusuf to Mallam Sulaiman. Yusuf is giving away his daughter in marriage to Mallam Sulaiman's son. The inclusion of the Arabic language and a direct quotation from the Quran at the beginning of this letter is evidence of the Islamic significance that the writer attaches to the subject of the letter. There are many non-uniformities in representing some Yorùbá sounds in *Ajami* script (e.g., [gb], [p]). An Ilorin scholar had his name transcribed from *Ajami* into Latin script as [al-Iluri], thereby practically changing the original pronunciation of the name *Ilorin* to *Iluri* in his own name (this scholar appears many times in Camara (1997), and in Abubakre and Reichmuth [1997]). Obviously, there is no conformity about which letter to use for the Yorùbá [o] as in 'orange,' Some Yorùbá *Ajami* writers might use something like [al-Ilaori], thereby adopting a diphthong [ao] for the sound [o] as in 'orange.'

The *Ajami* writing system in Hausa and Yorùbá languages continues to face problems do to the fact that since colonization, nothing much has been done to develop a standard *Ajami* orthography for any Nigerian language. Nigerian universities have not done much to promote this writing system. The department of Nigerian Languages at Bayero University, Kano, has a great potential to standardize *Ajami* writing for Yorùbá, Nupe, and many indigenous Nigerian languages in which native speakers are interested in using *Ajami* for their languages.

ORAL INVOLVEMENT IN ARABIC WRITING IN ILORIN

One characteristic of writing in Ilorin and in many Hausa and Yorùbá commuities is its involvement with oral traditions. We have already discussed the *Ifá* script among the Yorùbá and how it derives its function and thematic essence from the Yorùbá ritual of divination. The indigenous Yorùbá writing is not just the graphic representation of thoughts to the Yorùbá people, especially to the *Ifá* worshippers; it attains a spirituality of the gods. It is transmitted through a process of knowledge given by the Yorùbá god of knowledge. The *Ifá* priest bears this knowledge to his clients and clients who have been initiated into *Odu Ifá* are themselves able to chant the orality of the graphic transmission. The *Ifá* priest chants simultaneously as he throws down his *Oplele*, or divination chain, and renders the graphic foretelling on the *Ifá* board or sand.

Arabic writing attains a level of spirituality and metaphysicism in some Ilorin quarters. It is not uncommon to see some people put some Arabic passages, sometime taken directly from the Qur'an, but other times just renditions of their own, in animal skins or leather pieces which are then tied neatly and wrapped around their hands or buttocks. Sometimes, they are put in pockets for some magical and spiritual essences. The most popular of these uses is the one made into what Yorùbá call *Onde* and which are often tied around the buttocks. Often, verses extracted from the Qur'an or some Arabic lines composed by local spiritual priests, called *Aafa*, are chanted as the bearer invokes the metaphysics of the *Onde*. This occurs usually when he or she is in trouble and needs immediate assistance. Islamic preachers often condemn such practices, which are seen as *Shirk*, associating partners with Allah. However, the Yorùbá or Hausa person involved in this practice still explores the relevance of the Arabic writing to his or her traditional oral culture and spirituality.

The importance of oral recitation of the Quran in Islam[16] has further allowed the Ilorin Muslims to explore their oral skills in their practice of the Islamic religion. The following are times when Muslims generally recite the Quran:

1. During five daily *salat*
2. During Ramadan fast, or any day, for meditations, or as a righteous practice
3. Anytime for preaching its verses to Muslims or non-Muslims
4. Anytime earmarked for purposes such as after someone dies, like an important Muslim scholar or leader, etc.
5. When teaching the Quran, especially its correct recitation.

Recitation of the Quran is a big event in Ilorin. All the *Imams* who lead daily prayers in Ilorin, especially the head of the Imams called the Chief Imam of Ilorin who leads at Friday Juma'a prayer at the Ilorin Central

Mosque, compete in Quranic recitation. There are several notable Ilorin Quranic recitation voices, occassionally a new Chief Imam or any notable Imam in any of the area mosques creates a new recitation voice-pattern. Each voice is recognized as a special pattern of rendition and is named after its chief architect. One of the Ilorin recitation voices is however unique. It is seen as an Ilorin community voice and is popular among every Ilorin household or Quranic school. Any Ilorin person can freely use this voice anytime. However, some Ilorin people use two other voices that are not traditional to Ilorin: (1) the Arabian style/voice where recitation follows strict Arabian *tajwid* pronunciation and can be easily heard on tapes bought from Saudi Arabia during pilgrimage, and (2) the Sudanese voice, most common in Quranic recitals in Kano and Bauchi areas of northern Nigeria. The majority of those who recite in strict Arabian voice in Ilorin are those who have attended Islamic and Quranic schools in Arab countries (e.g., Egypt, Saudi Arabia, Iraq, and Libya) or sometime those who went to Ilorin Islamic schools with similar Arabian orientations. The following seven can be identified as popular Ilorin recitation voices:

1. The traditional Ilorin Voice
2. Imam Fulani Voice
3. Imam Bashir Voice
4. The Adabiyya Kamaliyya Voice
5. The Jabata Voice
6. Kokewu Kobere Voice
7. The Makondoro Voice

Further research will be useful in locating other voices and perhaps in recording them for phonological descriptions. Several ones might have gone into oblivion, and some others not mentioned above might be limited to household or local streets.

Once every year on the 28th night of the Ramadan fast, Ilorin holds a Quran recitation festival where the traditional ruler of Ilorin (called the Emir of Ilorin) hosts the community in his palace. Young reciters compete for honors and the best ones win important awards donated by the Emir. Often at this festival, new voices attain community-wide popularity, and some reciters become community stars. Before the introduction this Quran recitation competition, the *Were* oral singers[17] had competed at this annual twenty-eighth night Ramadan festival. It was not uncommon to see the *Were* singers also include some Quranic verses in their songs so as to reflect on the religious occasion and impress the Muslim audience.

This festival, either as *Were* songs or as Quran recitations, therefore, celebrates the indigenous oral form in Ilorin. Specifically speaking, the Quran recitation festivity is to show the pride of the Ilorin community as it demonstrates its oral voices in the rendition of the written Quran. It is also an important demonstration of how public oral performance becomes a feature of important religious practice among Muslim Ilorin. Oral traditions are a common feature in contemporary religious and non-religious practices among all ethnic groups in Nigeria. Modern Hausa and Yorùbá language writers, whether writing in Arabic or Roman script, constantly demonstrate strong interest in exploring the oral forms from their traditional cultures as marks of their cultural identities.

4 *Horses of Memory* and *The Word is an Egg*
Osundare's Poetic Voices

My first attempt to present Èlàlòrò to an international audience was at the first ever International Comparative Literature Association (ICLA) congress to be held in Africa,[1] at the University of Pretoria, South Africa. My paper was titled, "Èlàlòrò: A (Pan-) African Theory for Critical Discourse." I revisitd the issue of racial biases in critical process and African writers during and immediately after colonization and Black American writers, especially before Harlem Rennanssance had firsthand experience of what I call racist criticism. But what might his be? Chinua Achebe (1989) simply calls it colonialist criticism (79–90). It is the kind of criticsm where White critics reject literary projects for simple reason that it did not look like European form, or where Anglo-American critics side with a White author when he or she demonstrated racist tendency by portraying non-White people as lesser than White. In my paper, Niyi Osundare and Chniua Achebe feature prominently because of their vocal voices against racist criticism. I submitted Èlàlòrò as a discourse paradigm, and, although it embraces cultural originality, it is antithetic to racist and myopic tendencies.

My South African paper is relevant here because my intention in this chapter is to conduct a cultural originality reading of two important poetry volumes by Niyi Osundare (1998),[2] and show that the Èlàlòrò preoccupation is only to give voice to cultural meanings and affirm aesthetic origins regardless of what culture involved. In other words, an Èlàlòrò reading of William Golding or Ernest Hemingway would not shy away to celebrate literary philosophies of these writers from their British and American roots, respectively. The Èlàlòrò framework is introduced with the belief that African indigenous theories must take important stages in world literary discourses as a mark of world's diversity and critical pluralism. Èlàlòrò presents a chance for a vibrant cross-cultural critical polemics because it is a call for a true representation and dignity for every world culture, language, and philosophical thought in the face of a massive globalization of western culture to the detriment of world's cultural plurality. Èlàlòrò calls for the application of every world culture's literary, philosophical, and creative ideas to understanding world's diversity. Èlàlòrò, although a phrase coined from Yorùbá cultural thought, calls for linguistic conceptual liberation where every concept, from whatever cultural origin it may be, is presented and safe-guarded in the language of its origin. We may find this to be often the case within European discourses where, for example, a treatise written in English still retains the French traditional concepts in the French language, rather than surrender it to the English language of the treatise's composition. Èlàlòrò recognizes that thinkers from every part of the world must retain their concepts in their own original mother languages even where colonization and the new drive for global reach may "force" people to write in English, French, Italian, German, Spanish, or Portuguese languages. Osundare's poetry represents a poetry written in English but which refuses to surrender its Yorùbá cultural identity (Arnold 1996) to the English traditions. Like Wole Soyinka, the 1986 Nobel laureate in literature, Niyi Osundare is a Yorùbá man from Southwestern Nigeria. He is among leading writers of his generation and is often called the poet of the marketplace, a name that reflects his populist poetics.

Osundare won the African area award of the Commonwealth Poetry Prize and was joint winner (with Vikram Seth of India) of the overall Commonwealth Poetry Prize for his poetry book *The Eye of the Earth*, in 1986. He was the 1997 Forlon-Nichols award by the African Literature Association. He won the Noma Award in 1991, the most prestigious award for African literature, for his poetry book, *Waiting Laughters*. Osundare's poetry, as the poetry of Nigeria's Tenure Ojaide and Ghana's Kofi Anyidoho, is most deserving of the kind of indigenous theorizing that Èlàlòrò paradigm is designed to achieve. This chapter demonstrates how Niyi Osundare, through poetry, exerts community strength, cultural morality, and creative vibrancy.

DISCUSSING HORSES OF MEMORY: MEMORY, MEMO-FROM-BIRTH REALMS

> I am a poet:
> my memory is a house
> of many rooms.
>
> (Osundare 1998, 95)

Omoeke Amao, an Ilorin Dadakúàdà oral singer, often sang the beautiful Yorùbá adage, *Owe lesin oro, oro lesin owe, b'ogbon ba sonu, owe laafi wa*, meaning that "proverbs are speeches' horses, and speeches are proverbs' horses. Whenever wisdom seems lost, a horse-proverb is set loose for its search." Niyi Osundare's (1998) *Horses of Memory* reminds me of Amao's use of this important Yorùbá adage. Amao and his chorus group repeat uncountable times, *owe lao fi wa, owe lao fi wa, ogbon to so nu-un, owe lao fi wa*: (we will use proverb to search for the lost wisdom!).

Osundare (1998), in *Horses of Memory*, is setting the horse loose for the memory of his youth, his culture, and his parentage. The collection is a dedication to his father, and every poem shows the wisdom he has learned from his parents. As Osundare opens the volume, he states that "This volume owes its inspiration to the memory of my father, Ariyoosu, Osundare, poet, singer, drummer, and farmer who left fertile hoemarks on the open page of earth when ... he danced to the other side of the river." He continues, calling his father, "this man of song and memory," and he says his collection intends to "achieve full celebrative energy and with the accompaniment of singing and drumming" (vii). Thus ushers in a superb poetry of cultural memory and artistic visions. In *The People's Poet: Emerging Perspectives on Niyi Osundare* (Na'Allah 2003), three contributors, Doug Killam, Shiyu Louisa Wei, and Kamau Kemayo, writing seperately from Canada, Japan, and the United States, concord with the notion that this book is among the poet's most successful collections.

Horses of Memory (Osundare 1998) contains 67 poems unevenly distributed into eight sections. The section with the largest poems is Section V, with 26 poems. Section VI has 19 poems, Section III has 11, and Section II has five and Section VII has four. The least number of poems, not the shortest in length, are in Sections I and IV, with one poem each. However, even with this distribution, Osundare stays true to his people's tradition where the drummer or singer allows his or her mood and performance-circumstance to dictate the course of songs in a spontaneous outfit, rather than force songs towards extraneous or predetermined causes. Number can have a spiritual or metaphysical essence,[3] but so can the artist's surrendering to commandments of spontaneous artistry.

Section I, "Settled Dust," is as metaphysical as it is metaphorical: dust stirs to keep at par with air and move at the freedom of light. The settling, as the poem here shows, is to enable the energy of the departed to concentrate its potentials for the guidance of his children and relatives still remaining on earth. The poem "For the One Who Departed," is therefore a dedication to the poet's father and a celebration of his attainment of ancestral status. The poet wants this poem to be chanted to the accompaniment of "heavy drums and occasional ululations" (see Osundare 2000, performance notes, p. 5). This marks this poem as a celebration of life in this world and at the ancestral world. The departed aged, was very useful to community, and he left children behind. The Yorùbá do not cry at such transition to the other life, for only the "untimely" deaths of young persons and the ignominious departure of failed souls are tragic deaths! The occasional ululations are exclamation of victory over worldly life. Any performance of this or any Osundare's poem without recourse to the poet's prescribed notes would fail to capture the beauty and essence of an African poetic culture intended by the poet. In 13 pages, the poet celebrates the passing of his father. Style changes, refrain changes, and words—heavy words change to atune to mood and cultural meanings, *b'orin ba yi, ki ilu naa yi* (once songs change, the drum has to change)! In this celebration of the rite of passage, there is harmony among earth, human and non-human, in paying homage to homely transition: *aye l'oja, orun nile* (earth is a market, ancestral world is home) says a Yorùbá adage:

> The moon moans in the closet of the sky
> Stars wring their hands in sparkless grief
> The lake wears a shawl of ash and adamantine mist
> The noonmard sun strikes a gong from the tower of clouds (5)

Again, Osundare's (1998) great talent is shown in the ways he weaves the objects showing their sorrowful expressions for losing a worldly company, the moon moans, the stars sparkless, the lake mists, the sun beclouded! Even the cock-roaster, the announcer of time, crows sorrowfully, "behind the man!" This refrain tells the performers and their audience that someday the cock will crow behind each of us all. In The Dance Theatre of Harlem's (1997) rendition of John Henry legend, the lamenting voice of the narrator-poet sings, ringing deeply and movingly into our hears just after John Henry falls on the ground and dies, similar to the narrating voice of Osundare's poems for his father: "John Henry was nothing but a man-an, John Henry was nothing but a man!" The legend John Henry was eulogized. For Niyi Osundare's father, "the matchet is the man / the man is the matchet" The poet asks, challengingly, "Who says the cock has crowed behind the man?" (17). The cock never crows for a farmer, a singer, and drummer of words, the poet. He lives forever.

This first poem is rich in many other ways. Divided into seven parts, each part takes its turn in contributing to the story about this death and in celebrating the passing of the farmer-poet. The first part announces the parting, every earth's element participates in the dirge, "the grass carried its dew to the furnace / Of the sun / The sun has eaten the dew, eaten the dew / With teeth sharpened on singing day" (Osundare 1998, 6). Only a master poet can commandeer words and sew them so richly with all the particles of earth's riches as Osundare (1998) has so effortlessly done here. Indeed, the farmer, closest to the earth, deserves earth's evocation at death. Songs and refrains, in Yorùbá and in English, contribute to the wealth of this performance. The farmer-poet "broke his word" or "Now that a sudden twilight has broken the farmer's word / Who breaks the earthworm with the hoe of dawn?" One of the successes of this poem is the way Osundare links the two arts, artistic creativity and farming creativity, the mouth and the hand, always meeting in the farmer-poet's home. A song is a seed. It germinates throughout life. One of the greatest praisings of the departed farmer-poet is the first stanza,

> The farmer broke his word
> And not the pod which once crackled
> Into a thousand songs in the earthly orchestra
> Of his gathering hand,

> Each song a seed flying up a thousand mountains,
> Threshing the weedy saddle of the harvest wond;
> The farmer broke his word
> And the grass carried its dew to the furnace
> Of sun. (6)

The second part of the poem laments about the society's losses with the passing of the farmer-poet (Osundare 1998). *Niwoyi esi la j'akasu bi ogofa / Baba lo akasu o kan wa ooo* (this time last year we ate sixty wraps of food, now he's gone, not even one is available to us!) Every close friend of the farmer grieves, the matchet is "blunt with grief", and is lying with neglect, already "fraught with fungi." Places where last year, "Yam raised a song and cassava caught the tune," "Now revel weeds . . ." Everyone of the farmer's farming tools spoke, the hoe asks after his hoer, the matchet laments at the absence of the wielder, and the clay misses the moulder as the body ill the breath.

The third part continues with yearning for and the celebration of the departed farmer-poet (Osundare 1998). The matchet is the man! Again, this legendary farmer reminds me of John Henry (Dance Theater of Harlem 1997), the African-American legend, who with his matchet competed with machine. Matchet is an image of productivity, strength, courage, and bravery. This section is a direct address to the farmer; to let him know that his work while on earth continues to prosper after his departure:

> The yams you planted last season
> Have burst into bloom:
> Efùrù has sprung muscular tendrils
> From the womb of a faithful soil;
> Ewùrà sprawls in fields and furrows
> Like a royal python with a million limbs;
> Aro eléwé is sky-bound, its leaves screening
> The sun like a properous grove. (10)

Osundare (1998) is one of his father's yams blooming all over the world, and we all are eating the yam to assuage our poetic hunger!

The next part continues this trend of directly addressing the departed farmer-poet (Osundare 1998). Again, starting with the refrain, "The matchet is the man." Clearly, the voice of the praise poet evokes to the ancestor farmer: he did well on earth, served humanity well! He respected the earth, and the earth, in turn, was his confidant![4] The next part continues its praise invocation, "You were a season for all men / You were a man for all season" (13). Again in this part, the synthesis of the farmer and the poet is achieved. He's the man for all the "Seasonings / of blade which sharpens the tongue / of tongue which marries the mouth / in the temple of splitting words" (14). As if reminding the farmer-poet, "The word was your horse!" Again,

60 *African Discourse in Islam, Oral Traditions, and Performance*

> You were the Word which fell from the sky
> And, touching earth, broke
> Into a thousand truths
>
> You were the Word
> Which shot the deer
> Before the hunter's gun (15)

The last two parts reassess death's meaning to the family of the departed: "Silence" (Osundare 1998). As the poet celebrates the legendary drummer, he uses the drum, the various types of Yorùbá drums, to show how emotion flows among friends closest to the drummer. "Bàtá wept all night, / Omele could not snail the sea of wailing waters, / Ibembe broke down like an orphan, / The stick crouched like a shrivelled twig / And everywhere, the swollen lips of the leather / Silence" (16). Everywhere is mourning, silence, from the stone's belly to leopards' grasslands to Oke Ubo to Osun's billows; silence! Perhaps it's intentional, and effectively so, that the last refrain in this part ends in smaller font-size, "The cock has crowed behind the man"! (16)

The concluding part of "For the One Who Departed" is like an *orin idagbere* (farewell or closing song), common in Yorùbá chants (Osundare 1998). It not only wraps up a befitting perfomance for a departed soul but also reintroduces the Yorùbá concept of death: The belief in continuity through the ancestral word. The palm tree is not dead, its spear is "Stalking the antelope of the sky." Despite the sorrow felt by siblings that their aged loved one is physically leaving them, *od'arina ko, otun d'oju ala* (until their paths cross [on the road], or in dreams). They still are joyful realizing that he or she is taking up a greater position as an ancestor who will always be their guiding spirit. Reconnecting the poem's last lines to its beginning, Osundare asks, "Who says the cock has crowed behind the man? (*Ope o ku e wo mariwo ope ooo!*) The palm tree did not die; its articles are everywhere! The farmer-poet did not die; we only have to look at Niyi Osundare! From personification, onomatopoeia, irony, repetition, to other metaphorical colorations, Osundare explores innovative techniques to present a thrilling and culturally relevant homage to his departed father. He provides endnotes to help non-Yorùbá performers and readers. This first poem sets a pattern for remaining poems in this collection. It is the *Olu orin* (the prime song) for the collection.

The six remaining sections resemble the first in many ways (Osundare 1998). Each poem is an orchestra of songs, drums, dance and resonant memory. Five poems in Section II, "Long Gallop:" (1) "Memory's Road," (2) "Memory Street," (3) "Scars of Unremembrance," (4) "Stilldancers," and (5) "We shall Remember." As their titles show, each flows unto the other in a thread of continued souvenir, continuing the lane of synthesis of earth, human beings and animals, living and non-living, concrete and abstract! "Memory's Road" starts with a union of style and theme: the

"Chariots of dew," the "horses of hills," the "hoofs of woolen clouds," the "spurs of fire," the "thread of hair," the "cacle of rain and thunder," the "whisper of sea and sand," the "tail of liquid lanes," and the "fire of heel and hoof." Still, "the road wears trousers / of uncountable legs," "the earth marries sky / and the sun locks his horn/ with twilights of prancing knights" (p. 23). Continuing the theme, the second part of this poem tells the story of the metaphorical snake and its offsprings. The third part continues the story and description of the passage: the "Passage / of latticed visions," "of bows and bends," "of mamba ditches," "of white shadows," "of tear-drawn hearses, of headward burdens," and "of wit and wind" and "of images wrestling words in mind-tunnels." The poem ends with a dialogue among Road, River, Sky, and Mother Earth, all "flowing" unto each other. "Memory's Road" is indeed many voices, unison in celebrating the memory of life and of age. Other poems in this section continue this dialogue of recollection.

Section III, "Running Kicks," explores memory from another perspective (Osundare 1998). "Africa's Memory" sings about Africa's stolen treasures to Europe and America and insists that Africa is poor because it is exploited. The last poem in this section is "New Drum," dedicated to Tanure Ojaide, Osundare's contemporary.[5] It asks for new steps to usher Africa into new waters, new sky of greatness: "A new drum rumbles in our skies / we shall dance to the memory of the moon" (54).

Section IV, "Memory Chips," is another one long poem cast in seventeen parts resembling what might be called 17 chips, each separated by a star (Osundare 1998). Most of the chips are quite simple: few lines stanza (at most four) with one- and two-line stanzas. Each of the chips is a wise saying; each a pot of memory! Some show a display of language and or literary gymnastics. At some levels, a few resembling exercise last seen in Osundare's *Moonsongs* (1988). Others bear far reaching, heavier and sharper messages than the few lines that carry them. Perhaps, the one I love most is the poem that defines words, so characteristic of Osundare (1998):

> Words, too, have memory:
>
> A pinnaful of verbs labouring
> Up the precipice of the head
>
> A canoe of nouns in the promontory
> Of forgotten seas
>
> Silence's echo is
> Louder than thunder. (57)

Osundare's (1998) every poem shows him as the grand weaver of elegant language; master of its ornamental colors. He's one the Ilorin Dadakúàdà singer would call, *ap'ede bi eni n jeko* (sings [writes] as if eating a most delicious food) He blends and uses words in ways that make listeners reflect and say "how true, poet!" Isn't it true that words, after having spoken them, revisit their hearer through words' own memories? Isn't it true that silence is actually a thunderous memory of words? Don't some people run their heels off from silence, because they hate to face words' memories?

Section V, "Soft Canters," contains a web of beautiful memories, and sometimes coins of wishes, prayers, and invocations (Osundare 1998). Other times, the poems are about love, hope, and laughter. The first poem, "Earth Will Not Tremble Under Our Feet," is a prayer, motivation, and a resolution. The title soon becomes the refrain line and is invoked stanza after stanza. It is like invoking one's ancestral spirit, "it won't turn distasteful in their time; it didn't with our ancestors!" While reading Osundare's poems, one feels thrilled from the inside, especially for a reader who recognizes the flavor of Osundare's people's literary aural. Earth is the mother; the aged mother under whose eyes we have all grown to full colors. Sometimes the prayers assume incantatory modes:

> The scorpion under the rock
> will find no victim
> for its fiery tail;
> the lion's dream will be a den
> of blunted claws. (65)

As deadly as scorpion is, without a prey, it lives to waste. The lion, despite power to capture smaller animals for food, remains harmless if his claws are unsharpened! Such scorpion and such a lion may eventually die of frustration! One remarkable talent of Osundare (1998) is his nearness to the earth and his eagerness to explore elements of nature in his work. "Green Memory" is one of the poems with very powerful reach to nature:

> Memory, too, is
> the footsteps of ants
> in the corridors of the forest,
> the winged termite's fleeting frolic
> in the wake of the first rains
> the squirrel's fly-wisk tail
> in the province of nutty seasons
>
> Memory is
> the penetrating touch
> of the January dew
> the dusken fluff of the homing eagle . . .
> Shake hands with a tree today
> Share the memory of a river. (82)

Interesting how Osundare (1998) links memory to the ants' daily schedules and to the termite's and squirrel's sessional engagements. He finds a way to make human beings share in these of blossoming and fertilizing memory! As I have shown from the beginning, Osundare's perfect moment is whenever ants, forest, termite, rains, squirrel, dew, eagle, human beings and the river come together in one poetic piece! He is true to the African oral traditions where nature, life, and blood are joint platforms to poetic creativity.

Section VI, "Memory Tracks," has 19 poems, each a songtrack about the richness of the poet's memory (Osundare 1998). Osundare declares in the last stanza of Testament (1):

> I am a poet:
> my memory is a house
> of many rooms.

Every poem seems just a tiny view of a smallest portion from his numerous rooms (Osundare 1998). You farther, you go, the deeply enticed you are to meaning and beauty. There are many great poems here: "On Reading Senghor, Again" (105–6), and "For Festus Iyayi (115). My most favorite poems in this section are "Who's Afraid of the Proverb?" (99–101) and "Peopled Imagination" 1–4 (109–12). The Yorùbá proverb-song appropriately provides the poem background music. The poet defines proverb as memory, and whoever is afraid of one is afraid of the other! Yorùbá wisdom permeates these poems. I wonder why anyone would perform Osundare's poetry without adequate preparation for the kind of atmosphere the poems would need in order to leave everlasting effects. For example, performing "Who's Afraid of the Proverb" (99) without the author's suggested background song is a loss to the essence of the proverb-poem! It is like silencing the echo of an agidigbo drum and, thus, compromising its wisdom and the learning it will bring upon the earth. "Peopled Imagination" showcases the voice that Osundare represents: "mine is a Peopled imagination," declares the poet. "Of voices from forgotten seas / whose spices sweeten the steps / of passing moons" (112).

Section VII is the last section of the collection carries the title of the volume (Osundare 1998), "Horses of Memory." Its four poems reflect clearly the preoccupation the poets so richly executes on every page of the volume. "I Met History Today" (119–23), "The Beard of the Griot" 1 & 2 (124–6), and "Horses of Memory" (127–31) each define memory as history, memory as the poet (the griot!), and memory as everything that the ear hears, the eye sees, the mouth speaks, and the body feels: "the desert is / the memory of the sea" (128), "the egg, is / the memory of the hen; / every chick there is / is memory of the yolk that was" (129), "Oh memory, / eye of the road, / nose of running rivers/ hooftrong of departed horses!" (130). Clearly, the poet achieves his ambition of celebrating the memory of his father, "the man of song and memory" (vii). And true to the Yorùbá poet's occupation as a teacher of culture and custodian of community well-being, Osundare has truly mobilized us to understand that "Every dawn is a memory / Of a night that was" (86).

THE WORD IS AN EGG: A PHILOSOPHICAL HARVEST IN CULTURE AND LANGUAGE

Niyi Osundare's newest harvest, *The Word Is an Egg* (2000), recaptures his arrival as one of the world's blossoming poet. Just after being conferred with the Forlon Nichols award in the United States by the African Literature Association and an honorary doctorate by France's University of Tolouse-Le Mirail, Osundare's appropriate response comes in *The Word Is an Egg*. A philosophical poetic treatment by the performer-poet, philosopher-poet in which he continues to define modern African poetry for Africa and the world.

This fine book, published by Nigeria's Kraft Books Limited, gives Osundare's (2000) readers across the globe opportunity to understand the concept of "word" from outside Eurocentrist and postmodernist contentions. Osundare uses this volume to continue his cause of defining African ideas through poetry. As a performer poet, he casts his songs in such a way that as his readers and audience perform them and throw their bodies and minds into their rhythms, they imbibe through physical and mental acts, the Yorùbá and African philosophical interpretation of the human, the non-human, the environment, and their relationships to the supernatural. It is from all these levels that I shall review *The Word Is an Egg*.

The volume, with a total of forty-seven poems, is divided into five sections (Osundare 2000). Section I, "Abuubuman," has one poem, "Invocations of the word." Section II, has 17 poems, with the prime poem, "The word is an egg," at the beginning. Section II "Silence," contains 16 poems while Section IV has 13 poems, and Section V has one poem. This volume is similar to *Horses of Memory* (Osundare 1998) in many ways. In *Horses of Memory*, the horse is associated with words and with memory! However, more significant is the dedication of this volume to Osundare's mother, "Fasimia, my Mother, / Indigo fingers/ Weaver of fabrics and fables; / Iya Onisuuru: / Indeed, "the patient eye will see the nose" (Osundare 2000, 5). As he celebrates his father's passing in *Horses of Memory* (1998), he celebrates his mother's life and living in *The Word Is an Egg* (2000). The volume's title comes from a Yorùbá idiom, *Eyin l'oro*, pronounced [Eyin loro], meaning egg is (like) word or speech—once broken may never be repacked. This adage beats the cautious drum regarding the use of speeches and warns speech makers or word users to be sensitive to how they use words or give speech because words or speeches break: Once egg falls and breaks it cannot be repacked into a whole. Once word or speech is spoken and hearers have heard them, they may not be unspoken! It also points to the importance or value attached to speech or words; they are treasures and must always be guarded.

Both *Horses of Memory* (Osundare 1998) and *The Word Is an Egg* (Osundare 2000) show Osundare's dedication to his parents, whom he frequently quotes in his writings, interviews, and several other scholarly engagements. The poet lives true to Yorùbá parents' typical wishes in popular songs:

> Omo mi ni o sinmi
> Omo mi ni o sinmi
> Ti mo ba d'agbalagba
> Ti mo ba d'arugbo
> Omo mi ni o sinmi

> My child will conduct my burial rites
> My child will conduct my burial rites
> When I become old and aged, and pass to the world beyond
> My child will (be alive to) conduct my burial rites.

Parents from all cultures wish their children a long life (Osundare 2000). The Yorùbá parents also pray for prosperity for their children. They pray for their cultural and spiritual strengths. *B'okete ba dagba omu omo re ni -n mu* (the rat that becomes old and aged, lives on her child's breast). The Yorùbá parent asks, as perhaps any parent would, that any death that would take their children take them instead. It's the Yorùbá tradition that a successful parent is one whose children are strong and supportive in their parents' old age and who give their parents befitting burial in their passing. This is another volume that affirms Stewart Brown's assertion that "Osundare does not dance to the thresholds between English and Yorùbá, but celebrates the thresholds in Yorùbá" (Na'Allah and Rice-Miximin 1999, 63). In many ways, as one considers Osundare's (1998, 2000) writings, one is well served to understand that their greatness results from his Ikere-Ekiti Yorùbá uprining! One needs a knoweldge of Osundare's Yorùbá culture.

Section I, "Invocations of the word," starts with a declaration: "In the Beginning was not the Word / In the Word was the Beginning" (Osundare 2000, 10). In many ways, this is anthetical to Eurocentric perception of the word. The word is even more powerful from the Osundare African perspective. The word is the spirit, the god, and the power that creates itself. *Enu agba lobi n gbo* (Kolanut attains maturity in the mouth of the elder). As in the coverpage of this volume, the mouth, the tongue, and the egg all symbolize the word! This poem is performed with "full musical accompaniment," (11) and the poet is celebrating the power of word:

> I see the Word
>   plumbing distant clouds for echoes of golden idioms

I see the Word
> shaving mountainheads with razors ofd reason

I see the Word
> on the lips of the gun, animally red

I see the Word
> in parliaments of contending tongues

I see the Word
> with ears of joy, stalks of swaying rapture

I see the Word
> in the dream of a dream
> in the dream of a drean
> in the cloud which gathers the rain
> in the rain which unchains the earth. (11)

Osundare sings praise of "word": "Fish of the Sea, Fish of the Legon, A joy to have in the mouth, Dreadful to have around the neck" (11). When one is in trouble, the Yorùbá says *o da oran* (he or she has broken the words!) or *oran wa lorun re* (he/she has tied words around his or her own necks). In both expressions, the person has a case to answer. Invocations of the Word is indeed a celebration of word, and all aspects of word is invoked: the drum, the metaphysic, the metaphors, and the sound. The repetition of "Araba ponmbé ponmbé ponmbé / Araba ponmbè ponmbè ponmbè" is to bring about the synthesis; to show the place of sound in the realization of Yorùbá words and its poeticity. Yorùbá as tonal language often explores the musicality of the tone. Again, this poem carries the philosopy of word among the Yorùbá:

> The Word is rain
> The Word is dust
> > The Word is a rainanddust
>
> The Word is black
> The Word is white
> > The Word is blackandwhite
>
> The Word is life
> The Word is death
> > The Word is lifeanddeath. (12)

Word is treated here the same way the Yorùbá treats philosophical or abstract World, *aye*, or Human being, *omo enia*, which can be good or bad (see Gbadegesin 1991). The Yorùbá believe that both *aye* and *enia* metamorphose like chameleons change colors. Not only is there another side of word, as in word and its opposite, but also a third realization, where two meanings share a single word: "word is rainanddust," "it's blackandwhite!" (Osundare 2000, 12). Contemporary parents who want in their chidlren and in themselves a bedrock of African tradition should take Osundare's poetry as daily companion!

Section II is a mixture of short and long poems, all continuing the themes already developed in Section I (Osundare 2000). Each title is as metaphorical as every word of every line of the stanzas. Such poems as "Dinning words," "The Kingdom of the tongue," "The future is a word," and "Falling off the tree of words" are all very catchy poems. Another one "Words which" (26) (performed to "Music; various voices), is especially spectacular:

> Words which go to war to find peace
> Words which go to war to find war
>
> Words which mew like a cat
> Words which roar like a lion
>
> Words which pouch their young with marsupial care
> Words which go to bed each night with a proverb under the pillow
>
> Words which die every dusk into the sea rising every dawn a golden eagle
> Words which burrow into the sun at noon prospecting for hidden silver
>
> High words.   Low words. (26)

A Yorùbá adage very relevant to the theme developed in the above poem is *Oro ni n yobi lapò, Oro nii y'ofa ninun apó* (word can bring forth kolanut from the pocket, or bow and arrow from the case) already discussed in this book (Osundare 2000)! This poem shows the potency of word to make or mar issues, and encourages the explorer of word to be mindful of how he or she uses it. How great it is, to enjoy poetry and learn African philosophy at the same time!

> Words which germinate like a seedcorn in the rains
> Words dust-brown like locusts on green plunder
>
> Words which bleed when hurt
> Words which fore-sound the idiom of unborn drums
>
> Words which guard the truth with an arsena of oaths
> Words which touch the earth with dew and dance

Words ambivalent like the atom
Words mercy-ful like penicillin

Words die.   Words live. (27)

Osundare (2000) is no doubt a very smart poet. As a super stylistician, he knows what to say and how to say it, knows what words to combine and in what order to protect the poetic flavor, and can retain the touch of African cultural milieu. Full of personifications, abstract object, human and non-human images, often assume plausible human characteristics, and his words have teeth with which they bite hard on the ears of hearers, yet sooth the sight of seers as music and voices join in the rendition of poetic melody. It was on Osundare's *Moonsongs* that I once queried[6] the overwhelming beauty that might distract readers from the important social message. However, this poet has a lured "message" so powerfully on "beauty" that both now answer to the same name (Osundare 2000, 27). The ideas of "word germinating like seedcorn, or bleeding when hurt" (27) are so beautiful just as they are so meaningful and socially relevant!

Section III, "Silence," has such poems as "Trapped words," "Serpent of silence," "Apocryphal thunders," "ABD," "I have learnt," "Pregnant words," and a number of other very pregnant titles (Osundare 2000). One of my favorite poems in this section is the one dedicated to four Nigeria news print, *Tell, The News, Tempo,* and *The Punch,* which are "locked in costly combat with Nigeria's brutal dictatorship . . ." (53). Most of the poems here address the military junta's attempt to suppress freedom of speech, and to drive opposition into oblivion. As the poet shows, the word is mysterious and cannot be imprisoned by the Nigerian emperor.

Section IV, "Thunderwords," contains 13 poems (Osundare 2000). "Words catch fire," the longest of them, is performed in many voices, in orchestra."Words catch fire" is in seven parts. From the title, this poem creates an image of a total chaos within a reality that words fail to hold, and the speaker of words loses credibility. *Enu opuro kii s'eje* (the mouth of the liar does not bleed) and this is because he or she has mastered lie telling that no one may be able to get him/her red handed. However, by saying "Words catch fire," the poet seems to successfully portray an enormous amount of lies and a ferocious suppression of truth, so ferocious that the counter forces of truth could no longer ignore. Osundare states,

> Words catch fire
> Words catch fire on the Emperor's lip
> Truth explodes
> Dreams disintegrate into twinkling ashes
> there is a surfeit of chains in the imperial furnace
> The gag is grim; gallows groan from moon to moon
> òdàrà máa gbá tì wón lo, òdàrà. (59)

"Ashes" here represents the destruction visited on the suppressor of words, as he or she gags other people's aspirations (Osundare 2000, 59). Esu Odara, the Yorùbá god of the crossroad, is employed to pursue word destroyers such as the Emperor (meaning dictators like many African leaders) and to punish them! Throughout this poem, we can see the negative impact of suppression of words: poet cannot sing, earers have their ears removed, everyone becomes a beggar carrying around bowls "empty of metaphors" (59). Whenever words suffer the entire society is in disarray! The poem shows that there is incessant repercussion from the misuse of words, of authority, and of order. This is a highly philosophical poem, and it is very relevant to contemporary African leaders, the sit-tight leaders, who act as if political positions are their birth-right. The poet states, "The hyena which vows to raid forever, / Let it remember the vigilant gun / In a bend in the bush" (61). It shows that power itself is fragile! This is a very rich poem; perhaps one of the book's richest. The poet at times "compares" to the emperor, and from the refrains and the songs, we can hear the powerful movements and the meanings deriving from a serious juxtaposition. Ending the poem, Osundare says,

> Words catch fire
> Words catch fire on the lips of the poet
> The blunt verity of pointed things
> The sting in the song
> The winged warrant of sleeping idioms
> The lyrical touch of raindrops on banana leaves
> Fluid frontiers, vision beyond the eye
>
> I am a poet
> Who feels intenselligently
> I call evil by its hidden name

Koko gba koko di / Koko didi koko di. (61)

Osundare (2000) would not let the Emperor gets away, and he is not afraid of the dictator. Osundare here defines the writer as one who challenges the lies in Emperors mouths, and stings the emperor with the bluntness of his poetic bees! The emperor is evil, but the poet is not afraid so, he "call(s) evil by its hidden name" (66). When the Yorùbá say, *O pee loruko t'onje*, he or she calls him or her by his or her name, or when impression is given that someone knows a person's hidden names, that means he has enormous power and he's a match for the foe's evil machinations. The refrain song itself sounds like a war song; the poet is armed to the teeth as he faces the emperor. This poem, as others, is not only rich in powerful metaphors and philosophical underpinnings, it creates an air of community performance in an orchestra of many meanings. No word is too small or too big for the poet's usage, and the poet explores any and every word to defend his and his people's rights. All the remaining poems in this section are as powerful, as philosophical, and as cogent as this poem. The use of ironies, onomatopoeia, rhetorical questions, repetition, and paradoxes are among the poet's most effective tools.

The last Section of *The Word Is an Egg* (Osundare 2000), titled, "Omoleti," contains one poem stretching across 11 pages. It continues the thesis began in the very first poem of the book and completes the circle began by the following refrain: "In the Beginning was not the Word / In the Word was the Beginning" (10). Omoleti tells the story of how the "Word begets" and the poet challenges anyone to tell him, "By whom was the word begotten?" (83). Here again, the poet is true to the Yorùbá creation story while also exploring what seems to me the biblical or Quranic stories about creation:

> In the Word was the beginning
> In the spoken Clay before the first Fire
> When the Wind, tremulous around the Void,
> Bided the lettered lore of the primal Tree
> Footless echoes spelt the blank
> The Universe loomed in myth and matter,
> Waiting for a Name. (82)

In a clearly oral narrative technique, Osundare (2000) unwraps his creation myth; he plucks "the imagination of parting lips / Unborn tonalities grappled with Space" (82). What a superb way of ending a superb collection. As the poet defines the Earth and the universe, he defines even God, saying it is word that gives them birth!

> In the Word was the Beginning
>
> And the Word named the Sea
> And the Sea named the Sky
> And the sky named the Sole
> And the Sole named the Palm
> And the Palm named the Womb
> And the Womb named the Tomb
> And the Tomb counted Silence in Digits of Seven
>
> The Word named God
>
> And the Word gave Fire its flame
> And the Word gave Water its mercy
> And the Word gave the Wind its wings
> And the Word gave the Cat its claws
> And the Word gave Dove its peace

And the Word left a Will on orphaned lips
And the Word counted Silence in Digits of Seven. (82)

Again, repetition, invocation, and poetic narrative unearth the story about Word, showing how tongue, sound, and syllable were born. Only a master poet—a poet deepened in his people's "lore and legend" (86) can be so gifted, so truly the people's poet!

CONCLUSION

Horses of Memory (1998) and *The Word Is an Egg* (2000) are used here only as examples of his poetic voices. This powerful poet has successfully demonstrated that even poetic voice so far removed from Anglo-American aesthetics can capture the world quite easily and mount its reign to global admiration. There is little doubt that Osundare is on his way to greater glory. He displays a rare talent as a poet and as a critical thinker. He contributes greatly to enriching a cross-cultural poetry heritage of our global century. Writing in the English language, he ensures that his creativity does justice to his Africanness, his Yorùbá heritage, and his Ikere-Ekiti ancestry. Exploring his people's literary philosophy, Osundare shows poetry as people's property, which must be used to represent their life meanings and aspirations. In a global village century, Èlàlòrò paradigm expects creativity to affirm a writer's ancestral flavor so that any community's identity, however localized, is not lost to an alien "super-culture" identity; so that "global village" can be truly defined as a "village" of many voices, not one with only one voice: a truly rainbow global village. A rainbow village will enable cultural thinkers to see human similarities and differences, and theorize on cultural pluralism where every cultural perception deserves respect and retains its authenticity. Èlàlòrò's global village is a comparatist village.

Critical periscope, whenever it involves two cultures, must not be adulterated with favorable or unfavorable biases toward any one culture. As I hope my discussion of Osundare's (1998, 2000) poetics has shown, comparative poeticism must help a world brought together by an instant message delivery electronics to exercise restraint in the interpretation of unfamiliar cultural messages and to learn to understand, respect, and possibly accept connotations from original source orientations. Èlàlòrò analysis is, therefore, always eager to discuss any literary work from that work's remotest socio-cultural perspectives. Author's social, cultural, and political backgrounds are as important as the literary work.

Again, Osundare refuses to subsume his people's cultural bearings under any Eurocentric tradition even as he continues to write in the English language (Na'Allah and Rice-Maximin 1999, 63). He does not surrender it to any Nigerian almighty-figure syndrome either. A Yorùbá adage summarizes this when it says, *Teni nteni, tekisa ntaatan*, meaning, "What belongs to you is yours, rags belongs to the garbage!" Osundare's Yorùbá culture is as strongly Yorùbá as his Ikere-Ekiti ancestry portrays its Yorùbáness; as his Ariyoosu father's and his Fásìmíá mother's Yorùbáness. Yet, it is easy for critics worldwide to locate similarities in Osundare's ideas and creative prowess with important writers from across the world. Augus Calder (1992) compares Osundare's poetry to the writings of Okigbo, p'Bitek, Aime Césaire, and Pablo Neruda (27–28). Calder rightly observes that Osundare is a writer ready "to put himself and his talent directly in the frontline" (27) when it comes to matters that concern his people and country. Ademola Dasylva (1997) concludes in a tribute, stating that "Osundare is the raw, pure gold. The more intense the fire of age and the rage of harsh reality of the times in the inclement furnace of poetic forge, the brighter this gold shines, and richer the value" (35). When Osundare featured recently in the West Indies, Barbados's *Sunshine* newspaper described him as "Nigeria's most celebrated poet after Nobel laureate Wole Soyinka" (Standiford 2000, 4). The paper quoted Osundare as defining his populist agenda as responsive to the position his people put the poet, "There are people who look up to you. Without mincing words, they say, 'Speak for us'" (4). Osundare added, "Social consciousness was part of my inspiration; I was raised to ask questions" (5). In one of such battles on behalf of his people, Osundare wrote poetry and essays confronting the Abacha military regime in Nigeria. He would not see why any right thinking person would condone a regime as heartless as the Abacha military government in Nigeria.[7] Osundare asserts, "It is a monumental contradiction that a country that produced a Soyinka and an Achebe would also produce an Abacha . . . And those Nigerians who joined him, who connived and collaborated with him stand condemned by our present realities and history. They see hunger in the streets and say it's religious abstinence, when they hear protests of dying people they say it's the national anthem" (quoted in Olayiwola 1999, 8).

Without doubt, we'll find similarly talented poets around the world, working on similar motif and political ideas in their poetry, regardless of the culture they write from. The Italian Giacomo Leopardi (1798–1837) is a poet I can compare to Osundare in terms of both writers responsiveness to humanity. Leopardi says a person can gain human dignity by fully "recognizing and accepting" their own "common vulnerability" with other human beings. He talks about the greatness and strength of humankind as showing "greatness in suffering, refusing to add to / The angers and hates of his brothers," and believing in the "brotherhood of men" (646). Poets, like Osundare and Leopardi, who use their poetry to fashion respect for the environment, for human dignity and culture, are poets indeed!

5 Cultural Poetics, African Diaspora, and the Global World
Tanure Ojaide's *I Want to Dance and Other Poems*

Tanure Ojaide (2003) is without doubt among the most prolific modern African poets, and his collection, *I Want to Dance and Other Poems,* is the 13th of his poetry volumes. Ojaide has discussed in several places his life history and his experience as a writer. His autobiography, *Great Boys: an African childhood* (1998), and his scholarly book, *Poetic Imagination in Black Africa* (especially Chapter 9) (1996), present very rich information about his birth, childhood, youth, and community upbringing. Ojaide was born on April 24, 1948, in a rural area called Okpara, in present-day Delta State of Nigeria. He became a Catholic as an elementary school boy: ". . . went to a Catholic school, was baptized and later confirmed in the Roman Catholic Church, but returned to serve as a priest or acolyte at the native shrine" (Ojaide 1996, 121). As if he knew he had to prepare to become a major poet of modern Africa, he grew up imbibing very deeply the two worlds of Western/Christian education and culture and the African native education and religion. Ojaide: states that "I think my poetry began from those days of going to school and learning to tell stories and going home to listen to my grandmother sing songs and tell folktales, myths, and legends of the Urhobo people" (121). In his 2005 book, *A Creative Writing Handbook for African Writers and Students*, Ojaide declares:

> To be a poet is to live life to the full. Have my relationships with my grandmother, father, and "Ita" not been the source of so many poems? Friendship with Joe and Ezekiel has been the harbinger of many poems. When Ezekiel died, I wrote many poems in his honour; some appear in *Delta Blues* & *Home Songs*. (53)

Each one of his poetry volumes carries a powerful evocation of Ojaide's personal and community experiences, and he speaks the voices of the common person of his Delta community of Nigeria. Even when he moved from home to study and later to live and teach in the United States, Ojaide remained closer to his grandmother and his people's traditional art and performances. Some of his poetry collections include *Children of Iroko & Other Poems* (1973), *Labyrinths of the Delta* (1986), *The Eagle's Vision* (1987), *Endless*

Song (1989), The *Fate of Vultures* (1990), *The Blood of Peace* (1991), *Cannons for the Brave* (1996), *Daydreams of Ants and Other Poems* (1997), *Invoking the Warrior Spirit: New and Selected Poems* (1999), and *In the Kingdom of Songs: A Trilogy of Poems, 1995–2000* (2002).

Yet, *I Want to Dance and Other Poems* (Ojaide 2003) is most significant for being both a metaphor for Ojaide's life journeys, from Africa to the Diaspora, "the farther the journey, the closer to home" ("Preface" and back cover). It is also a symbol of Ojaide's embodiment of his Urhobo roots.

The front cover (Ojaide 2003) shows images of unity of family and community through dance and social embrace: pregnant woman; women carrying children on their backs; other cultural items and artifacts; and symbols of traditional beauty, happiness, contentment, and solidarity. Although Ojaide is Urhobo and writes from the womb of his local Urhobo traditions, his poetics easily speaks to the indigenous African idea of art as life. A Yorùbá's description of and immediate response to a newborn baby is, *Ayo ab'ara tintin* (a joy in a tiny body)! The emphasis is not the size of the baby, but the fact of the baby being a buoyancy of joy for family and community: building lineage connections, family strength, and longevity. The African family constantly welcomes its new additions, not because it already has plenty of food to feed them but because children mean wealth, health, lineage expansion, and ancestral linkage.

Ojaide's (2003) first outing in this volume is a quotation from one Memerume, an Udje oral poet and performer from Urhobo community of Edjophe. Ojaide quotes from Memerume's Urhobo language song and provides its translation in English:

> *Owhorakpo je ya vwerie,*
> *sievo k'ota r'unu-u.*
>
> Humans branch here and there,
> and so do words of the mouth. (3)

Ojaide (2003), in adopting this poetic statement as an epigraph, invokes the metaphor of space, movement, reach, interconnectedness, and relationship—similarities between words and humans. Through words, the traditional Urhobo poet, like an African god of creation, also creates interconnectedness of life and meaning. As a modern African poet, Ojaide embraces this Urhobo oral poet as he does his muse and the Urhobo god of memory, *Aridon* ("Preface" 6). Ojaide states that:

> Memory is very important to the poet. Among my Urhobo people, poets and singers worship Aridon, god of memory, and Uhaghwa, god of inspiration and charming performance. Aridon is represented by a thread, which is meant to take one back to the source of past experiences. To me as a poet, childhood is vital, because it is the repository

of memory. That is why the Delta area has been so important to me. I had quite an extraordinary youth, which still bubbles in my memory and writing. (1996, 122)

Ojaide (2003) says his muse, Aridon, is a passionate one who constantly works to get him into his dancing feet (perhaps in what looks like a dancing competition with the god who is also a god of art and dance!), and his singer's mouth readily bursts into the melody befitting the dance of the gods. In a way, Ojaide uses this epigraph to show the focus of his poetry collection: "a song in three parts: surreal and mystical, . . . practical experiences and . . . memories of the poet's travels" ("Preface" and back cover). This poetry is described as the "movement from the surreal and mystical to the human and physical . . . " ("Preface"). One of the important ways many Nigerian poets have sought and attained connections with their African traditions is their alliance with African gods and legendary figures that they take as their heroes, guides, and poetic muse. For instance, to Wole Soyinka (1976), it is Ogun, the god of metal and of creativity; to Christopher Okigbo (1986), it is Idoto; to Osundare (1992), it is Osun, the river goddess. Ojaide (2003) similarly takes poetic inspiration from an Urhobo god, *Aridon*, and thus declares in the "Preface":

Once Aridon, muse and god of memory, possesses one, there is compulsive grip of the hand to record what is literally frothing in the head and heart. The possessed one becomes restless. At that time nothing else matters until the spell runs out; that is, after the poet has put down what he or she has witnessed personally. Of course, the gift of the god comes with a price—the poet has to present it to the world in a creatively attractive manner, and that demands labour. (6)

Ojaide (2003) is giving the credit for his poetic aura to both his creative god under whose power he writes and to his personal creative skills and labor through which his words and metaphors get molded. Like T.S. Eliot (1999), who describes the process of creative writing in the drafting, revising, and redrafting and of carefully choosing "best words" rendered in "best order" as a process of "critical labor . . . " Eliot and Ojaide (2003) love to post this poetic merit to the poet just as they each recognize the god muse!

Yet, the African poets' "collective awareness" of their Africanness—their historical, ethnic, sociological and experiential factors—constantly reverberates into their aesthetics and poetic choices (Irele 2001, 10–11; Na'Allah 1987; Ojaide 1996, 1–15), including what Ojaide (1996) describes as the inter-relatedness of literature and morality in African culture.

My discussion of *I want to Dance and other poems* (Ojaide 2003) will be conducted from Èlàlòrò paradigm. Èlàlòrò is a performance discourse theory derived from a rhetorical strategy for critical examination of a cultural material, speech, or text using community wisdom in local proverbs and adages. As a performance theory, Èlàlòrò, a Yorùbá phrase, "speech for operation or surgical analysis," calls for indigenous cultural affirmation of a work of art, especially in the light of Èlàlòrò's concept of global pluralism in which language, styles, and manners are important bases for measuring cultural identity and representation.

Èlàlòrò thus propounds for a linguistic liberation and liberalization in formally colonized nations of the world in which, regardless of the language of composition of a work of art from that community because of colonial experience or drive for global reach, indigenous or native concepts should be retained in the writer's own original or mother tongue. One of the crucial roles of literary critics in the global world, therefore, is to recognize indigenous colorations and local concepts in literary works even when written in European or any other languages that are foreign or non-indigenous to the writer's native community.

The use of Èlàlòrò paradigm in this review is intended to encourage further exploration of this critical framework by contemporary critics who are concerned about the disappearance of non-western indigenous voices from contemporary literary scenes of the 21st century. Thus, the author's background, including his mother tongue and his people's history and cultural values, are important factors in unearthing his or her literary project. The African text is a cultural and historical product and sometimes even born out of a cultural pluralistic experience (Ojaide 1996, 17–31). It is also a product for functional and didactic essences. The cultural analysis expected in Èlàlòrò would therefore insist on the polished critic locating those backgrounds and cultural anecdotes throughout the reviewing or critical process. The critic is also a researcher who would need the tools of field and library work, and someone who would not shy away from interviewing the author or people from the author's nativity if that is what it takes to explore his pedigree. The Èlàlòrò literary philosophy is rooted in the belief that phonological and morphological parameters of any text, including the text's syntactic structures, are informed by cultural, physical, and metaphysical formations and, therefore, could not be fully understood from the kind of abstract renditions of a text-based criticism or a postmodernist parlance where the author is already declared dead and buried. In reviewing *I want to Dance and Other Poems* (Ojaide 2003) and as one who does not speak Urhobo language, I searched for any material I could find by Ojaide, sought after him for an interview, reviewed a website by an Urhobo organization, and spoke to another native Urhobo.

From the opening pages of *I want to Dance and Other Poems* (Ojaide 2003), Ojaide connects the traditional African spirit of his Urhobo home to his new Diasporic feet abroad when he uses, as a second epigraph, a quotation from Edward Kamau Brathwaite's *Arrivants*:

>   To the best
> of my dreams
>   I will sing (9)

Brathwaite's (1973) popular linkage with and exploration of Black ancestral traditions in his poetry (see *The Arrivants* and *Middle Passages*, and *Black + Blues*, for example) explains Ojaide's invocation of Brathwaite and his work as a metaphor for his Diasporic muse, thus completing for him the duality that he now finds himself as a poet of Africa and its Diaspora. Memerume and Brathwaite to Ojaide, the African poet, symbolize the flow from Africa to the Diaspora and represent the human inter-connectedness and the space that he celebrates. It represents the dreams of life and of living that he sings about as he travels in and out of his Urhobo, Nigeria and Charlotte, North Carolina, United States home to places around the world, that of rendering the universality in a humanistic parlance that is so always important to the poet as he "moves from the surreal and the mystical to the human and physical" ("Preface") and captures the entire world in his palm.

With a total of 51 poems, *I want to Dance and other Poems* (Ojaide 2003) is divided into three sections. Section 1 contains 18 poems, Section 2 contains 18 poems, and Section 3 contains 15 poems. Each of the sections explores some unique features that paint the images of the "surreal and mystical atmosphere, practical experiences and their fresh memories and travel" and all the three sections combine together to project themes of movement, humanity, African inter-connectedness, celebration, hope, and achievements. The predominant theme here is life experience and travel. The poet seems to be projecting the Urhobo proverb, "Oroyare mre ne orotore," meaning "The person who travels wide experiences more than the sedentary old." From Africa to the African Diaspora, Ojaide shares experiences of life and living and celebrates the history and challenges of the African person in a global world. Yet, it seems that the poet's unconsciousness responds to his muse more than to his consciousness. It seems that the poet had surrendered to Aridon the voice to speak directly through his pen. In my interview, Ojaide seems marveled at the feat his poems have attained and some crucial meanings they might connote. Only Aridon, Ojaide's creative god, would tell how he commandeers the poet's mind and endears his creative mind to bring forth poetry even beyond his own personal imagination. The theme of travel in *I Want to Dance and Other Poems* is a metaphor for the Middle Passage of trans-Atlantic slavery as well as for contemporary travels of contemporary African away from his exploited and poverty-ridden homeland in search of a better life in the economically booming West.

The first poem, "Daily Worship" (Ojaide 2003, 11) is an opening or homage poem. The traditional African performer is always conscious of his or her homage to the gods and the elders. His "Daily Worship" is in two stanzas. The first stanza has 13 lines and the second has only three. Here's how that poem starts:

> A bird flies into the open house of words
> where I am cloistered by command of the caste.

> I who daily dance the mask decked with feathers
> raise arms to embrace the messenger from afar—
> the bird wants for a nest the swaggering tower
> I carry on the head and the perches for the season.
> In the town's gathering place I will have
> to open the gift that Aridon wrapped for me,
> delivered by the bird become companion.
> To the bird that raises the song I sing
> I first give abundance before I ever taste
> of the sweet berries that fall into my lot. (11)

The metaphor of the bird is carefully chosen and it represents the mobility, the travel, and yet the creativity and long, deep insight of the poet. The bird not only flies and migrates from place to place, it sings melodiously through its titillating voice. This reminds one that the *uty* bird was Ojaide's (2003) muse, and he has explained in his writing about how the bird inspired many of his songs (53). This poem talks of the gift of poetry, "I will have to open the gift that Aridon wrapped for me," to show and talks of being "cloistered by the command of the caste" (Ojaide 2003, 11). The poet is eager to give credit for his poetic feat to his creative muse and god of memory, Aridon. He uses different metaphors for poetry and poetry performance: "open house of words," "the mask decked with feather," "the swaggering tower," "the gift that Aridon wrapped for me," "the song I sing," and "the sweet berries that fall into my lot" (11), all showing the deeply rooted way that Ojaide believes his poetry is connected to his ancestral culture and the relationship between the poet, his poetry, and the function or important place for poetry in society. At the second stanza, the poet beckons on the sun to accompany him in his journey to carry out the biddings of Aridon. He asks "the sun that warms my dance" to "Come and worship with me" (11). The poet here is performing the ritual of opening so that the day can be sweet for him so that he can eat from and share his "sweet berries" with all that like to take from it. He performs his opening ritual so that his berries would not turn sour!

The second poem in Section 1 (Ojaide 2003, 12), "My Company," talks about the "bonfire that opens up another world." The poet is in tune here with the traditional closeness of the African oral griot who is one with his earth, with nature. "The glowing moon" embraces the poet. Yet, this three-stanza poem gives hints of some strange occurrences in the contemporary world of the modern poet, "infidels chant alleluia at dawn of holidays" (first stanza) and the bird's experience of being caged (second stanza). To be caged is not necessarily limited to the idea of losing one's freedom; it might also portray the world where the contemporary poet and the modern people suffer from the harrowing experience of the exploitation of the poet's community and the poverty of vision and ideas displaced by the society's exploiters, which mercilessly affects the poet! Yet, the poet celebrates the freedom he attains, in ideas and in physical release of his being "into the air." "The bird flies back, only to leave, and return." This is a physical flight, between his home and the Diaspora. This modern African person flies away and he is being compelled to return but soon again to fly away and return soon again! It is a familiar narrative of the contemporary African migrant that Minthia Diawara (2004) in *We Won't Budge* discusses as the pull he has to his native home only to want to leave it but to return "home" again once he has left. For Ojaide (2003), the god is closely linked to and responsible for the restlessness of the poet's drive to return to his native home. The last stanza shows that even Aridon is restless here; wherever the native African goes abroad, "the angel must report at home for the night." For me, this explains to me what I have sensed is Ojaide's belief that the African person cannot be too far detached from the African land; he must regularly touch the African earth and, more so if he's a writer, swim in the flesh of the African waters.

Ojaide (2003), in my discussions with him, frowns at an attitude in which a modern African poet, simply because he now lives in the Diaspora, forces the western post-modern identity, his personal and societal upheavals in the so-called First World on his African poetry. He calls such poets dubious! It is like asking them to learn the lesson of the Urhobo proverb, "Edje ogo k'orhua-a," meaning, "You don't show the antelope where cultivable land is." They must all be antelopes that know the African land well enough and are experts on how to cultivate it. Ojaide believes that African poets and persons in the Diaspora must, out of necessity, constantly return to their homes even if they would soon leave again.

The remaining poems in Section 1 (Ojaide 2003) convey many experiences of travel especially the poet's travels, and his life performances at home and around the world. Life is a performance and every space, a performance space. The poems in this section vary. In "Eastward-Bound," where he portrays the anxiety of preparation, the process of setting out from home and arriving at a destination, and the experiences both when *en route* on a journey and after arriving at destination. The quest motive is to acquire the knowledge, to see the face, and "visit her mantled in the mist of the east" (14). In "I string The Kora" the poet, already in the East, portrays an early morning performance in which the poet's duty is to "wake the world" to the new brilliant day from their previous night's sleep of lapping on to the lap of moonlight. The poet beats the musical Kora and "clears the throat with alligator pepper" (14) The poet here paints image of the wayfarer, the sun is on his way back home; the sunbird is the process of dipping into ocean; and the poet, the pilgrim, is still on his journey to see the person whose face he is dying to see. The poet is already imagining her face and creating an image of her smiling on his arrival: "I see through the chasm eyes open and close, / I see a mouth laurelled with smiles, / a nose peaked by divine craft; / I see through mountains the cheeks / and hair I seek to touch with reverence" (14). The "magic" of art and creativity, the poet's major power, is what he hopes to deploy in announcing his presence before his quest and seeking to taste her "tasteful dish"! The poet here explores from African folktale and the image of the trickster and calls himself Ananse, and he will display his wits and would find the "hidden gift" he is after! The poet employs very strong personal characters, from Pilgrim, to bird, to Ananse, he journeys from human to the surreal to the mystical!

Other poems continue this tradition, telling stories, painting personal and community experiences. Some are long, like "A Bird's Tale" (Ojaide 2003, 17) being 11 stanzas and eight different divisions (the longest poem in the section). "Swimmer," in one stanza and 12 lines, is the shortest (25). The other poems are "To the Bird of the East," "You Will Appear," "The Suitor Is Dancing," "Moon Phase," "To my Realist Friend," "Airspace," "Healing Song," "Island Residence," "Roaming the Lightscape," "You Defy Capture," and "Ten Pieces, Birdsong."

Section 2 (Ojaide 2003) starts on page 39 with an epigraph from Homer's *The Iliad*, "But the gods give to mortals not everything at the same time," and thus opens a section that continues the poet's dance from one world to the other, and from the physical to the metaphysical, from the real and the mystical to the surreal. By invoking *The Iliad*, the African poet is affirming the interconnectedness of both (the African and the Homer) worlds in their perception of the cosmos and their understanding of the place of human beings in it. Milman Parry (1928) and Albert Lord (1960) in their studies show that Homeric songs share such features and performance essences that contemporary African scholars identify in African traditional oral performances. Isidore Okpewho's *The Epic in Africa* also discusses similar characteristics between African epic and the Homeric epics, and the universal human connections that Ojaide seeks to show by choosing Homer's *Iliad* as epigraph to Section 2 can never be lost. The invocation of gods and goddesses and the explorations of community and human interconnectedness displayed in Homer's *The Iliad* are similar to explorations by traditional African singers in their performance of African traditional poetry.

Yet, Ojaide (2003) always starts from the local and sets out to the global. His first poem in Section 2 is titled, "Following the Minstrel's Trail." It is a narrative poem, a story of his hero and role model, Ojaide's teacher, Paul Orovwigho of Okurekpo, whose life also presents a definition of a poet and an artist. A poet, like his teacher's nickname, is "the wonder of our world;" he or she is the "lord to whom we fell captive with delight" (40). A poem worth its salt is a tiger that does not need to proclaim its tigritude. The poet is a vehicle through which the muse or the god of creativity sends messages to the world, and the power of poetry would draw out its audience from their closet: "the waves of the song should / drown the clattering of the far-flung crowd" (40). Thus, Ojaide invokes "the god of melodies, the great dispenser" to enable him perform his art at the time that it is most effective. "Following the Minstrel's

Trail," therefore, pays homage to Ojaide's teacher, as well as presents an indigenous concept of artistic power. Many of the poems in Section 2 tell stories from the poet's personal experiences, reflects on cultural or philosophical issues, and invokes or celebrates individuals or even concepts. "My Father's Eyes" celebrates the skills, wits, and intellectualism of his father, which were never affected by the mishap of his father's loss of his right eye. This poem explores lineage history and family tradition as it is done in traditional African praise poetry, through references to mannerism, actions, physical traits, personal skills, and philosophy. The poet celebrates his father's fatherhood and establishes a personal connection with him as his connection to both his ancestry and to his present world, to whom he says, "the world he didn't know still lives/ on the fiction and fact of his fatherhood" (42). The loss of an outer eye does not affect his father's inner vision of the world. Other homage, celebration, and invocation poems in this section include "Three Mami Wata Poems" (52–53), "To My Feminist Friend" (54), "A Child Holds the Lamp" (55), "Guest of the Forest" (56–57), "Tobi" (60), "Anthill Residence" (61–62), and "Night" (63). Some of his poems are highly philosophical and presents his way of looking at our present world, sometimes merging it with a vision drawn from his strong Urhobo cultural upbringing. An example of such poems is "Entering the New Millenium" (44), where the poet describes the ripeness of a century as "everybody's fear," saying "The snake lost its tail and grew a second head!" (44). It is as if we the people are at a loss whether to celebrate the end of a misery year or the beginning of one which gives no promise of being better than the departed: "If we celebrate the hatching of toxic eggs, / we must prepare against poisonous birds / whose droppings will burn the air we breathe" (44). The metaphors of snake and its second head, of toxic eggs, poisonous birds, "the elephant trampled farms," and "dynasties of nightmares," are examples of how the poet presents people's perception of their lives from the ending century to the beginning of a new one.

An Urhobo proverb says, "Ekpere owhe, j'owhe wa," meaning, "you can't stop the seasons." Yet, you can understand your experience from the previous one and have an idea of the new season knocking on your door. "Asa r'adia, oye avwe ebe r'oye vware oko" It is leaves that you find where you live that you use to wrap what you have! Another example is the star poem, "I want to Dance," (Ojaide 2003, 45) where "She danced to life, despite the strap!" Several other poems describe sheer struggle, exploitation of poor people, and destruction of our common earth. Another such poem in this section is "Four Pieces" (46), which presents the Niger Delta, the oil rich soil that is personified and exploited, harassed, and killed. The poem talks of "Her jewelry of honor / sold to stave off drought/ in their inland capital." One can feel the wailing in this poem; the poet is crying out, giving vivid picture of the coldness of the murder and the heartless of the robbery of the Niger Delta: "The Delta bleeds; disrobed." Crying further, "Within seven days of / its prowling, / the water turned cold / and blood-toned. E-e Ogiso! / Ogiso! / e-e Ogiso!" Other very interesting poems in Section 2 includes "Three Mami Wata Poems" (52–53), "To my Feminist Friend" (54), and Anthill Residence" (61).

Section 3 starts with two epigraphs. The first is a quotation from Sudanese Taban lo Liyong's *Homage to Onyame*, and the second is from Haitian Edwidge Danticat's *Breath and Memory*. It is interesting that Ojaide (2003) chooses to quote from these two poets, both of whose lives represent history of migration, Taban, within East Africa, from Sudan to Kenya, Uganda, and South Africa and for Edwidge, first, ancestor forcefully removed as slaves from Africa to the Diaspora, and as a young girl of four, her parents had moved to New York leaving her with aunt and uncle in Haiti, and at 12 she moved to Brooklyn to join her parents. The two epigraphs center around knowledge, action, and freedom or lack of it.

This section contains 15 poems. The first poem, "From This Soil That Hurts" (66), is a strong poem that, like many before it, explores elements of nature, soil, grass, crop, tongue, fruit, vegetable, and more to address issues of community and national exploitation and survival. The next one is "Women Writing Africa, in Fez" (68), which focuses on African women's determination, power, and consistence in reasserting self and community in the face of patriarchal exploitation. The last stanza presents some rhetorical questions:

> What are men doing that drive women from
> the file that leads to the exchange counter?
> Why are flowers not always sunlit in their seasons;
> why are hunters deaf to the antelope's cry;
> where are the women whose rooms are vacant?
> And what men are hearty when crushed
> with fat bills, possessing but dispossessed? (69)

This poem shows the illusion of patriarchal supremacy and shows that women, rather than men, in voice, body, and wits rule and deserve acknowledgement. The poet asks: "What empire on earth of men is not vulnerable to herstory?" (68).

The poems in Section 3 (Ojaide 2003) are all powerful, many addressing issues of place, community, travel, experience, art, and other life issues, sometime philosophical and other times real. Poems include "The Size of Manhood" (72), "Rivera's Brush" (75), "Santa Maria" (76), "Discovering Lands" (77–8), "The Open Spaces of My Life" (84), and more. The last poem of the collection is "When the Migrant Returns Home" (87–8), which appropriately sums up the preoccupation of the entire collection: a celebration of migration; of human and community solidarity; and, most importantly, of homecoming and rediscovery, and of reconnection to communal and ancestral roots. Now at home after journeying around the world, the migrant contends with his new status as a stranger in his native home and yet, a citizen of the world. Despite his tales of the New World and his

Cultural Poetics, African Diaspora, and the Global World 83

fantasies of its reaches, he knows all too well that he must "shed borrowed accents" and return to be the same as the native *udje* music; he needs to get to the ground and dance the dance of his ancestors:

> *Udje* music doesn't lose
> its edge despite its age
> unlike *igoru* and others
> it stays in hearts and heads—
> it's the native bound to the soil. (87)

6 African Cultural Revival as an Important Message in *Death and the King's Horseman* and *The Lion and the Jewel*[1]

Soyinka's *The Burden of Memory, The Muse of Forgiveness*, where he acknowledges Negritude's fight to reclaim African cultural glory, it was not common to suggest that Wole Soyinka's literary work projected a drive towards African cultural revival such as seen in Langston Hughes's Harlem Renaissance poetry. Yet, a cultural understanding of both *Death and the King's Horseman* and *The Lion and the Jewel* (1963) would reveal that primary voices coming from these plays are unmistakably those of African revival and cultural pride in the face of western colonial pomposity.

Twice I heard audience members ask Soyinka about who among his characters in *Death and the King's Horseman* spoke for him. I have always believed myself that an author sometimes chooses a character in his work and builds them to represent his personal views and vision of the world, and I strongly think that Soyinka has done the same in these two plays. This question supports the thesis that an author often creates at least one character that represents his vision and argues his views in a novel or play. The first questioners were at the University of Toulouse in France, where Soyinka had a rendezvous with students who were then studying *Death and the King's Horseman* in their courses. Soyinka agreed that Olunde spoke many views he shared and championed visions dearest to his heart. The second questioners, asking a similar question, still on the same book, were at Knox College in Gailesburg, Illinois, United States. Soyinka responded with some humour. He did not name Olunde this time. He declared that Elesin showed some traits and talents to which he, Soyinka, was reputable! Soyinka said he was the real "bushrat with [the] restless eyes!"

In Soyinka's (1963, 1975) plays and in his novels and poetry, there are always unmistakable voices of the playwright's dialogue with his audience. In this short piece, I will consider two of those voices that show his consistent portrayal of the strength and capability of the African community to move forward in the face of conflict. Soyinka seems to have a consistent theory about how Africa would survive the colonialist and postcolonialist denigration of African life and culture. Just as he enjoys having fun with his characters or the various issues they engage in, it is always bell clear whenever Soyinka wears his boxing gloves. He punches directly at spots where spectators would find themselves drawn into the debate. Nadine Gordimer (1994) has many words for Soyinka, who she says always, "went further than words" (40). She discusses how Soyinka often goes beyond his writing and takes physical actions about issues he is concerned about. Using Soyinka's activities during some political crisis in Nigeria, crisis which Soyinka himself connected to the Nigerian civil war as an example, she says that Soyinka "tried to stop the war,"[2] and adds,

> Literally with his body, by physical intervention, attempting to take over the broadcasting station. [. . .] Soyinka is the supreme and splendid example of the writer meeting the demands of his time beyond intellectual obligations as they are generally understood. (40).

Two very interesting Yorùbá adages help to explain Soyinka's vision in the two plays I shall be discussing here. This is a recurring adage about cultural ownership, identity, and feeling of possession, which we have touched upon at least in two previous chapters: (1) *Naaní naanì naaní, tara eni laa naaní* (if one will love anything, one should love what one has), and (2) *Teni n teni, t'ekisa nt'aatan* (one's property should be dearest to one; what is dearest to the garbage is the rag!). Both containing traditional wisdom, expect a fight whenever a person's culture and identity is challenged. They expect every culture to put forth a polemic of self-love and recognition. *Eni* or *ara eni* (self) here does not necessarily means a singular self. It means a family, a community, a nation, and people. It means humanity. In describing Soyinka as a talented explorer of African oral art, Bernth Lindfors (1993) observes:

> Soyinka frequently weaves them so intricately into the fabric of dramatic action that they become a vital part of the total artistic design, a part which could not be altered or eliminated without destroying the complex patterns of human interaction upon which the drama itself depends. In other words, they are not meaningless exotic decorations but elements central to the intense theatrical experience Soyinka attempts to create. (27).

My priority in this chapter is to show that beyond the cultural and artistic interface (in terms of the use of Yorùbá dance, mime, and linguistic flavour) that easily cajoles readers' attention in Soyinka's work, the playwright is often concerned with putting forward his theory of African emancipation in the face of Eurocentric delineation. Soyinka's theory of the revival of community strength and the vision for Africa to forge ahead in the face of the unceasing colonial and postcolonial denigration are part of the playwright's exploration of his people's wisdom. Soyinka seems to fight, as does Achebe, against Western primitivists' slander of the African experience—what Gordimer describes as their attempts to "relegate it to anthropology or, at best, regard it patronisingly as a quaint anachronism in modern life" (Gordimer 1994, 38). In other words, while Soyinka's tigritude[3] opposes romanticising black beauty as is done in Negritude, it does propound a theory to frustrate Eurocentric myopism about Africa, exactly as done by some of his characters in the two plays I shall be discussing in this chapter.

The two plays, *Death and the King's Horseman* (Soyinka 1975) and *The Lion and the Jewel* (Soyinka 1963), will show that in addition to great dramatic innovations, Soyinka shows a tendency to engage in critical polemics championing issues that would normally have taken charge in his essays. Olunde in *Death and the King's Horseman*, and Bale Baroka in *The Lion and the Jewel*, are two intriguing characters that readers would find memorable in the sense that they clearly articulate Soyinka's vision of African cultural revival.

THE DEBATE AND THE LECTURE

In *Death and the King's Horseman*, Soyinka (1975) creates two levels of foreigners, each making inroads into the other's territory. The first and the most ferocious foreigners are the Pilkings. Jane Pilkings is often by her husband's side and represents "the softest his heart can get" when it comes to African issues. The second is the young African, Olunde, who is a foreigner in Britain. He was born into the crisis of the European colonization of Africa. As would be his fate,[4] the second foreigner is in Europe in quest for Western education.

Soyinka (1975) gives the foreigners, the Pilkings, and Olunde opportunities to interact with their hosts. He allows them to reveal to us, through their utterances and actions, how far they will go in understanding their hosts. They are both obviously deeply rooted in different ancestral traditions, each representing the core of his people's socio-cultural expectations of the time. Apparently, each of them has deeply rooted ideas or philosophy about life and about human dignity. Each also has potential, due to their quest motifs, to develop further, explore new forms and to test his beliefs and ideas from a new cultural periscope. How far does each character go in *Death and the King's Horseman*? What is the basic revival theory the author proposes to his people through the various actions or the lack of thereof by his characters? What do the utterances of these foreigners tell us about each of them, and, in particular, how does Soyinka's mouthpiece, Olunde, represent Soyinka's message for African revival?

In the second play, *The Lion and the Jewel* (Soyinka 1963), also, there are also two important characters, one representing the new European (or Western) order, and the other representing the African cultural values. The first is Lakunle, the village schoolmaster, and the second is Bale Baroka, the Ilujinle Village Chief. For different and sometimes similar reasons, both characters want the same village belle for a wife and both engage in competition to marry her. Perhaps much more important to them than the marriage is that both profess opposing ideologies about African development, and each is bent on carrying out his plans. Again, how does the playwright equip each of these characters with words and wisdom to represent his own views and vision of the African development? What is the theory that Soyinka propounds through *The Lion and the Jewel* characters? In particular, how does Bale Baroka represent Soyinka's message for African revival?

THE DEBATE: OLUNDE VS. THE PILKINGS

In representing Soyinka's views about African revival, Olunde and Baroka are made to inherit primary responsibilities for leading their respective communities. Olunde is destined to become the next Elesin, after his father's passage. He is, therefore, being prepared by his people to stand up to the responsibility of an Elesin when it is his turn to do so. It is for this purpose that his people protest the colonial officer's decision to send Olunde away from home. The following discussion about Elesin's position, and the messages of two villagers to Mr. Pilkings regarding Olunde throw light on how important the Elesin's role is to his people:

AMUSA: The chief who call himself Elesin Oba.

WOMAN: You ignorant man. It is not he who calls himself Elesin Oba, it is his blood that says it. As it called out to his father before him and will to his son after him. And that is in spite of everything your white man can do.

WOMAN: Is it not the same ocean that washes this land and the white man's land? Tell your white man he can hide our son away as long as he likes. When the time comes for him, the same ocean will bring him back. (35).

The Elesin's position is deeply cultural and people have the strong belief that nothing can destroy it. True to the villager's prediction, therefore, the ocean brings back Olunde at a time when he needs to succeed his father. Although not yet an Elesin, he adequately articulates his people's views and argues fervently in favour of their way of life, comparing it with what he has seen of the British way of life. He chooses to *naani* (love) his own culture in preference to the British culture!

Amongst Soyinka's (1975) important messages in *Death and the King's Horseman* is that some African cultural events, often confused with the

European, are rooted in a most logical, humane, and sensible African perspective, if only the European foreigners would care to understand. Specifically in this play, an actual event that took place in Oyo city of Nigeria in 1946 has been recast by Soyinka and "set back two to three years while World War II was still on, for minor reasons of dramaturgy" (5–6). The King of Oyo Yorùbá (presently southwestern Nigeria) was transiting to the ancestral word,[5] and the King's Horseman was expected to die and accompany his king and master to the ancestral world. This is how one of the native characters (now a converted Christian) explains it:

> It is native law and custom. The King dies last month. Tonight is his burial. But before they can bury him, the Elesin must die so as to accompany him to heaven. (28)

While calling it a "barbaric custom" Mr. Pilkings says in response to his wife's suggestion that he must stop Elesin's ritual death:

> I don't have to stop anything. If they want to throw themselves off the top of a cliff or poison themselves for the sake of some barbaric custom what is that to me? If it were ritual murder or something like that I'd be duty-bound to do something. I can't keep an eye on all the potential suicides in this province. And as for that man believe me it's good riddance. (31).

Finally the playwright allows these two characters to face each other and to argue out their respective positions from the experience they have gathered living in the other's culture. Olunde (Soyinka 1975), who had been to Britain to study and become a medical doctor, represents the first side; the African side. It was during World War II, so he followed the war very closely. He took interest in the British media, following reports filed from the war front. He had constant discussions with people at various levels—friends, neighbours and colleagues at the hospital—and, as a student doctor, he was involved at the hospital, responding to the killed, the wounded, and the sick.

Conversely, Mr. and Mrs. Pilkings (Soyinka 1975) were colonialists in Nigeria, living among Olunde's people. Mr. Pilkings was in charge of the local police and was also responsible for other important aspects of the administration of the colony. The playwright shows that Olunde, the foreigner with an open mind who moves beyond his myriad myopism, ends up understanding the new culture and respecting his own people and traditions more than he had ever done. The other way around happens to the foreigner with a closed mind. Even his own culture, which he thinks is superior, he never actually respects let alone recognize the foreign ways of life. It does not appear that Mr. and Mrs. Pilkings are interested in understanding the African natives beyond desecrating their gods and cultic essences. Conversely, Olunde, living

African Cultural Revival

in Britain as a foreigner, found himself understanding the British culture in ways he had not done before. In hospitals where he trained and among the people he mixed with, he ended up learning about some important British attitudes, especially with regard to the war.

Soyinka (1975) uses Olunde to explain to and debate with Mrs. Pilkings about the African ways that the Pilkings have dubbed "pagan," "horrible" (Soyinka 1975, 28–29) and "barbaric" (31). The Pilkings choose *egungun* dress, the African community's highly revered ancestral cult dress, and wear it as entertainment outfit for a visiting English Prince, and this is despite the many protests from Amusa: "Mista Pirinkin, I beg you sir, what you think you do with that dress? It belong to dead cult, not for human being [. . .]." "Mista Pirinkin, I beg you, take it off. Is not good for man like you to touch that cloth" (24). He then wonders: "I cannot against death to dead cult. This dress get power of dead" (49).[6]

Now, let us go into the issues debated over by Olunde and Mrs. Pilkings (Soyinka 1975). In Section 4 of the play, while the party organized for the visiting British royal is on, Olunde, who just returned from Britain, comes to the Residency Hall in search of Mr. Pilkings. He has heard about his attempt to interfere in his father's ritual rites and hopes to convince him to respect his people's sentiments. The Pilkings themselves do not know that Olunde is in Town. Their first dialogue is about the *egungun* dress, which Mrs. Pilkings is obviously wearing:

OLUNDE (*emerging into the light*): I didn't mean to startle you madam. I am looking for the District Officer.
JANE: Wait a minute . . . don't I know you? Yes, you are Olunde; the young man who . . .
OLUNDE: Mrs. Pilkings! How fortunate. I came here to look for your husband.
JANE: Olunde! Let's look at you. What a fine young man you've become. Grand but solemn. Good God, when did you return? Simon never said a word. But you do look well Olunde.
OLUNDE: You are . . . well, you look quite well yourself Mrs. Pilkings. From what little I can see of you.
JANE: Oh, this. It's caused quite a stir I assure you, and not all of it very pleasant. You are not shocked I hope?
OLUNDE: Why should I be? But don't you find it rather hot in there? Your skin must find it difficult to breathe.
JANE: Well, it is a little hot I must confess, but it's all in a good cause.
OLUNDE: What cause Mrs. Pilkings?
JANE: All this. The ball. And His Highness being here in person and all that.
OLUNDE (*mildly*): And that is the good cause for which you desecrate an ancestral mask?
JANE: Oh, so you are shocked after all. How disappointing.

OLUNDE: No I am not shocked Mrs. Pilkings. You forget that I have now spent four years among your people. I discovered that you have no respect for what you do not understand.
JANE: Oh. So you've returned with a chip on your shoulder. That's a pity Olunde. I am sorry.
(*An uncomfortable silence follows*).
I take it then that you did not find your stay in England altogether edifying.
OLUNDE: I did not say that. I found your people quite admirable in many ways, their conduct and courage in this war for instance. (50).

This is a very interesting discussion! Obviously, both of them are very smart at the verbal pyrotechnics, each clearly understanding what the other implies. Olunde clearly comprehends what Jane means when, on seeing him, she says he has "become" a fine young man, emphasising his "look" by stating "you look well." This is the pattern of the colonialist's notion: "We have saved you from the savage custom, we have now helped to civilize you." Earlier in Section 2, the same kind of language has been used to address Joseph, their servant who converted to Christianity. Interestingly it is the same *egungun* issue:

PILKINGS: Joseph, are you a Christian or not?
JOSEPH: Yessir.
PILKINGS: Does seeing me in this outfit bother you?
JOSEPH: No sir, it has no power.
PILKINGS: Thank God for some sanity at last. Now Joseph, answer me on the honour of a Christian—what is supposed to be going on in the town tonight? (27)

Representing the author's voice (Soyinka 1975), Olunde, unlike Joseph, adequately responds to the colonialist's primitivist stand: "You have no respect for what you do not understand" (50). We can sense the disappointment in Jane, that Olunde is not Joseph, and that they have failed in their bid to get him to abandon his culture! *Teni n teni, t'ekisa n t'aatan*! By making Olunde speak those pinching words, Soyinka reiterates the vision of holding onto one's cultural values and suggests that even when Africans travel to European lands, they must keep their minds and hearts intact. This is demonstrated when Olunde talks about his experience at a British hospital where he trained during World War II. Jane responds with disbelief and shock, occasionally trying to play him like Yorùbá children play okoto, the snail shell, but Olunde proves surprisingly smart for the game. The second discussion is about war and sacrifice, centring on the colonialist's interpretation of the community's need for Elesin to perform a ritual death to accompany the deceased King to the ancestral world:

JANE: Ah yes the war. Here of course it is all rather remote. From time to time we have a black-out drill just to remind us that there is a war on. And the rare convoy passes through the occasional bit of excitement like that ship that was blown up in the harbour.

OLUNDE: Here? Do you mean through enemy action?

JANE: Oh no, the war hasn't come that close. The captain did it himself. I don't quite understand it really. Simon tried to explain. The ship had to be blown up because it had become dangerous to the other ships, even to the city itself. Hundreds of the coastal population would have died.

OLUNDE: Maybe it was loaded with ammunition and had caught fire. Or some of those lethal gases they've been experimenting on.

JANE: Something like that. The captain blew himself up with it. Deliberately. Simon said someone had to remain on board to light the fuse.

OLUNDE: It must have been a very short fuse.

JANE (*shrugs*): I don't know much about it. Only that there was no other way to save lives. No time to devise anything else. The captain took the decision and carried it out.

OLUNDE: Yes . . . I quite believe it. I met men like that in England.

JANE: Oh just look at me! Fancy welcoming you back with such morbid news. Stale too. It was at least six months ago.

OLUNDE: I don't find it morbid at all. I find it rather inspiring. It is an affirmative commentary on life.

JANE: What is?

OLUNDE: That captain's self-sacrifice.

JANE: Nonsense. Life should never be thrown deliberately away.

OLUNDE: And the innocent people round the harbour?

JANE: Oh, how does one know? The whole thing was probably exaggerated anyway.

OLUNDE: That was a risk the captain couldn't take. But please Mrs. Pilkings, do you think you could find your husband for me? I have to talk to him.

The debate gets heated up. Olunde, representing the playwright's voice (Soyinka 1975), juxtaposes between the sacrifice which the community requires of the aged, spent Elesin, and the one the British captain offered for his society, and the sacrifices thousands of the dead British soldiers made during the War. Soyinka uses Olunde to bring home to Jane the foolishness of the primitivist's thoughts. He knows how to drive home the truth. The Yorùbá say *Otito koro* (truth is bitter) and Jane is uncomfortable dealing truth:

OLUNDE: Mrs. Pilkings, I came home to bury my father. As soon as I heard the news I booked my passage home. In fact we were fortunate. We traveled in the same convoy as your Prince, so we had excellent protection.

JANE: But you don't think your father is also entitled to whatever protection is available to him?

OLUNDE: How can you understand? He has protection. No one can undertake what he does tonight without the deepest protection the mind can conceive. What can you offer him in place of his peace of mind, in place of the honour and veneration of his own people? What would you think of your Prince if he had refused to accept the risk of losing his life on this voyage? This . . . showing-the-flag tour of colonial possessions.

JANE: I see. So it isn't just medicine you studied in England.

OLUNDE: Yet another error into which your people fall. You believe that everything which appears to make sense was learnt from you.

JANE: Not so fast Olunde. You have learnt to argue I can tell that, but I never said you made sense. However cleverly you try to put it, it is still a barbaric custom. It is even worse—it's feudal! The King dies and the chieftain must be buried with him. How feudalistic can you get!

OLUNDE: (*Waves his hand toward the background. The PRINCE is dancing past again—to a different step—and all the guests are bowing and curtseying as he passes*): And this? Even in the midst of a devastating war, look at that. What name would you give to that?

JANE: Therapy, British style. The preservation of sanity in the midst of chaos.

OLUNDE: Others would call it decadence. However, it doesn't really interest me. You white races know how to survive; I've seen proof of that. By all logical and natural laws this war should end with all the white races wiping out one another, wiping out their so-called civilization for all time and reverting to a state of primitivism the like of which has so far only existed in your imagination when you thought of us. I thought all that at the beginning. Then I slowly realised that your greater art is the art of survival. But at least have the humility to let others survive in their own way.

JANE: Through ritual suicide?

OLUNDE: Is that worse than mass suicide? Mrs. Pilkings, what do you call what those young men are sent to do by their generals in this war? Of course you have also mastered the art of calling things by names which don't remotely describe them.

The argument now is about which is primitive; ritual suicide of an aged, spent person or mass suicide of young military officers? As can be seen, Jane twists Olunde all the way, but the playwright is a master of his art. He initiates an interesting debate reflecting every type of logic that the primitivist often proffers to justify his "superiority." He does not, however, allow them to get away with it; his character, Olunde, confronts Mrs. Pilkings with yet another bitter truth:

OLUNDE: Mrs. Pilkings, whatever we do, we never suggest that a thing is the opposite of what it really is. In your newsreels I heard defeats, thorough, murderous defeats described as strategic victories. No wait, it wasn't just on your newsreels. Don't forget I was attached to hospitals all the time. Hordes of your wounded passed through those wards. I spoke to them. I spent long evenings by their bedside while they spoke terrible truths of the realities of that war. I know how history is made.

Jane cannot deal with naked truths and goes round and around, trying hard to pretend that Olunde is not even talking about what actually happened. This kind of debate is what Soyinka (1975) obviously prefers to an outright endorsement of one's culture, as it happens in Negritude. Soyinka uses Olunde to show how to get behind the skin of the primitivist thinker. When Jane understands she cannot counter the sharp criticism of Olunde, she resorts to a different defence strategy—that it was not Britain's best of times when Olunde lived there:

JANE (*after a moment's pause*): Perhaps I can understand you now. The time we picked for you was not really one for seeing us at our best.
OLUNDE: Don't think it was just the war. Before that even started I had plenty of time to study your people. I saw nothing, finally, that gave you the right to pass judgement on other peoples and their ways. Nothing at all.
JANE (*hesitantly*): Was it . . . colour thing? I know there is some Discrimination. (54).

It is interesting and rather ironic that a people who practice racism could claim cultural superiority over those who see humanity at equal levels of engagement and co-existence. Olunde makes his point on behalf of his creator that sacrifice cannot be clothed in any other language, and that mass murder of innocent people, civilians, and army officers is worse than the sacrifice the Yorùbá community demands of the aged Elesin. Eldred Durosimi Jones is right when he says that Olunde's eventual decision to take the place of his father shows "the society's hope of regeneration and of continuity" (quoted in Booth 1993, 128). Olunde is therefore an excellent example of the kind of African that Soyinka projects as Africa's future—the African who will be proud of his culture, mentally sharp enough to defending his people and their views, and ready to give his life to ensure regeneration and continuity for his community.

THE LECTURE: BALE BAROKA AND SIDI

The Lion and the Jewel (Soyinka 1963), as has been already pointed out, is the story of Sidi and Bale Baroka. After having successfully tricked Sidi to come to his palace, Baroka engages her in two over-powering processes. The first is making her to see his wrestling match with a very muscular wrestler to prove his physical capabilities as a man and to show that his old age does not affect his physical prowess. Sidi nitially turns down Baroka's invitation, saying he is old and spent, proudly telling Sadiku:

> See how the water glistens on my face / Like the dew-moistened leaves on a Harmattan morning / But he—his face is like a leather piece / Turn rudely from the saddle of his horse, [*Sadiku gasps.*] / Sprinkled with the musty ashes / From a pipe that is long over-smoked. / And this goat-like tuft / Which I once thought was manly; / It is like scattered twists of grass— / Not even green— / But charred and lifeless, as after a forest fire! / Sadiku, I am young and brimming; he is spent. / I am the twinkle of a jewel / But he is the hind-quarters of a lion! (22–23).

So when she later decides to visit Baroka, it is to mock him for what she thinks is his impotence. Sidi cannot, therefore, believe her eyes when Baroka throws the muscular wrestler on the ground. She is too excited, and exclaims: "You won, you won!" and breaks into dance and song: Yokolu Yokolu. Ko ha tan bi / Iyawo gb'oko san'le / Oko yo'ke" (Pride, and high mindedness, all is now over! The wife has thrown her husband to the floor, the husband develops a hunchback!) This is a popular victory song among the Yorùbá! For the second over-powering process, Baroka engages Sidi in a witty dialogue, ensuring that he gets her rapt attention, and eventually her conviction about his intellectual and physical puissance. He seeks to dazzle her and through his words, work her into a trance of submission. He shows Sidi evidence that he is not the anti-progress type that he has been portrayed to be. After proudly showing Sidi the printing press that he has caused to be made at the palace, he says, and Sidi responds, truly dazzled:

BAROKA: The work dear child, of the palace blacksmiths
    Built in full secrecy. All is not well with it—
    But I will find the cause and then Ilujinle
    Will boast its own tax on paper, made with
    Stamps like this. For long I dreamt it
    And here it stands, child of my thoughts.
SIDI: [*wonder-struck*] You mean . . . this will work some day?
BAROKA: Ogun has said the word. And now my girl
    What think you of that image on the stamp
    This spiderwork of iron, wood and mortar?
SIDI: Is it not a bridge?
BAROKA: It is a bridge. The longest—so they say
    In the whole country. When not a bridge,
    You'll find a print of groundnuts
    Or palm trees, or cocoa-trees, and farmers

Hacking pods, and workmen
Felling trees and tying skinned logs
Into rafts. A Thousand thousand letters
By road, by rail, by air,
From one end of the world to another,
And not one human head among them;
Not one head of beauty on the stamp?
SIDI: But I once saw Lakunle's letter
With a head of bronze.
BAROKA: A figurehead, my child, a lifeless work
Of craft, with holes for eyes, and coldness
For the warmth of life and love
In youthful cheeks like yours,
My daughter . . .
[*Pauses to watch the effect on Sidi.*]
. . . Can you see it, Sidi?
Tens of thousands of these dainty prints
And each one with this legend of Sidi.
[*Flourishes the magazine, open in the middle.*]
The village goddess, reaching out
Towards the sun, my daughter!
[*Sidi drowns herself totally in the contemplation, takes the magazine but does not even look at it. Sits on the bed,*] (50-51).

Representing the playwright's voice, thus (Soyinka 1963), Baroka lectures Sidi, and through her all readers and viewers, that development for Africa needs not be just any type of development or by just any means. Technology transfer or importation of technology is clearly out of question for Baroka. Still addressing Sidi, he says:

BAROKA: . . . For a long time now,
The town-dwellers have made up tales
Of the backwardness of Ilujinle
Until it hurts Baroka, who holds
The welfare of his people deep at heart.
Now, if we do this thing, it will prove more
Than a single town has done!
. . . I do not hate progress, only its nature
Which makes all roofs and faces look the same.
And the wish of one old man is
That here and there,
[*Goes progressively towards Sidi, until he bends over her, then sits beside her on bed.*]
Among the bridges and the murderous roads,
Below the humming birds which

Smoke the face of Sango, dispenser of
The snake-tongue lightning; between this moment
And the reckless broom that will be wielded. (52).

Baroka reiterates to Sidi that he cares for his people and labours daily for his community's development. His refusal to allow the railway into the town does not indicate a lack of desire for progress, and his suspicion of Lakunle, the schoolteacher, is not a fear of new ideas. He explains: "The school teacher / And I, must learn one from the other" (Soyinka 1963, 54). He then adds,

BAROKA: Those who know little of Baroka think
His life one pleasure-living course.
But the monkey sweats, my child,
The monkey sweats,
It is only the hair upon his back
Which still deceives the world . . .

[*Sidi's head falls slowly on the Bale's shoulder. The Bale remains in his final body-weight-down-by-burdens-of-State attitude.* (54)

It is clearly the author, Soyinka, speaking here through his character. Leadership should be about caring for people and working for them. Development in postcolonial Africa must not be merely through technology transfer, but through exploration of local ingenuity and know-how. As Baroka says, Western knowledge is not an enemy, but each side must "learn one from the other," and that development must be truly relevant to the African people's needs and realities.

CONCLUSION

In presenting a tigritudist theory for Africa's development, Soyinka (1963, 1975) does not reject contributions that Western knowledge can make it to Africa. He feels, however, that African thinkers and leaders must labour hard and plan for their community's regeneration. As an Ogunian theorist, and speaking through Baroka, Soyinka (1975) emphasises the qualities of our creative and metaphysical deities that can be harnessed for the technological, cultural, and scientific development of Africa. Africa incidentally has enough cultural thinkers to make this happen. Both Olunde and Baroka praise Western wisdom but refuse to be enslaved by it. They identify its weaknesses and strengths and see no difference in the way humans desire to give their lives for their people's peace and security. The case of Olunde is very relevant to contemporary Africa because increasing numbers of Africans are now living in exile in Europe and America. Soyinka's suggestion, through Olunde's actions, is that Africans must be ready at all times to answer the call of their homelands. They must not relinquish their cultural and social responsibilities and identities. During Soyinka's public address in Toulouse, he reiterated this belief as he said about himself that he had never "arrived" in exile. I have given below the relevant extract from my summery of the speech:

> Going into exile is one thing, arriving there is another," he said. He insisted further that there was a process of "going, but never arriving there [in exile]." Soyinka said exile was "simply a state of mind," and that he had "not arrived in exile" (Na'Allah and Rice-Maximin 1999, 62).

Olunde's response to the telegraph about the King's death clearly proves Soyinka's (1975) point about exile, and it is clear that even as Olunde trains at the British hospital, his mind is at home, with his people. James Booth definitely misses the point when he concludes: "the sacrifice of Olunde [. . .] is [. . .] essentially religious" (Booth 1993, 133). Olunde's response to his people will guarantee their physical, political, social, and economic welfare, as well as ensure the spiritual health of the community. The chaos, which may result in case of a failure to perform it, will have huge implications for society's progress.

7 Language and Culture in an African Adaptation of Sophocles' *Oedipus Rex*[1]

Language and Culture are definitely among most important factors to think about when literary works are considered for adaptation from one tradition to another. There is no doubt that Ola Rotimi (1971) must have given a lot of thought to his decision to embark on an adaptation into an African culture from a European one. He seems to have justified his selections by two important reasons: (1) the African elites are familiar with many European cultures having been widely educated under European colonization; and (2) it might interest many Africans, even amuse them, to consider how a European story may fit into an African way of life. Apart from Soyinka (1976), who later wrote discussing parallels between Yorùbá deities and Greek gods in his *Myth, Literature and the Africa World*, it is not surprising that many African scholars would embark on such task if only to satisfy their cultural and political curiosities. This chapter, therefore, intends to look at how Rotimi (1971) handles the difficult tasks of "protecting" languages and cultures of both Yorùbá and Greek (or is it English?) as he embarks on this very valuable venture. Sophocles's masterpiece, *Oedipus Rex,* has for ages attracted a great attention from around the world. European colonization in Africa brought about centuries of contact with Western culture. At independence, many African nations had firmly rooted in their school systems a legacy of education fashioned after the European styles. The Nigerian national curriculum remained British until the beginning of the 1980s, when a new National Policy on Education ushered in a new education tradition that largely projected Nigerian culture.

For many years in Nigeria, therefore, the *Oedipus Rex* was a title familiar to literature students and many elites who are all products of colonial and (the immediate) post-independence education. The play successfully projects Greek's socio-cultural and religious values. It focuses on politics, the Greek feudal-cultural and religious traditions, and the literary elements of the Greek systems. Although this chapter will examine many aspects of language and culture in Rotimi's (1971) adaptation of *Oedipus Rex* (1982) and, in many ways, even compare the two works; I do not intend to discuss structural and epistemological differences between the two plays.

Though scholars have expressed difficulties in placing most of Sophocles' works at particular authorial dates, it is certain that *Oedipus Rex* (also called *Oedipus the King* in English translations) was first staged during the early years of the Peloponnesian War, which began in 431 BC. Rotimi's (1971) adaptation of *Oedipus Rex* into an African culture, therefore, provokes many questions from many fronts: In what ways has he transplanted Greek's sociocultural, religious, and political practices into his Nigerian Yorùbá setting? How does he twist or create language in achieving what many scholars regard as a booming success in the transformation of *Oedipus Rex* into *The Gods Are Not To Blame* (Rotimi 1971) (hereafter simply called *The Gods*) [(see Badejo 1970; Olaniyan 1988; and Owusu 1998)]? It is amazing that three decades after Rotimi's book was published and despite the fact that it was first released in 1971 by the famous Oxford University Press in London, the work, which also qualifies in every respect as an African masterpiece, has not been cited in scholarly circles in North America, much less around the world.[2]

Sophocles was born around 496 B. C. He played prominent roles as a public administrator/treasurer of the imperial league and later served as an army general (*The Norton Anthology* 1987, 306). He fought to protect the territorial sanctity of Athenian League. Sophocles was mainly a playwright and a director. He won many first prizes, once even over Aeschylus, his senior contemporary. History shows that he never came third in any competition. Some of Sophocles' works include the *Ajax*, the *Trachiniae*, *Antigone* and *Oedipus at Colonus*.

Rotimi (1971), on the other hand, is a popular Nigerian playwright, who has attained fame, at least in Africa, through his Nigerian version of *Oedipus Rex*, first performed in 1968 and later published in 1971. He was born in 1936 in Sapele in the Nigerian Niger Delta. He attended Boston and Yale Universities. As a Research Fellow at the University of Ife in Nigeria, Rotimi founded the Ori Olokun Acting Company. *The Gods* had its first performance during the Nigerian Civil War at the Ife Festival of the Arts in 1968 at Ile-Ife in Nigeria. It was awarded first prize in the African Arts/Arts d'Afrique playwrighting contest in 1969. Rotimi's popular comedy, *Our Husband Has Gone Mad Again*, was premiered at Yale in 1966. His other works include *Kurrumi* (1969), *Ovonramwen Nogbaisi* (1971), *If* (1983), *Holding Talks: An Absurdist Drama* (1979), and *Hopes of the Living Dead* (1988) (see Banham 1994, 81–2).

This chapter will examine the unique features of Rotimi's (1971) adaptation. It will show what basic changes and additions he makes and how he explores African oral traditions in re-writing *Oedipus Rex* in a way that hardly betrays its Greek origin. We want to see whether Greek oral tradition that is the bedrock of the Oedipus story (*The Norton Anthology* 1987, 307) finds a common ground in an African oral culture. Perhaps more importantly, we want to see how, despite the infusion of African traditions into the story, the written work has continued to remain "foreign" in the grassroots of the Yorùbá communities.

SOME STRATEGIES IN THE ADAPTATION TRADITIONS: THE GODS' EXAMPLE

It is interesting to examine the linguistic status of the source text, *Oedipus Rex*, in the late 1960s when Rotimi (1971) conducted his adaptation. This is helpful because of an easy presumption that an adaptation of this kind is generated from an original source in terms of language and cultural origin of the source book. However, it is doubtful whether *Oedipus Rex* was available in its original Greek text in the late 1960s when Rotimi decided to clothe it in African regalia. Rotimi, a theater graduate well grounded in Greek classical drama conventions (see Banham 1994, 81), was not literate in Greek to the extent that he could read the work in its original language. There was enough literature on Greek culture written in English, and *Oedipus Rex* was available in English translation. Rotimi's adaptation of *Oedipus Rex* was, therefore, based on an English translation, *Oedipus the King*. Although neither the 1971 edition of *The Gods,* nor any commentary thereof, tells us whose translation Rotimi used (one of the popular translations of *Oedipus Rex* today is Robert Fagles's), the fact remains that his adaptation is based on a second-hand text. This certainly is no fault of Rotimi's, since, as Maynard Mack (*The Norton Anthology* 1987) says, "no one in a lifetime can master all the languages whose literature it would be a joy to explore" (2651). My curiosity about this matter, yet, is burning. I would like to know whether Rotimi's transplantation would have been different if he had done it directly from the Greek text. From Mack's submissions in his "A Note on Translation," one might easily answer the above question in the affirmative. The example Mack gives of the different translation renditions of Andromache's appeal to Hector in Book VI of Homer's *Iliad* (2651–2) shows that many factors are responsible for what words or sentences the translator chooses. One of the factors is what Mack calls "the linguistic characteristics of the language into which it is turned: the grammatical, syntactical, lexical, and phonetic boundaries which constitute collectively the individuality or 'genius' of that language" (2652). However, would it be correct to say that an English translation of Greek work portrays a hundred percent of Greek context? Or is Rotimi's (1971) work simply an adaptation of an English version of a Greek story? Questions might never end.

The second factor is the cultural reality of the age in which the translation is made. Mack (*The Norton Anthology* 1987) asserts, "The fact about translation which emerges from all this is that just as the translated work reflects the individuality of the language it is turned into, so it reflects the individuality of the age in which it is made, and the age will permeate it everywhere like yeast in dough" (2653). He gives an example of how a translator might attempt to color a word in a way he "thinks" it is rendered in the source language. Speaking about how Hector's wife addresses him which

Chapman in 1598, translated as "O noblest in desire . . ." and which was subsequently translated differently by Dryden in 1693, Alexander Pope in 1715, William Cowper in 1791, Lang et al. in 1883, Richmond Lattimore in 1951, etc. (2651-2), Mack concludes that, in general, the translators of our century will be seen to have abandoned formality in order to stress the intimacy, the wifeliness, and, especially in Lattimore's case (i.e., "dearest, . . ."], "a certain chiding tenderness, in Andromache's appeal . . ." (2652). In some instances, there may be no equivalent word or concept in a target language.

The point of our above discussion, therefore, is that an adaptation based on a translation cannot adequately represent the true reality of the source text, not only because of the time gap between them and the need to conform to the structural situations of the target language, but also because a translation is, in itself, a transformation of the original body-text into a different one. Even-Zohar (1990, 45–51) correctly sees translated literature as a literary system different from its source form. He submits that translated literature "may possess a repertoire of its own, which to a certain extent could even be exclusive to it" (46). One important question is, "What does Rotimi intend to achieve from his adaptation of an English *Oedipus Rex* into a Yorùbá world of English expression?" Gadamerian hermeneutics (see Palmer 1969) also believes that a translated work has a "world" that is different from that of the original text. Though an adaptation is not the same thing as a translation, and I shall return to this issue toward the end of this chapter, my contention here is that the importance of an original source (e.g., language and text) to both forms cannot be over emphasized.

Rotimi (1971) strategically creates a departure from the Greek tradition even while proving, by his adaptation, the commonality between the Greek culture and the Yorùbá tradition. On the commonality side, this work helps to demonstrate Soyinka's (1971) explanations in "The Fourth Stage" (140-160) where he traces the African meaning of tragedy from the Yorùbá oral traditions. He asserts:

> Our course to the heart of the Yorùbá Mysteries leads by its own ironic truths through the light of Nietzsche and the Phrygian deity; but there are the inevitable, key departures. "Blessed Greeks!" sings our mad votary in his recessional rapture, "how great must be your Dionysus, if the Delic god thinks such enchantments necessary to cure you of your Dithyrambic madness." Such is Apollo's resemblance to the serene art of Obatala the pure unsullied one, to the "essence" idiom of his rituals, that it is tempting to place him at the end of a creative axis with Ogun, in a parallel evolutionary relationship to Nietzsche's Dionysus-Apollo brotherhood. But Obatala the sculptural god is not the artist of Apollonian illusion but of inner essence. The idealist bronze or terra-cotta of Ife which may tempt the comparison implicit in "Apollonian" died at some now forgotten period, evidence only of the universal surface culture of courts and never again resurrected. It is alien to the Obatala

spirit of Yorùbá "essential" art. Obatala finds expression, not in Nietzsche's Apollonian "mirror of enchantment" but as a statement of world resolution. (40–1)

Soyinka (1976) says Yorùbá gods, *Ogun*, *Obatala*, and *Sango* have many similar features with the Greek gods Dionysus, Apollo and Prometheus, while also emphasizing some "key departures." He describes *Ogun* and *Obatala* as gods of creativity. He calls *Ogun*, whom he describes as his personal god, "the first actor" and *Obatala*, a "plastic artist" (142–3). He reproduces in a very visual and creative way the Yorùbá oral traditional account of the creation myth and explains how the gods emerged into this "universal womb," with *Ogun* making the first appearance:

> Ogun, the first actor . . . [h]is spiritual re-assemblage does not require a "copying of actuality" in the ritual re-enactment of his devotees, any more than Obatala does in plastic representation, in the art of Obatala. The actors in Ogun Mysteries are the communicant chorus, containing within their collective being the essence of that transitional abyss. But only as essence, held, contained and mystically expressed. Within the mystic summons of the chasm the protagonist actor (and every god-suffused choric individual) resists, like Ogun before him, the final step towards complete annihilation. From this alone steps forward the eternal actor of the tragic rites, first as the unresisting mouthpiece of the god, uttering visions symbolic of the transitional gulf, interpreting the dread power within whose essence he is immersed agent of the choric will. Only later, in the evenness of release from the tragic climax, does the serene self-awareness of Obatala reassert its creative control. He, the actor, emerges still as the mediant voice of the god, but stands now as it were beside himself, observant, understanding, creating. At this stage is known to him the sublime aesthetic joy, not within Nietzsche's heart of original oneness but in the distanced celebration of the cosmic struggle. This resolved aesthetic serenity is the link between Ogun's tragic art and Obatala's plastic beauty. The unblemished god, Obatala, is the serene womb of chthonic reflections (or memory), a passive strength awaiting and celebrating each act of vicarious restoration of his primordial being. . . . His beauty is enigmatic, expressive only of the resolution of plastic healing through the wisdom of acceptance. (143)

Soyinka (1976) explains that gods are to the Yorùbá "the final measure of eternity" (143). He quickly adds, however, that this concept of eternity is not the same eternity in Christianity or Buddhism. He explains that the Yorùbá believe in contemporaneous existence. To them, the present life "contains within it manifestations of the ancestral, the living and the unborn" (144). While celebrating the unity of the cosmic and earthly worlds, the Yorùbá person distinguishes between "himself and the deities," "himself and the ancestors," and "the unborn and his reality" (144). He recognizes the gap between one existence and another and knows the lots of his eternal essence of being. He conducts ceremonies, sacrifices, and ritual rites and indulges in symbolic transactions constantly to bridge those gaps and to "recover his totality of being" (144-5). Soyinka, therefore, describes tragedy in traditional Yorùbá drama as "the anguish of this severance, the fragmentation of essence from self" (145). He says further:

> Its music is the stricken cry of man's blind soul as he flounders in the void and crashes through a deep abyss of a-spirituality and cosmic rejection. Tragic music is an echo from that void; the celebrant speaks, sings and dances in authentic archetypal images from within the abyss. All understand and respond, for it is the language of the world. (145)

Despite the exploration of the similarities and the efforts to radically change some areas to reduce the differences between Greek and Yorùbá traditions in terms of metaphysical and religious characteristics, it may not be correct to claim that Rotimi's (1971) transplantation enjoys easy acceptance in Yorùbá culture.

As parts of his adaptation strategies, Rotimi (1971) makes slight changes in Oedipus story (i.e., theme and characterization) and shifts emphasis in time and space, manipulating the dramatic structure in order to make his story more Yorùbá. For example, he changes some specific setting details and greatly reworks the language to make his story exclusively African. He leaves no evidence for an innocent reader/audience to suspect that his work is an adaptation from a foreign culture. Specifically, he introduces a prologue and adopts an oral tradition of a narrator-audience technique. As the narrator tells his story, the actors play out the actions through miming. He introduces background singing and drumming to keep the tempo and maintain well-calculated climactic moments. He replaces the Greek gods with Yorùbá deities. He substitutes local characters for Greek ones and shifts roles from their original actors to others at some crucial points to allow for plausible Yorùbá situations. The playwright successfully transforms a Greek legend into a modern African drama. He creates a Yorùbá equivalent of the Greek story. Though there is no Yorùbá folktale, legend, or myth with theme and story-line similar to the Oedipus story,[4] Rotimi's skillful transformation of this Greek story is so completely "Yorùbánised" that many unsuspecting natives easily argue that the story has a Yorùbá origin. An anonymous reviewer of an earlier draft of this work describes, in a well-written analysis, how Rotimi's *The Gods* is a radical transformation on a Greek drama into Yorùbá culture:

Even while following the Oedipus plot-line quite closely, Rotimi has performed a really radical transformation on the Greek drama. The notion of "Destiny" is different: Yorùbá cosmology is human-based. (Individual human souls actively choose their own "Head" (Ori) before coming to earth; and their life-course is a process of striving to bring a good "Head" to fruition, or to ameliorate a bad one through sacrifice and work. Ori—often translated as "Destiny"—refers to each individual's own personal potential for success in the world, which is emergent and meliorable, not remote, impersonal and implacable.) The Oedipus-character, Odewale, makes the centrality of human agency eloquently clear at the very end of the play, when he asserts that it is not gods who are to blame, but himself, who because of his choleric disposition and excessive "tribal" patriotism killed the stranger at the crossroad.[5]

It is interesting, however, that the Oedipus story, now the King Odewale story, neither spreads nor attains the same level of popularity among the Yorùbás as it does among the Greeks because the adaptation is not able to penetrate the Yorùbá grassroots. It circulates mainly among people who have attended Western education schools, especially literature students in high schools and at post-secondary institutions. Yet, the author has done so well to ensure that his adaptation fits into a traditional Yorùbá folktale, exploring the fact that, as in the Greek culture, the Yorùbá people also enjoy many oral legends and myths. Says Robert Fagles (*The Norton Anthology* 1978):

> Sophocles used for his tragedy a story well known to the audience and as old as their own history, a legend told by father to son, handed down from generation to generation because of its implicit wealth of meaning, learned in childhood and rooted deep in the consciousness of every member of the community. (307)

However, despite the exploration of a legend that has several similarities to Yorùbá oral legends (e.g., being told by mouth, from father to son, generation to generation), the adaptation fails to penetrate the Yorùbá world. Could it be because the Oedipus story was not conceived, born, and nurtured from the Yorùbá culture? After all, the Oedipus/Odewale story is not one of the tales the Yorùbá parents or grandparents tell to their children across generations. We shall attempt to answer this question before the end of this chapter. However, at this point as we examine *The Gods* (Rotimi 1971) and compare it to Fagles's (*The Norton Anthology* 1987) translation of *Oedipus Rex*, we shall try to appreciate how Rotimi, while satisfying the classical conventions (see Aristotle 1982), conducts his transplantation into an African world and enriches the African literature in English.

THE GODS ARE NOT TO BLAME:
THE TEXT AND THE CULTURE

As this chapter has already argued, Rotimi's (1971) *The Gods Are Not to Blame* takes a notable departure from the play, *Oedipus Rex*, which it seeks to transplant. Our intention here is to show how Rotimi introduces to African literature a new form and reality. In a manner reminiscent of storytelling (as the Oedipus legend is originally an oral story), I shall, in summary form, narrate the two works[5] one after the other, beginning with Fagles's (*The Norton* Anthology 1987) Oedipus *the King* (1977) translation:

Summary of *Oedipus the King*

A procession of priests and others carrying tree branches ascend the alter in King Oedipus's palace. They are agonizing over the biting starvation that engulfed their city, Thebes and are supplicating to the gods and to King Oedipus for a solution. King Oedipus comes in and is visibly moved. He tells them that he has sent Creon, his wife's brother, to Delphi to consult Apollo's oracle. As the king continues his discussion with his subjects, Creon returns from Delphi with a message from the oracle: "Drive the corruption from the land, don't harbor it any longer, past all cure, don't nurse it in your soil—root it out" (314). The oracle says that a person living freely among them had killed the former king, Laius. He must either be banished or killed before life can return to normal in the city. The king, acting on Creon's cue, finally invites Lord Tiresias, a blind man and a priest of Apollo, to help untie the knot. Tiresias is unwilling to do this, for he knows well the "dreadful secrets" (321). Because King Oedipus exerts pressures and makes accusations against him, he reveals that King Oedipus is "the curse, the corruption in the land" (322). He says Oedipus is also a bed-sharer. The king levels a charge of a conspiracy against Creon. He says Creon colludes with Tiresias to dethrone him:

You plotting to kill me, kill the king—
I see it all, the marauding thief himself
scheming to steal my crown and power! (327)

The king banishes Creon from Thebes for life. While trying to persuade King Oedipus not to rely on Tiresias's prophecy, Jocasta tells him:

Well then, free yourself of every charge!
Listen to me and learn some peace of mind:
no skill in the world,
nothing human can penetrate the future.
Here is proof, quick and to the point. (332)

Jocasta narrates as unfulfilled, an oracle's prophecy to Laius, her late husband and King of Thebes, that their son would kill him. She says Laius was killed" by strangers." She adds that her son "wasn't three days old and the boy's father fastened his ankles, had a henchman fling him away on a barren, trackless mountain" (332–3). As Jocasta continues her story, she reveals, paradoxically, the truths about the birth of her son and the death of her husband, King Laius. She thus becomes the means by which Oedipus discovers the truth. From then on, events quickly roll by. Oedipus summons before him the "henchman" who flung Laius's son away to the mountain. Almost at the same time, one messenger brings the news of the death of King Polybus from Corinth. The messenger says, "Death has got him in the tomb" (339). This is a relief to King Oedipus. He announces to the people of Thebes that unlike an oracle that told him in Corinth that he would kill his father (Oedipus still believes that Polybus who brought him up is indeed his father), Polybus is now dead peacefully on his bed, "not murdered by his son" (339) as predicted by the Oracle. However, this relief is short-lived as the messenger from Corinth confirms that King Polybus was not King Oedipus's father. Both the messenger and the shepherd (the henchman) confirm that they exchanged Oedipus between themselves in the mountain while he was a baby. The shepherd explains that he decided, out of pity, to save Oedipus's life instead of killing him as instructed by King Laius. King Oedipus thus finally confirms the truth of his birth. It becomes clear to him that he indeed is the killer of his own father and the husband of the person who bore him in her womb. He accepts this truth despite his intellectual analyses, intelligence, investigatory prowess, and his many efforts to prove the contrary. The evidence is now overwhelming, and Oedipus accepts his error of judgment. Jocasta hangs herself, and King Oedipus plucks out his own eyes. As he has previously vowed to do to the culprit whenever caught, he sets out to wander on to the mountains. He is not allowed to take his children with him. The chorus, which has all along been active, asking questions and reconciling Creon and Oedipus, Jocasta and Oedipus, now pities Oedipus. It proclaims the weakness of human intelligence and the limitation of rationality. As King Oedipus walks away in exile, the chorus addresses the audience directly:

> People of Thebes, my countrymen, look on Oedipus
> He solved the famous riddle with his brilliance
> he rose to power, a man beyond all power.
> Who could behold his greatness without envy?
> Now what a black sea of terror has empowered him,
> Now as we keep our watch and wait the final day,
> Count no man happy till he dies, free of pain at last. (358)

Before the summary of Rotimi's (1971) work, I should establish that he makes some replacements often expected in literary adaptations concerning settings and characters. The following are examples:

Oedipus the King (The Norton Anthology 1987) *The Gods are not to Blame* (Rotimi 1971

Place Settings:

Thebes	-	Kutuye
Sphinx	-	Ikolu (a neighboring village)
Phocis	-	Ede (the town where king Lauis/Adetusa is killed)
Delphi	-	Ile-Ife (the town wherein is Apollo/*Ifá*'s shrine)
Corinth	-	Ijekun-Yemoja (where Oedipus/ Odewale grows up)

Characters:

King Lauis	-	King Adetusa
Queen Jocasta	-	Queen Ojuola
King Oedipus	-	King Odewale
Creon	-	Aderopo
Priest	-	Ogun Priest
Priests of Thebes	-	Chiefs (traditional chiefs of Kutuye)
Tiresias	-	Baba Fakunle (a blind prophet)
Messenger from Conrinth	-	Alaka (a messenger from Ijekun-Yemoja)
Shepherd	-	Gbonka (King Adetusa's special messenger)
Guards and attendants	-	Body Guards
Antigone, Ismene,	-	Daughters of Oedipus and Jocasta
Adewale, Adebisi, Oyeyemi, Adeyinka	-	Children of Odewale

The following summary reflects the above replacements, but also shows other important changes introduced to make the adaptation of the Oedipus story into a Yorùbá world in *The Gods Are Not to Blame* (Rotimi 1971) successful:

Summary of the Odewale story

King Adetusa and Queen Ojuola are blessed with their first baby, and as is customary in Kutuye, they invite an *Ifá* priest to divine the child's future. The priest, Baba Fakunle, tells them that the gods have willed it that "[t]his boy, he will kill his own father and then marry his own mother!" (3). The parents weep so much for the unhappy future forecast for them. They resolve to take immediate action to forestall it, saying, "but to resign oneself to it is to be crippled fast. Man must struggle. The bad future must not happen" (3). They decide to "kill the boy" (3). So, the priest of *Ogun* ties the boy's feet with a string of cowries, symbolizing a sacrifice to the gods. He gives the baby to the king's special messenger, Gbonka, to get rid of him in the bush. Unknown to King Adetusa and Queen Ojuola, Gbonka takes pity on the baby and gives him to Alaka, a hunter he meets in the bush. Alaka, in turn, gives the baby to his master, Ogundele who, with his wife, have no child of their own. Ogundele names the baby boy Odewale, meaning, "the hunter has come home," and takes care of him as their only child. Odewale grows up to know and love them as his parents. One day as he is working on the farm, a person whom he has known all his life as his father's brother looks down at him, spits, and says: "the butterfly thinks himself a bird" (60). This statement provokes Odewale and makes him wonder why "his uncle" uttered such words to him. "Am I not who I am?" (60) he asks. He consults a priest of *Ifá* for an answer, but the priest reveals to him, "You have a curse on you, son. You cannot run away from it, the gods have willed that you will kill your father and then marry your mother!" (60). Determined to struggle against such calamity, he resolves to run away. He says to himself, "Continue to stay in the house of my father and mother? Oh, no, the toad likes water, but not when the water is boiling" (60). He flees home and first settles in a town called Ede. He buys a piece of land and farms it for years. One morning, he arrives at his farm to meet an elderly man with a caravan of bodyguards and slaves digging out his crops. This stranger claims the land belongs to his (the stranger's) mother. Although Odewale does not want to fight, he is unable to control his anger after listening to several insults thrown at his ethnic group: "That is the end. I can bear insults to myself, brother, but to call my tribe bush, and then summon riff-raff to mock my mother is tongue! I will die first" (46). He employs his tortoiseshell talisman pendant mesmerizing the bodyguards and puts them to sleep (47). He engages in combat and a show of talisman power with the old man (48-49). He strikes the old man dead with his hoe and immediately flees from the town.

After many days on the road, he comes to a spot where two tribes, Kutuje and Ikolu, are engaging in a devastating war. There is nobody to lead Kutuje because its king, according to reports, was recently killed by thieves who laid ambush for his entourage during a visit to his late mother's town. Ikolu has the upper hand, and Kutuje is almost ready to give up. Odewale decides to take sides with the weaker side. He mobilizes them and encourages them to victory. He himself takes the forefront and fights all the way. The tides change and Kutuje people suddenly defeat the Ikolu. Odewale becomes a hero, and, though he is a stranger, the Ikolu people unanimously make him their new king. King Odewale thus inherits all the properties of the former king, including houses and slaves. According to custom, he also marries Ojuola, the late

King Adetusa's wife, and over 11 years of marriage, she bears him four children. The people of Kutuje enjoy peace and plenty. Unfortunately, these good times suddenly end. Drought, sickness, and death take over Kutuje. The people can no longer cope. One day they descend upon the palace, moaning, agonizing, and supplicating for an end to their misery. They demand swift action from their king. Odewale explains that he has already sent his stepchild, Aderopo, to consult the oracle of *Ifá* at the shrine of Orunmila in Ife. He (Odewale) promises to do whatever *Ifá* demands to end their suffering.

However, *Ifá* speaks in riddles: "there is a curse in this land [on a man], and until that curse is purged, our suffering will go on," (19–20) reports Aderopo. The oracle claims that a person who killed the former king, Aderopo's father, lives in Kutuje, and until the person is banished or killed, the suffering will continue. Odewale swears to track down this person, saying, "we will kill him slowly, so that he spends the rest of living days dying with each moment that passes" (21, 25). On Aderopo's own suggestion, he is sent to call the most popular *Ifá* priest from Oyo to help untie the *Ifá* oracle's knot. Baba Fakunle, on arrival, senses the truth and does not want to reveal it: "the truth smelled stronger and still stronger as I came into this place. Now it is choking me. . . . choking me, I say. Boy! Lead on home away from here" (27). However, no one can stop King Odewale's inquiries. He insists that Baba Fakunle must tell the truth. He castigates Baba Fakunle for having taken a bribe to shut his mouth, saying Baba Fakunle sells his honor "for devil's money, then let[s] pigs eat shame and men eat dung" (27). Baba Fakunle, now provoked, reveals loud and clear that King Odewale is the murderer. He says he is also a bed-sharer. Odewale suspects that Baba Fakunle colludes with Aderopo against him and thus banishes Aderopo to exile. Soon, however, the hunter slave from Ijekun appears in the palace. He has traveled many miles to break the news of Ogundele's death to Odewale. Feeling vindicated, Odewale narrates the reason for his flight from Ijekun to the people (i.e., so that he would not kill his father as predicted by the oracle). But, Alaka quickly breaks in: "The hunter Ogundele and his wife Mobike—you think they gave you life?" (61). He reveals that, on the contrary, he picked up Odewale in the bush of Ipetu village (See 61–63) during a hunting expedition with his master Ogundele. Alaka says, "A man brought you there, wrapped up in white cloth like a sacrifice to the gods. Your arms and feet were tied with strings of cowries" (63). Even though Ojuola pleads with Odewale at this point to discontinue his search, the king is more determined to unearth the root of his birth. Alaka reveals further that a man, a short man who "limps on the left leg . . . [h]e told us that his late wife came from Ikoti" brought the baby there. This description fits Gbonka, King Adetusa's special messenger. When King Odewale summons Gbonka to the palace, he hesitantly confirms the story. He identifies the then baby as the now King Odewale. Gbonka says the Priest of *Ogun* had ordered him to kill the child. It finally dawns on King Odewale and his wife (and mother) that Odewale indeed killed King Adetusa and married his mother as the gods willed. It is more than they can stand. Ojuola stabs herself to death with a dagger. Odewale plucks out his own eyes with a knife in fulfillment of his earlier curse. He calls his four children, asking each one to hold the other's hand. With his eldest son, Adewale leading the way, they wander into the wilderness. As the chiefs attempt to stop them, Odewale charges:

Let no one stop us and let no one
Come with us or I shall curse him . . .
When
The wood-insect
Gathers sticks,
On its own head it
Carries
Them. (72)

I have taken more time and space to narrate the Odewale story because the *Gods Are Not to Blame* (Rotimi 1971) is less popular than the *Oedipus the King* translation. By rendering the play into a tale, we are, in a way, returning it to its original narrative form. (Robert Fagles [*The Norton Anthology* 1987] describes the Oedipus story as "a story well known to the audience [in Greece] and as old as their own history" (307).

A juxtaposition of the Oedipus story with the Rotimi's (1971) adaptation reveals few fundamental changes. Regarding characterization, Creon is Jocasta's younger brother. Says King Oedipus, "I sent Creon, my wife's own brother, to Delphi—Apollo the Prophet's oracle—to learn what I might do or say to save our city" (*The Norton Anthology* 1987, 313). It is Creon's idea to invite Tiresias, the blind Apollo priest. However, this character appears in *the Gods* as Aderopo, the queen's second child by her former husband. Ogun, the priest, said "We have sent Aderopo to Ile-Ife, the land of Orunmila, to ask the all-seeing god why we are in pain" (Rotimi 1971, 12). This little change might initially seem insignificant; however, it helps to embellish the ironic trends in the play. For example, like Creon's idea, it is Aderopo's suggestion to invite Baba Fakunle, the blind *Ifá* Priest from Oyo. The king, therefore, is able to say to Aderopo, while accusing him of plotting with Baba Fakunle to oust him from the throne, "Is Aderopo jealous that I am sharing a bed with his mother? Very well then, let him come and sleep with his mother" (31). At another point, King Odewale adds "So, let him [Aderopo] marry his own mother. And not stopping there, let him bear children by her" (31).

Another striking change is the reason Oedipus (now Odewale) is made king. In *Oedipus the King* (*The Norton Anthology* 1987), it is when he successfully answers a riddle and thus saves the city of Thebes from the constant terrorism from the winged female monster (See footnote, (312). This feat makes Oedipus a hero in Thebes because all Thebeans who attempt the riddle fail to solve it, and the monster continues to kill them unabated. On the other hand, the Oedipus character in *The Gods* (Rotimi 1971), Odewale, reaches Kutuje when the death of their King, Adetusa, exposes them to incessant harassments from the neighboring village, Ikolu. This is vividly explained by the narrator in the Prologue to *The Gods:*

> The land of Kutuje
> had known peace and seen quiet
> for some time
> until
> the people of Ikolu
> taking the advantage of death in the palace,
> attacked Kutuje.
> They killed hundreds,
> they seized hundreds,
> they enslaved hundreds more,
> and left behind in the land of Kutuje
> hunger, and thirst, and fear. (5)

To the Kutuje people, Odewale is the messiah who saved them from extinction. They crown him king to fill the vacant throne as a reward for his heroic feat. Odewale himself elucidates:

> I heard their wailings,
> first as rumour;
> I heard them, far, far away
> in the course of my countless wanderings
> from land to land, town to town, village to village,
> seeking peace and finding none.
>
> I came to this land of Kutuje
> to see for myself
> the truth of the rumoured wailings.
>
> Crossing seven waters
> a son of the tribe
> Ijekun Yemoja,
> found my way,
> to this strange land
> of Kutuje. I came

to see suffering,
and I felt suffering.
"Get up,
Get up," I said
to them; "not to do something
is to be crippled fast. Up, up,
all of you;
to lie down resigned to fate
is madness.
Up, up, struggle: the world is
struggle."

I gathered the people of Kutuje
under my power
and under my power
we attacked the people of Ikolu,
freed our people,
seized the lands of Ikolu,
and prospered from their sweat.

So it is—
he who pelts another with pebbles
asks for rocks in return.
Ikolu is now no more,
but Kutuje prospered.
In their joy,
the people made me
KING,
me, of Ijekun tribe.
They broke tradition and made me,
unasked,
King of Kutuje. (Rotimi 1971, 5-7)

In each case, however, the Oedipus character achieves his heroic status by saving a community from death and thus, becomes a king as a reward. Rotimi's (1971) story fits a true life situation in Yorùbá culture. Yorùbá history shows that approximately around the 16th to 18th centuries, the Yorùbá empire recorded history of such incessant wars wherein many warlords attained heroic positions. A good example here is Ogedengbe among the Ijesha, and Alfa Alimi in Ilorin who was invited to be king as a reward for helping to defeat the Alafin of Oyo (Olaoye 1984, 6–11).

There is also a difference concerning those whom the king regards as his parents. In *Oedipus the King* (*The Norton Anthology* 1987), the characters are King Polybus and Queen Merope of Corinth. The tragic hero's "parents" in *The Gods* (Rotimi 1971) are no royal figures. Ogundele, the father, is a lead hunter, and his wife, Mobike, is a housewife. However, Ogundele is a famous and rich hunter. He himself has a slave/messenger. Rotimi's choice to replace a king with a hunter does not diminish the effect or importance of Odewale's parentage. He does not fail to satisfy the classical conventional requirement of a noble birth for the tragic hero. Nobility among the Yorùbá includes great occupational successes and heroic communal services. Farmers, hunters, blacksmiths, pot-makers, and traditional rulers all have equal chances to earn nobility status for their families through selfless service to the community.

Rotimi (1971) also makes changes on the Chorus as it appears in the original text. The role of the chorus is very important in Greek drama; it represents the community. The chorus in *Oedipus the King* (*The Norton Anthology* 1987) is particularly active. It asks questions and sometimes substantiates the superiority of the gods. At one point it also denounces the prophecy and appeals to the gods to reveal the truth. Rotimi (1971) creates "townspeople" to replace this device. However, he does not give as much place to the townspeople as Sophocles does to the chorus. "Townspeople" play only some of these roles. In Act 1, Scene 1, for example (Rotimi 1971, 12), the townspeople wail a dirge as children and elderly people die of hunger and malnutrition. The townspeople also ask questions and, at times, echo the people's anguish over the plague: "We are suffering my lord, we are" (12), the townspeople tell King Oedipus. We however do not see the townspeople throughout the play. Unlike the chorus, it does not appear at the end of the play to make philosophical statements and project the "catharsis" generated by the tragic action.

The last example[6] appears at the end of *The Gods* (Rotimi 1971). In *Oedipus the King* (*The Norton Anthology* 1987), Oedipus has two children, and he is forbidden to take them with him in exile. The following dialogue between Creon and Oedipus, and the information in the stage direction, makes this clearer:

Creon. Come along, let go of the children.
Oedipus. No— don't take them away from me, not now! No no no!
[Clutching his daughters as the guards wrench them loose and take them through the palace doors.]

Conversely, in *The Gods* (Rotimi 1971), Odewale, who has four children, does not only request to take them with him as he wanders into the wilderness, but he also gets them lined up in a row, each holding the hand of the other. He threatens to curse whoever stops them:

Odewale. I thank you. [calls] Adewale.
[CHILDREN run in.]
Adewale. This is me, my father.
Odewale [touching a child]. Dewale—

114 *African Discourse in Islam, Oral Traditions, and Performance*

>Adebisi. No, it is me, Adebisi.
>Odewale. Oh, where is Adewale?
>Adewale. Here I am, father.
>Odewale. Take Yemi by the hand.
>[OYEYEMI hands him/her left hand.]
>Adewale. No, not your left hand! [Hits OYEYEMI's hand.]
>Oyeyemi. Leave me alone!
>Odewale. Ssshhh! Do not fight, do not fight. [He links the children's hands.] Where is Adeyinka?
>Abero. Here she is my lord.
>[He reaches out and takes the baby.]
>Odewale. Adewale, you lead the way.
>Adebisi. To where, father?
>Adewale. To where?
>Odewale. Anywhere. . . . [W]herever we get tired, there we rest to continue again.
>[CHIEFS rush to stop him.]
>Let no one stop us and let no one come with us or I shall curse him . . .
>When
>The wood-insect
>Gathers sticks,
>On its own head it
>Carries
>Them.
>[They start on their journey, passing through a mass of Kutuje townspeople who kneel or crouch in final deference to the man whose tragedy is also their tragedy. Soft choral dirge]. (71–2)

In Yorùbá traditional royal family structure, the number of wives and children is significant. Traditional African Kings are polygamous. The King's wives, called *Olori* among the Yorùbá, strongly influence the palace and the community as a whole. It is probably easy to overlook the monogamy of King Odewale in *The Gods* (Rotimi 1971), but fewer children, especially one or two, will draw attention to the royal house. It is an abomination to allow such children to live in a Yorùbá tradition. It will most probably sustain the curse on the community. The chiefs who attempt to stop Odewale and his children from leaving are only moved by pity and emotion. As we can see from the text, instead of "wrenching loose" the children from him, they actually want to stop "all of them" from leaving for the wilderness. Hence Odewale's reply: "Let no one stop us and let no one come with us or I shall curse him . . ." (72). The destruction of all of them (unlike what happens in Greek tradition—a look at the final Oedipus play, the *Oedipus at Colonus*) is necessary in order to restore peace and tranquillity to the Yorùbá community.

On the whole, the changes and shifts in the story-line introduced by the playwright in *The Gods* (Rotimi 1971) do not distort in any way the classical tradition of the masterpiece, *Oedipus Rex* (*The Norton Anthology* 1987). They do not alter the important messages and preoccupations of the original Oedipus story. They do, however, help to localize the Oedipus story and make it more acceptable in the new Yorùbá setting.

THE GODS ARE NOT TO BLAME: EMBROIDERING AFRICAN DRAMATURGY IN A GREEK CLASSICAL MASTERPIECE.

Ola Rotimi (1971) cleverly weds the basic classical Greek techniques with traditional African dramaturgy in creating a unique modern African piece. *The Gods are Not to Blame* satisfies the classical conventions as identified in Aristotle's (1982) "The Poetics" (55–82) and as demonstrated in Sophocles' *Oedipus the King* (*The Norton Anthology* 1987). The following definition of a tragedy suits *The Gods Are Not to Blame* (Rotimi 1971):

> Tragedy, then, is an imitation of an action that is serious, complete, and of a certain magnitude; in language embellished with each kind of artistic ornament, the several kinds being found in separate parts of a play; in the form of action, not of narrative; with incidents arousing pity and fear, wherewith to accomplish its katharsis of such emotions. By language "embellished," I mean language into which rhythm, "harmony," and songs enter. By "the several kinds in separate parts," I mean that some parts are rendered through the medium of verse alone, others again with the aid of song. (Aristotle 1982, 59–60).

The strict observance of the unity of time and space and other classical theatrical traditions makes the play a true classical tragedy. Yorùbá proverbs, adages, and metaphors give the play a special poetic quality. But more than that, they help to Africanize the play in a way similar to what is today a popular modern African dramatic tradition. Rotimi's (1971) work shares features with plays written by Wole Soyinka, Ngugi wa Thiong'O, Olu Obafemi, Zulu Sofola, Mbogo Emmanuel, Hussein Ebrahim, Femi Osofisan, and Bode Sowande. Though most of these playwrights do not share the same sociopolitical visions, they all explore the African oral myths, legends, folktales, and other elements of orature in African drama. The elements of the total theater—mime, songs, dialogue, dance—are all blended together in *The Gods*. For example, in the Prologue, singing and drumming occur in the background. The rhythmic clinkings of metallic objects create the divine atmosphere that ushers in the Ogunian flavor. Even before the narrator tells his story, the stage, shrine, and communal involvement have given the play a strong Yorùbá stamp. The following stage directions demonstrate this claim:

Background choral singing, drumming, and symbolic sound-effects come up now and again to stress climatic moments.

Blackout on stage. Rhythmic clinking of metallic objects can be heard in the background, building up, then fading to a sustained softness: the rhythm of Ogun, the Yorùbá God of Iron and War.

Moments later, spotlights brighten downstage, revealing the shrine of Ogun in its stark simplicity: two upright palm-tree fronds supporting, horizontally, a third; a lone matchet is stuck in the ground within this frame.

Presently, NARRATOR appears on stage, briefly regards the shrine of Ogun from a distance, bows his head piously, then turns to address the audience. (1)

This initiation ritual is very symbolic in the play. It gives it the traditional authenticity. Right from the start we know that we are being called to witness a situation in which the gods and the people interact.

The use of the mime in the prologue (Rotimi 1971) (all actions in the prologue are in mime) and some other parts of the play brings to us the real-life ritual episodes at traditional Yorùbá shrines. The playwright incorporates effective stage direction. It becomes more highly useful in the production of the play. Through effective staging, we see the story even more vividly than the mouth can tell us. The adage, "action speaks louder than words," applies here. Apart from the very first stage direction introducing the play, there are 15 other stage directions in the prologue alone. The combination of miming with the narrative technique in the prologue makes a successful theatricality.

The use of the narrator gives the play an oral legendary mark. The narrator explores his great qualities of voice modulation, gesticulation, and generous emotional involvement by introducing the audience to a play that is about the overpowering will of the gods and the vain striving of humanity. It is very interesting to see the stage turned into a folktale arena, and the members of the audience are made to listen to a tale and participate in a tradition so familiar to them. This method gives the local African audience a sense of belonging and makes them feel part of what is taking place on the stage, for like in a traditional folktale domain, the narrator and the audience interact. Another thing the narrator technique does is help to raise the enthusiasm of the audience for the play. This introductory story helps to capture the audience as they are led into the "world" of the play. In other words, the prologue achieves two purposes. First, there is a different technique from the original text, *Oedipus Rex*. So in a way it gives the play local identity. Second, we have a method that generates our interest in the play. The characters are introduced to us by the narrator. Unlike the Greek audience to whom the Oedipus story was familiar, the African audience is meeting it for the first time. The spectator, therefore, wants to know the story as well as appreciate the technique of the theatrical performance.

The narrator technique has been a very important dramatic component of modern African plays. Femi Osofisan (1982) uses it in *Morountodun and Other Plays*, and Olu Obafemi (1987) adopts it in *Suicide Syndrome*. Also, it is an important technique in Ngugi and Micere Mugo's (1976) *The Trail of Dedan Kimathi*. These are all writers who are greatly influenced by the Brechtian epic tradition. While rejecting metaphysics and criticizing what has been described as the "unreconstructed view of myth and African history" in modern African drama (See Banham 1994, 79), the left-wing writers share the tradition of exploring dramatic techniques from traditional oral performances. They differ from Soyinka and Rotimi, who are less critical of traditional history. In *Morontodun*, for example, Osofisan (1982) reconstructs the popular Moremi myth in Yorùbá tradition and creates another Moremi, Titubi, who rejects her bourgeois parents and embraces the oppressed farmers and traders. Osofisan's contention is that the legendary Moremi of Ife whom Yorùbá history treats as a heroine for helping the Yorùbá in confronting the incessant raids of the Igbo actually saved the shameful face of the aristocratic rulers whose duty it was to defend the community. Having realized the heavy repercussion of their failures, Moremi offered herself to bail out the ruling class of which she was a member. So in Titubi, Osofisan creates a revolutionary figure who commits class suicide and identifies herself with the poor. This is unlike Soyinka's (1975) preoccupation in *Death and the King's Horseman*. Soyinka, therein, celebrates the Yorùbá tradition that requires the King's horseman to be buried along with the king so that peace, harmony, and progress can be ensured in the community. He actually compares it to the sacrifices of lives in the Western world where millions of military officers fight to defend their nation and where thousands of lives are lost. In the same vein, Rotimi's (1971) idea in *The Gods* is clearly uncritical of traditional culture. By titling his work *The Gods Are Not to Blame*, he is provoking an interesting debate on the role of the gods in King Odewale's tragic end. This title suggests that the sad spectacle, even though predetermined by the gods, cannot be blamed on them. Do we then blame Odewale for overrating his own intelligence and for allowing his temperament to lead him to committing murder and, consequently, incest? Is this a matter of free will or fate? It is certain that Rotimi, by all intents, celebrates the traditional classical culture like Soyinka and several African writers. The narrator in *The Gods*' Prologue is, however, not monopolistic. As he talks, actors mime out the actions. The following is a good example:

> Narrator. Baba Fakunle,
> oldest and most knowing
> of all *Ifá* priests in this world,
> it is you I greet.

> Mother waits, Father waits.
> Now, tell them:
> what is it that the child has brought
> as duty to this earth
> from the gods?
>
> [BABA FAKUNLE rises and moves aside. KING ADETUSA and QUEEN OJUOLA advance toward him, followed by the OGUN PRIEST, who carries the baby.]
>
> Now Baba Fakunle
> tells Mother, tells Father,
> tells the Priest of Ogun and aged keeper. (2)

At certain points, the narrator allows the actors to talk. Baba Fakunle, for example, makes his forecast:

> Baba Fakunle. This boy, he will kill his own father
>   and then marry his own mother! (3)

We also have examples on pages 5 to 8 of *The God* (Rotimi 1971) where Odewale acted out his roles. Thus, we have the narrator not only telling a story but also ensuring direct speeches from the characters. The author also incorporates a role for the traditional African towncrier in *The Gods*. King Odewale dismisses the people from the palace, challenging them to go for herbs in the bush to cure themselves of the illnesses that engross the Kutuje:

> Odewale. So may it be. [Roughly.] Up, all of you—into the
> bush! Go and get cutlasses—go on! Go and pick herbs
> from the bush, boil them. Get up, go on
> —in twos, threes, get up! (14)

Then, the Towncrier goes round to encourage people to come out for the task:

TOWNCRIER.

O ya	Come round everybody
E je k'alo	Let us all go, into the bush
E m'ada l'owo, e gbe	Get your cutlasses
koko	get cooking pots
Igbo ya, igbo ya.	get ready for work.
Ewe gbogbo l'ogun	All herbs are medicines
Ogun gbogbo l'ewe	all medicines herbs

Language and Culture in Oedipus Rex   119

O ya	so, come round everybody
E je k'alo	let us all go
E m'ada l'owo, e gbe koko	into the bush.
Igbo ya, igbo ya.	
	Landlord get up,
	Guests, join in too.
At'onile, at'alejo	Everyone, young and old
At'omode o, at'agba	into the bush.
Igbo ya, igbo ya. (17)	

The towncrier is an important artist in a traditional African society. He serves as the "newspaper" and the radio of the traditional community. He often helps to add color to the king's messages and takes these messages to all nooks and corners of the community. As we can see from the passage above, he not only announces the king's message, but also mobilizes the people to honor it. His word reassures the population that the herbs in the bush will cure them: "Ewe gbogbo l'ogun/Ogun gbogbo lewe (All herbs are medicine/all medicines herbs)" (Rotimi 1971, 17) This poetic rendition adds beauty to the message. The inversion and repetition in the lines just cited are examples of how much interest the towncrier generates. The repetition of "Igbo ya, Igbo ya (Get ready for work)" (17) in a soothing manner directly appeals to the spirits of the people for the work ahead. The inclusion of this character in the *The Gods* has helped to make the play plausible to a Yorùbá audience.

Another important element of the African drama is the inclusion of songs at certain points in the play. The songs conveniently suit all the occasions in which they appear. For example, as the men and the women move to the bush for the medicinal leaves, they sing and dance. It is customary among the Yorùbá to sing and dance in such instances. In fact, every occupation has a work song (see Ogunjimi and Na'Allah 2005, 91–7) performed by the workers to boost their morale and rekindle their energies while they work. A particular type of occupational song is the war song chanted among the Yorùbá by hunters and warriors. The following lines are from the songs performed by the Townsmen as they dance towards the bush:

TOWNSMEN.

T'eba ngbo gbe-gbe-gbe	When you hear our voices
T'ebe ngbo gbe-gbe-gbe	Brother, you better respond
B'osi gbe	to the call of duty
Ehinkule re	or you'll have yourself to
L'ao gbe si	blame.
T'eba ngbo gbe-gbe-gbe	
Awa l'omo ale'ku wonu ogan	We'll chase death back into its hole—

Awa l'omo aja'we so l'oko	We, masters of herbs.
Iku ogbe b'oduro	Sickness we dare you to wait
Arun o se ra re	and you, too, death. (Rotimi 1971, 17–8)

The people of Kutuje consider the drought and sickness that descend on them a declaration of war, and they are ready to confront them. Normally, in such circumstances, as they sing, they demonstrate their words through gesticulations. The people of Kutuje show bravery as they defiantly challenge death: "We'll chase death back into its hole." They call themselves "masters of herbs" (Rotimi 1971, 18) and metaphorically dare sickness to wait and face death! Their actual words in the last line quoted above, "Arun o se ra re," means "sickness will itself be sick," or "sickness will cause itself sickness." The drumbeats and dance accompaniments add more color to the scene.

Another traditional African element is the incorporation of a folktale session. At the beginning of Act 2, Scene 3 (Rotimi 1971), we are told Ojuola just told the Olurombi story to the royal children. The Olurombi story is very popular among the Yorùbá. It is about a barren woman who promises to offer her child in sacrifice to the gods if they give her one. Obviously, she is desperate and feels she will be satisfied only when she experiences pregnancy. In such circumstances among the Yorùbás, others would rather promise to sacrifice animals, food, or money. She attains popularity because of the enormity of her promise. The gods answer her prayer and she gives birth to a baby girl. She loves her daughter very much and does not want to sacrifice her. After many years, she dreams and sees a priest who reminds her of her promise to the gods. She disregards it but has similar reminders many times. She realizes she has no choice and finally embraces her fate and gives up the daughter in sacrifice. She obviously remains very sad about her action. The lesson here is that she had a choice to give a lesser promise, but she allowed herself to be led by her desperation. People must always be in firm control of their situations and not allow unnecessary pressure to make them promise something they may not be able to fulfill. Though this story is not itself reproduced in the play, we understand through the stage direction that Ojuola just finished narrating it. We see the children singing the chorus of the folksongs with Queen Ojuola (Olarotimi 1971, 36):

Onikaluku njeje ewure, ewure, ewure,	Everybody promises goats, goats, goats
Onikaluku njeje agutan, agutan gbolojo,	Everybody promises sheep, fat sheep
Olurombi njeje omore, omore aponbi epo,	Olurombi promises her child, her beautiful child
Olurombi o join-join, iroko join-join. Oh	Olurombi indeed, Oh iroko tree indeed.[7]

Language and Culture in Oedipus Rex   121

The incorporation of a Yorùbá tale helps the playwright to completely rewrite the play with "a full African agenda." For example, folktale sessions are highly fertile features of an African daily socio-literary life. Through folktales, children learn about the customs of their communities. The children master the moral codes and prepare for the difficult task of building their future lives (see Rotimi 1971, 52–64). They learn to sing and to develop great talents in the uses of their voices. It would have been un-African (or at least incomplete) to create an African play featuring African family life without a folktale session. The above folksong employs repetition, antithesis, and traditional religious ritual modes to transmit a special kind of beauty. The repetition of "onikaluku," "njeje," "ewure," "agutan," and "Olurombi" add flavor to the performance of the songs and make them linger on in the children's memories.

One important palace element which Rotimi (1971) explores in *The Gods* is the royal bard. No traditional African palace exists without the royal bards, who are the custodians of the "palace poetry." They praise and entertain the king and keep record of events in the palace. They remind the king of important historical events. The bards enjoy some immunity and sometimes rebuke the king publicly for bad policies. Soyinka's (1975) *Death and the King's Horseman* (see *The Norton Anthology* 1995, 2686–2738) shows the sociopolitical roles of the royal bard through the character of the praise-singer, Elesin. Rotimi (1971) produces a similar bard here for King Odewale. In Act 2, Scene 3, the bard showers some encomiums on King Odewale:

> ROYAL BARD. There are kings, and there are kings
> if you mean to hurt our king
> you will fail:
> the lion's liver is vain wish
> for dogs.
> [Drums.]
> Ehn . . . whoever thinks that he can
> rule better than our king,
> let him first go home and
> rule his own wives
> then he will know how hard to rule
> is hard. Meat that has fat
> will prove it by the
> heat of fire!

Generous praise songs, such as the one above, are intended to boost the image of the king among his people. The first line, "There are kings, and there are kings," obviously means to show that King Odewale is unique among all kings. This is powerful as much as it is ironic. He metaphorically calls Odewale's life "the lion's liver." By asserting that the liver is a "vain wish/for dogs" he is alluding to the immunity of Odewale by his enemies. The lion is definitely a mightier animal than the dog! The bard continues this contrast by talking about "whoever thinks that he can / rule better than our king." He says such a man must first try his luck ruling over his own family! Odewale is also the metaphorical "meat that has fat." In other words, he is not ordinary "meat": it is in difficulties (e.g., challenges of rulership) which he calls the "heat of fire" here that the test of the mightiness of Odewale can be seen. The royal bard talks in parables. His literary encomiums on Ojuola, though meant to accord the queen her pride of place as her husband's better half, comes to us as a powerful irony:

> Ojuola,
> Queen, daughter of Oyenike,
> You and your husband—
> two parts of the same
> calabash split equal
> by the gods. Indeed,
> what is the difference between the right ear
> Of a horse
> And the left ear of that same
> horse?
> Nothing. (37–8)

It will soon be clear to everyone that Odewale and Ojuola, as suggested by the Bard, are "the same calabash split by the gods." We shall soon come to know that, indeed, there is no difference between "the right ear of a horse and the left ear of that same horse" (Rotimi 1971, 38). The royal Bard adds color to the African palace, and an exclusion of this figure could have cost Rotimi's play its acclaimed place as "a plausible African piece."

More than all other African features woven into the Oedipus story to make it look truly African, the freshness of its language is the one magic that is mostly responsible for its success. The characters of *The Gods* (Rotimi 1971) speak in rich African idioms. Though the play is written in English, the ingredients cooked together in its linguistic platform are entirely African. In Chinua Achebe's (1989) popular tradition, Rotimi eats his words with the most delicious palmoil of the Yorùbá proverb corpus. Hardly is any sentence uttered without a proverb or some kind of powerful Yorùbá idiomatic embellishment. In an African way of obeying the classical conventions of a tragic play, the characters speak poetry, the king speaks kingly, and the queen speaks with all the regalia of royalty. Even the slaves' language does not lack the freshness of Yorùbá images. Our first example is a proverb from the Prologue. King Odewale, while talking of the turn-around defeat of Ikolu in the hands of the Kutuje people, says, "he who pelts another with pebbles/asks for rocks in return"

(Rotimi 1971, 7). In other words, the Ikolu had desired to exploit the Kutuje and should not complain now that the Kutuje people destroyed them. When Aderopo returned from Ile-Ife where he had consulted *Ifá*, he prefers to speak first to the king in person, drawing from a popular Yorùbá adage, "The secret of a home should be known first to the head of the home" (19). However, Odewale would not take that. He responds with a proverb, "a cooking-pot for the chameleon is a cooking-pot for the lizard" (19). In other words, the plague affects all Kutuje people equally, and the solution is the same for everyone. All the people should hear publicly together what Aderopo brings from *Ifá*. The metaphors of a cooking-pot, chameleon and lizard are used for metaphorical justification. Chameleon, and lizard, though significantly different, share strikingly similar characteristics.

After Aderopo delivers the message about the accursed killer of the former king, the first impression Odewale has is that King Adetusa was killed by one of his subjects. Several of the proverbs he uses in this circumstance are very significant. While expressing the callous nature of the act to the townspeople, King Odewale says, "When the frog in front falls in a pit, others behind take caution" (Rotimi 1971, 23). By this, Odewale infers that if a former king can be easily killed, the present one should not feel safe. He follows that with yet another proverb, "When crocodiles eat their own eggs, what will they not do to the flesh of a frog?" (23). Crocodiles that eat their eggs have eaten their own flesh. How can we be surprised, therefore, if the same crocodile eats the flesh of another animal? In this allusion, crocodiles are the people of Kutuje, and the egg they eat is the former king. Odewale's contention is that a killing of a stranger like himself will not raise any eyebrows. There are so many proverbs in this play that we cannot possibly analyze them all here. At the point when the king is ushering Baba Fakunle into the palace, he chants the *Ifá* priest's praise poetry. The following anecdote makes a reference to Baba Fakunle's blindness:

> A chicken eats corn, drinks water
> swallows pebbles,
> yet she complains of having no teeth.
> If she had teeth, would she eat gold?
> Let her ask the cow who has teeth
> yet eats grass.
> Baba Fakunle
> If you had eyes what would you see?
> Ask us who have eyes yet see
> nothing. (26)

The irony the playwright creates here is made vivid by the use of this double faceted anecdotal proverb. The blind man, Baba Fakunle, is the chicken who eats corn and swallows pebbles. Corn and pebble are metaphors for hardness and strength. These are a contrast to the grass, a much softer substance that should require fewer efforts to chew when consumed by the cow, a mightier animal. The blind priest contrasts with the people who have their two eyes. These sharp contrasts are clearly explained in the second stanza above. More and more proverbs contained in the play add poetic quality to it. Though King Odewale uses the greatest number of proverbs, virtually every character uses one proverb, adage, metaphor, or another device to achieve contrast. For example, some of the other proverbs used by six of the characters are listed below:

Odewale.	Because the farm-owner is slow to catch a thief, the thief calls the farm-owner thief. (46)
	The monkey and gorilla may claim oneness but monkey is Monkey and the gorilla, Gorilla. (51)
	The toad likes water but not when the water is boiling. (60)
Ojuola.	The horns cannot be too heavy for the head of the cow that must bear them." (20)
Adetusa.	No termite ever boasts of devouring rock. (48)
Aderopo.	Until the rotten tooth is pulled out, the mouth must chew with caution. (21)
Ogundele's Brother.	The butterfly thinks himself a bird (59)
Alaka.	Secrets of the owl must not be known in daylight. (62)

Though proverbs can be explained outside the context of their usage, their full meanings are realized only within their sociolinguistic environments. Every proverb above qualifies as a full sentence. Sometimes, they may also be used with other sentences. Both kinds of usage are found in *The Gods* (Rotimi 1971). There are instances where some of them are explored for metaphysical uses like incantations and magic. For example, the proverb used by Old Man (King Adetusa), "No termite ever boasts of devouring rock" (48), is meant to render Odewale's charm ineffective. He engages in a physical and magical combat with Odewale with intent to kill. The dramatic effect here includes the magical dimension of the actions. It is poetry in ritualistic performance. The Old Man's chants are full of proverbs, incantations, and metaphors:

No termite ever boasts of devouring rock!
I am your lord, your charms can do me
nothing.
Venom of viper does nothing to the back of
a tortoise.
The grinding stone says you must kneel
to my power;

Language and Culture in Oedipus Rex   125

>   the basket says you must tremble
>   when you see me;
>   mortar and pestle say you must bow
>   countless times to power.
>   The day the partridge meets the lord
>   of the farm
>   it jumps into the bush with its
>   back
>   or it drops dead. Drop dead, drop dead. (48)

The battle of words turns into a test of physical and metaphysical strengths. In several other lines that follow the above excerpt in the play, Old Man and Odewale are locked in a struggle for their lives. From Old Man's chant we have, "the grinding stone," baskets," "mortal," and "pestle" take on human characteristics: "the basket says, . . .mortar and pestle say. . ." This scene caps the success of Rotimi in projecting the different sociocultural structures of the Yorùbá life in *The Gods Are Not to Blame*.

BILINGUALISM IN THE GODS ARE NOT TO BLAME:

Bilingualism is a very important feature of *The Gods* (Rotimi 1971). Most of the songs are provided both in Yorùbá and English translations. In many ways, this reality helps the author to properly contextualize the original *Oedipus the King* (*The Norton Anthology* 1987) into Yorùbá traditional situations. One of the choices Rotimi (1971) has is to provide every element of the play in English. There are many experiences, by Soyinka and Achebe for example, that show that Rotimi can successfully provide Yorùbá images, proverbs, and songs in English translations. In many instances in *The Gods*, Rotimi does just that. However, he also ensures that Yorùbá songs accompany the English equivalents, because unlike many proverbs and traditional adages that he simply translates, songs carry some performance features that can only be realized in their original language forms.

The bilingualism of *The Gods* (Rotimi 1971) achieves two crucial additional points. First, it enriches the non-Yorùbá readers with some words of Yorùbá language and the rhythms of some of its songs. Second, it is certain that the author, though he includes Yorùbá texts, does not intend the play for a non-English literate audiences in Nigeria or beyond. A Yorùbá person who does not read and speak English cannot function within the world of the play. In short, this play is more of an addition to English culture than it may ever contribute to the Yorùbá tradition. For cutting out those who can function only in Yorùbá language, the play has itself limited its own influences among the local Yorùbá audiences.

The fact that Rotimi (1971) won first place in the African Arts/Playwrights contest in the 1969 production of *The Gods Are Not to Blame* shows that this play has been popularly acclaimed as African masterpiece, exactly the same feat achieved by the *Oedipus Rex* in the Western world. Thematically speaking, *The Gods* shares many similarities with *Oedipus Rex*. *The Gods* is as much about worldly politics as it is about the gods and the deadly games they play with the fate of people. We see how kingly affairs are conducted daily with pressures and pleasures. We witness how Odewale, the tragic hero, believing in the power of human intelligence, initiates thorough investigative strategies that later reveal drastic truths he least expects. We see how King Odewale, like King Oedipus, accepts the judgment of the gods without any bitterness. His statements in *The Gods* demonstrate a total acceptance of his fate. The way he places blame on his own shoulders is particularly striking:

> ODEWALE. No, no! Do not blame the Gods. Let no one blame the powers. My people, learn from my fall. The powers would have failed if I did not let them use me. They knew my weakness: the weakness of a man easily moved to the defense of his tribe against others. I once slew a man on my farm in Ede. I could have spared him. But he spat on my tribe. He spat on the tribe I thought was my own tribe. The man laughed, and laughing, he called me a "man from the bush tribe of Ijekun." And I lost my reason. Now I find out that that very man was my . . . own father, the king who ruled this land before me. It was my run from the blood I spilled to calm the hurt of my tribe, that brought me to this land to do more horrors. Pray, my people—Baba Ogunsomo. (71)

Oedipus, on the other hand, never blames himself. The title of Rotimi's play, therefore, becomes somewhat ambiguous, not just plain ironic.

However, beyond the issue of *The Gods*' (Rotimi 1971) resemblance to *Oedipus Rex*, we have discussed how *The Gods* breaks some new grounds in an effort to Africanize the Greek classical tragedy. While maintaining the Aristotelian conventions of poetry, songs, and diction as media of imitation in tragedy, Rotimi embeds *The Gods* with the freshness of African proverbs, images, rituals, magic, metaphysics, and many other elements of traditional Yorùbá idioms. He draws attention to the fact oral tradition shapes the play in its theme of the relationship between man and the gods. Our rendition of the play into a folk narrative at section three of this chapter, therefore, is meant to boost the oral material sensibility of *The Gods*.

The other changes Rotimi (1971) makes are also significant. Unlike *Oedipus Rex*, *The Gods* is split down into a prologue, three acts, and ten scenes. Act 1 has two scenes; Act 2 has four scenes; and Act 3 four scenes. *Oedipus Rex*, on the other hand, is a single, straight-forward unstratified play. As I also analyzed in this chapter, Rotimi conducts some basic changes in the story lines, settings, and characterization of the original story to make the play more plausible to the Yorùbá world. The playwright uses, with unique artistic excellence, cultural and language resources of his Yorùbá community, to bring forth a new dimension to the classical tragedy.

CONCLUSION

This chapter establishes the fact that Rotimi (1971) (in the traditions of Wole Soyinka, Chinua Achebe, and Ngugi wa Thiong'O) made an important contribution to African literature in English. Among very interesting issue in this adaptation is that although *Oedipus Rex* was originally written in Greek, Rotimi depended on the English translation for his African adaptation. For that fact alone, the English version (as well as the English language and culture) has a greater cultural and linguistic influence on his choices in the adaptation process. It is not sure how much, if at all, he actually considered Greek as a source of his original text while writing *The Gods Are Not to Blame*. It may be right, therefore, that instead of Greek, what might be considered a "source tradition" in terms if language, especially for the new play, is English and not Greek. Yet, his adaptation is also conveyed in English, but this time in a different type of English: Yorùbán English! But English all the same. It is in the same vein that one can clearly say that while bringing in a foreign tradition into African cultures, Rotimi enriches the English language with powerful diction from the womb of the Yorùbá traditions. Adding *The Gods Are Not to Blame* to reading lists in literature courses in Africa, Europe, and America would broaden the horizon of literature students and give them opportunity to appreciate how a highly talented African playwright successfully transplants *Oedipus Rex* into his own culture. This work will definitely enrich our Global World in understanding the prospect for and excitement in cultural transplantations, especially those done with sustained respect for the source culture and equal recognition for the right of the target culture not to surrender its identity.

8 Yorùbá Egungun
Some Critical Thoughts

My intention in this chapter is NOT to suggest that traditional Yorùbá abandon their preoccupations with ancestral worshiping. Yet, as a critical exercise, perhaps among the sharpest yet in Èlàlòrò tradition, I am challenging some of the scholarly materials I have come across that present Egungun as having a Yorùbá origin. That one can query cultural history in Èlàlòrò discourse shows that "origin" is a *primary locale* of an Èlàlòrò premise and must never be taken lightly.

What this chapter will show is that a process by which the Yorùbá embraces and nativises[1] other cultures into its own tradition cannot be overlooked when we consider some forms that are often identified as originating from Yorùbá culture today. The Yorùbá like to say, bi ewe b ape lara ose, adi ose (when the leaf [*ewe*] stays long on the soap [*ose*], it metamorphoses into a soap) while not being an *asipa owe* (wrongly performed proverb) it is important to also understand that this proverb only aims to embrace or abandonment of discrimination and division rather than to erase the true source of *ewe* (leaf) and make it entirely the same as *ose* (soap). Even if the ingredient that goes into making a soap comes from a leaf, the intent of this proverb is not to show such a "biological unity" at this time. Samuel Johnson (1973), a famous Yorùbá historian, posted that *Egungun*, the African cultic masquerade in Nigeria, originated from the Nupe country. He said the interaction between the Nupe and Yorùbá resulted in the introduction of the cult to the Yorùbá nation. S. F. Nadel (1954), another historian, believed otherwise. He said masquerade worshipers in Nupeland were the Nupe-ized Yorùbás. In other words, to him, the origin of the cult was rooted in Yorùbá religion. Olajubu (1970), a folklorist and Professor of Yorùbá literature, supported Nadel. He argued fervently that Yorùbá nation originated, owned, and spread the *Egungun* cult in the country. I will examine the various arguments put forward to seek the most authentic.

My interest in tracing the origin of this very important African traditional ritual performance is kindled by my recent discovery that *Dadakúàdà*, an Ilorin oral art, originated from the *Egungun* poetry, the Iwi (Na'Allah 1988). This is a controversial discovery in an ancient city that today is overwhelmingly Islamic; a city where, to this day, *Egungun* must not be displayed and where intoxicants of any kind has been outlawed by Government legislation.[2] Thus, as a follow-up to that discovery, an effort is here made to examine the discourse surrounding the origin of *Egungun* from a socio-functionalist point of view. My work, therefore, situates the Egungun myth where it truly belongs, in today's socio-cultural and political realities of African nations.

The Nupe are said to have migrated to Nigeria about a hundred years before the Uthman Dan Fodio Jihad (Nadel 1942). They first settled on the hills of Lokoja and later moved to the left of the bank of the new Lokoja (founded by the Niger Company) where they have remained since.

The Nupe are called by various names by various people. The Yorùbá called them *Tapa* and the Kankanda called them *Anupewayi*. Locally, however, the language is called *Nupe* and the people are *Nupeci* or, in the plural, *Nupecizi*. Like in all traditional African lives, the Nupecizi are very religious people. They believe in the all-mighty and all-powerful *Soko*, God, and commune with Him through the intermediary divinities (i.e., *Kuti*) (Awolalu and Dopamu 1979). As I discuss later in this chapter, no historic account presents anything in contrary to the widely held belief that the Nupecizi, before Islam, were worshipers of traditional masquerade divinities. They are also noted for powerful witchcraft. Today, however, 99% of them are Muslims. Islam, however, has not been able to completely replace the traditional religious practice. Many Nupecizi still stand by their solid allegiance to their gods and are still actively involved in *Egungun*, *Igunnu*, and witchcraft performances. During annual traditional festivals in Lafiagi and Pategi, for example, *Egungun*, *Igunnu*, and witchcraft performances continue to engage in public displays at community centers and King's palaces. Notable families as custodians of these deities still exist in all Nupe-speaking communities in Nigeria.[3]

There are several versions on the history of the Yorùbá. A myth has it that the forefather of the Yorùbá, Oduduwa, is in fact the creator of the earth (Awolalu 1975). Another popular tradition is that the Yorùbá sprung from Lamrudu, a King of Mecca (Johnson 1973). The king turned and attempted to transform the mosque of Mecca into "an idol temple." His effort met strong resistance. He was slain and all his children and sympathizers were expelled from Mecca. Some of his children went westward. Oduduwa, one of them, finally settled at Ile-Ife. His children spread and founded villages and towns around Ife. They frequently engaged in both intra- and inter-ethnic wars and were able to expand their territories. The ancient Oyo kingdom was the peak of the Yorùbá communal, cultural, and administrative entity, with King Alaafin, whose title meant "Owner of the Palace," as the political head of their nation.

According to Johnson (1973), Kori was the only object of worship among the Yorùbá. The head-shells of the palm-nuts were made into beads and were hung from neck to knees. The Yorùbá collectively worshipped Kori and depended on it for all divinations. Also *Ori* was often adored; it was regarded as the god fate, and it was often represented by 41 cowries strung together in the body of a crown. Later, heroes were defied and worshiped. Today, the Yorùbá have important deities such as the *Ogun, Sango, Oya, Orisa Oko,* and *Buruku.*

It is difficult to come by any written document explaining Nupe theory on the origin of *Egungun*. My interviews with three native speakers have revealed that the Nupecizi themselves have a very interesting existing oral tradition that presents the Nupe theory on the origin of masquerades. The community people I spoke to[4] Alhaji Muahmmad Ndagi Patigi 70, Malam Muhammad Liman Rogun 72, and Binta Ibrahim 35, have all narrated to me that long before the inception of the Nupecizi on earth, the men folk decided to plan strategies that would ensure security for the people and properties in the community. They wanted their strategies kept secret and therefore decided to meet at night. They kept women and children out of the meeting, believing that they could easily leak out their plans. However, each time a particular woman fought with her husband, she made a jest of him referring boldly to his submissions at the menfolk's secret deliberations. The news soon spread among the men folk and they decided to find out how the woman got their information. The oracle told them that this woman changed into a cat and always attended their meetings. True enough, the cat appeared during the following three meetings and all their efforts to kill it were abortive. Each time they attempted to capture the cat, it disappeared into thin air. The men changed their meeting schedule to once weekly. The day before the meeting, some men put on masques and covered themselves with dark (sometimes red or pink) clothes. They scared women and children away, some holding canes. Some of the men were tall and some were short. This developed into what now is a religious tradition of tall and short masqueraders among the Nupecizi.

Although Johnson (1973) did not recount the above tradition, he strongly asserted that the Egungun cult started from the Nupe country:

> The first Alapini with the other *Egungun* priests, the Elefi, Olohan, Oloba, Aladafa, and the Oloje, emigrated from the Tapa country to Yorùbá, joining the remnants returning from their Bariba Country. (160)

Alapini was the head in the hierarchy of *Egungun* priests, and together they came in a "colonization" expedition and found fertile soil in the Yorùbá country. Johnson (1973) said it was these priests that instructed the Yorùbá in the *Egungun* worship and that the Tapa must be given credit for the introduction of *Egungun* into Yorùbáland. The Nupecizi took over the Yorùbá country, forcing the Alaafin, the King, to escape to Gbere in the Bariba country.

In such an invasion, even if the Nupecizi had not intended it, they would still have left their imprints on the sands of Yorùbáland. The records of cultural domination of one nation by another are abundant during those years of incessant wars of conquest. One nation, in an expansionist ambition, would manipulate its way militarily and lord it over another. Even within a single ethnic group, speakers of one dialect did take up the sovereignty of the others. In the old Oyo empire, for example, the Kiriji was was one such examples.

So it is not surprising that the nupecizi would have seized the opportunity of their occupation of the Yorùbá nation to introduce their traditional religious practices, including the worship of *Egungun*.

Many arguments were often put forward to debunk the purported Nupe origin of the Egungun cult. Nadel (1954), for example, disagreed with the claim that the *Egungun* originated from the Nupe country. He argued that the only worshipers of *Egungun* among the Nupecizi were the Nupe-lized Yorùbá. Nadel had reached this conclusion after his various encounters with many Nupecizi who informed him that, "no . . . we have none of this, only Yorùbás do it . . . "

Olajubu (1970), in his writings on *Egungun* orature, supported Nadel's claims. He believed any opposite opinion was obscure and recounted various Yorùbá oral traditions that accounted for the origin of *Egungun* among the Yorùbá. The first was that it was traceable to Ile-Ife, and that "all *Awo*, that is all secret knowledge, had a common origin; they were all born at the creation of the world at Ile-Ife" (389). Another was a myth about two children (one farmer, and a singer/dancer) of the same parent. The singer/dancer's fine clothes attracted many people. He was embarrassed and would pull a veil over his face and clothes over his head. He thus became the *Egungun*. Another myth said that the Alapini,[5] a most senior chief in Oyo, had three children: (1) Ojewumi, (2) Ojesanmi, and (3) Ijerinlo. These children disobeyed him by eating the "Ihobia," a kind of Yam. They became thirsty, went to the stream, one after another, drank and fell dead. The *Ifá*, Yorùbá god of divination, agreed to reincarnate them. On the seventh day, they were back to life but had to veil their faces because they "were terrible to look at" (389). They entered town in beautiful costumes and thus became *Ogungun*. There were few other myths similar to the above ones. As Awolalu (1979) said, Yorùbá worshiped *Egungun* as "ara orun," the one from heaven, who came to look after his children. He cured them of illnesses and gave barren women children (65–6).

The literature presented above seem unable to sufficiently explain the origin of the *Egungun* cult. Johnson (1973), for example, has failed to provide any concrete proof other than a purported narration "on the hill Sanda at Kusu"[6] which presented a claim the *Egungun* was introduced to the Yorùbá world by the Nupecizi. However, it is not surprising for an empowered society to impose its culture and tradition on the victim nation; Examples abound in history. It was, therefore, quite possible that the *Egungun* cult was introduced to the Yorùbá nation after such a military domination of the Yorùbá by the Nupecizi.

The accounts given to support the Yorùbá-origin of the *Egungun* are not sufficient. These accounts lack rigid substance and unity. All information (on Yorùbá *Egungun* in general) just seems to have oversimplified his history in an effort to say "this mystery must be demystified." To me, it seems an exaggeration to expect, for example, a sudden appearance of a well-known (common) singer/dancer (however gorgeously dressed) to start a religion, cult, and an annual festival as strong as the *Egungun* cult and festival in Yorùbáland, just like that!

In the *Dadakúàdà* songs, any member of the audience whose ancestral origin can be traced to the Nupe country is praised as "omo Tapa ti o leegun nle," meaning "an offspring of Tapa who has no *Egungun* in his house." This is an irony. It is believed that every Tapa home must, of cultural necessity, have an *Egungun*. However, with the coming of Islam, this tradition gradually died out, and so today a good Nupe Muslim home is today without the *Egungun*. Such a Muslim is therefore praised as above to show the degree of his faith in the new religion. Such verse is evident in the following *Dadakúàdà* songs:

> Ayinla Olowo eniwa,
> Afinju Oniburedi ore mi,
> Omo Tapa ti o leegun nle;
> Omo Tapa, oko mi,
> Oni buredi tin dun yun gba.[7]

> Ayinla Olowo, our man,
> My friend the famous bread dealer,
> The offspring of Tapa who has no masquerade in the house,
> The offspring of Tapa, my husband
> The sweet bread dealer.

> Nijo'hun mo ro ree mi,
> Alhaji Abudu Omoluabi makudi,
> Omoluabi, atere kan sanma ti n wu yan
> Ore mi Abudu omo Tapa ti o leegun nle.[8]

> That day I saw my friend,
> Alhaji Abudu a decent rich man
> A decent slim-touching-the-sky man who we love
> The child of Tapa who has no masquerade at home

> Laila ila Allahu,
> Eman gbo bi oku ewure
> Bin ti n fohun bi eniyan
> Ejire oo
> Adisa agan
> Adisa omo Tapa ti o leegun nle.[9]

There is no deity worthy of worship except Allah
Do hear how dead goat
Speaks like a human being!
Ejire oo
Adisa agan
Adisa, the offspring of Tapa who has no Egungun in his house.

Such praises are equally popular in Ilorin:

Ilorin Afonja enun dun bi iyo
Ilu to bi to yen
Ko da won o leegun rara,
Esin leegun ilee won,
Oko loroo be (see Na'Allah 1988a, 5–7)

Ilorin Afonja, a mouth as sweet as salt
A town as big as that
Has no *Egungun* at all!
Horses are their *Egungun*
Sword is their custom

The town Ilorin is so praised because of her new position as an Islamic city among African religious towns of the Nupecizi, Yorùbá, and Ebira. Whereas *Egungun* display is basic to the socio-cultural activities of these towns, it has been outlawed in Ilorin.[10]

Ilorin is one of the closest Yorùbá towns to the Nupe country. Some Ilorin indigenes are of Nupe ancestral origin (Na'Allah, 1985). There are places in Ilorin today called "Koro Tapa" (Tapa Streets) and "Ode Alfa Nda" (Alfa Nda Area, with "Nda," a Nupe name). Almost every household in Ilorin today has some Tapa connection. So it is likely that the development of *Egungun* and possibly the subsequent origination of *Dadakúàdà* poetry has a Nupe influence.

Nadel's (1954) contention that *Egungun* originated in Yorùbá is not entirely reliable. Like most of the imperialist anthropologists, what he did was to speak to selected (Nupe) informants who, I suspect that, because of their new faith, denounced Nupe origin of *Egungun*. We encountered the same problem in our research into the Origin of *Dadakúàdà*. Some *Dadakúàdà* poets, despite strong and dominant positive evidence, dissociated *Dadakúàdà* from *Egungun* cult. Yet, when they were asked to explain how notable *Egungun* performers like Abe Numo and Ajibaye became *Dadakúàdà* poets, they had nothing to say. Nadel is not an African and may not have the same socio-cultural understanding of African sensibilities like Johnson (1973) and the researchers who have recognized enough evidence to trace the origin of *Egungun* to Nupecizi.

Olajubu (1970) declared in one of his findings that *Agan*, a spirit, carried by *Ijimere* (a part of the *Egungun* cult) "was a native of Ilodo somewhere in the Nupe country" (15). How could have such an important part of the *Egungun* originated from the Nupe country while *Egungun* itself took root from the Yorùbá nation!

The Nupe indigenes I interviewed traced the beginning of *Egungun* to "the Inception of the Nupe on earth." According to oral tradition the cult came about to satisfy the need of that moment (i.e. to scare women and children away). In contrast, Yorùbá religion, as we have discussed above, basically rotated around the *Kori. Buruku*, another Yorùbá divinity popular among the Egba was, according to Awolalu and Dopamu (1979), brought to the Yorùbá nation from the Ewe and Fon people of Sabe in Dahomey. All other Yorùbá gods were developed later through the deification of heroes (Johnson 1973).

Any one has never contested the historical interaction between the Yorùbá and the Nupecizi. Evidence abounds today that many Nupecizi have been Yorùbá-nized. In recent times, there have been disagreements among the Yorùbá political leaders; they have challenged each other's ancestral right to Yorùbá nation and to its leadership.[11] The allegation has always been that some Yorùbá political leaders descended from the Nupe country. However, we hardly hear of Nupe-lized Yorùbá, so even if there are, the population must be quite insignificant. Such massive Yorùbá-nization of the Nupecizi shows that many aspects of the Nupe religion have also been Yorùbá-nized. Certainly, the *Egungun* is one of them. Nadel (1942) talks of Nupe colonies in Yorùbáland. He discovers a large percentage of the Nupecizi that have been, in his words, "completely Yorùbá-nized today in language, customs and every habit" (16).

The word *Egungun* has every morphological characteristics of a Yorùbá word or name. However, the name alone cannot account for the true identity of such an important deity as *Egungun*. Even the *Igunnun* whose origin has never been contested (as belonging to any tradition outside the Nupe culture) is popularly known with the Yorùbá name, *Igunnun*. Still yet, it has the Nupe name of *Ndako gboya*. I believe the Yorùbá's earlier accessibility to Western education, its world, and propaganda, enable the Yorùbá names for these deities to spread ahead of the Nupe names. The degree of acceptability of the *Egungun* ritual among the Yorùbá, whose population definitely outweighs the Nupe's in the country, also accounts for the popularity of the Yorùbá names.

There are presently many contentions on the language of the *Egungun* among writers on Yorùbá literature and religion. Ulli Beier (Olajubu 1970, 8–14), for example, asserted that the *Egungun* language is a "ventriloquist trick" on the people. Olajubu disagreed with this view. He maintained that *Egungun* spoke in imitation of a brown monkey, *Ijimere,* and in true representation of "a dead one that is returning to the world" (8–14). I believe such contention is a result of the inability of the scholars to understand the *Egungun*. It must be emphasized here that this in not so with the *Egungun* in the Nupe culture. I strongly posit that the first *Egungun* in the Yorùbá country were pure Nupecizi and, hence, spoke Nupe, which the Yorùbá population could not understand. The few members of the cult who spoke Yorùbá, therefore, translated their messages. As a carry over of this tradition, a monkey-like language is adopted by the Yorùbá *Egungun*, and a member of the cult translates the messages to the audience. Thus, the original language *Egungun* actually spoke must have been Nupe.

CONCLUSION

It is clear in the history of Nupecizi that *Egungun* worship has been a very strong religion of the Nupe people. It is also unambiguous that both *Egungun* and *Igunnu* cults have been with the Nupecizi even before their interaction with the Yorùbá. It was introduced to the Yorùbá nation through the various close contacts that existed between the two cultures at ancient times. This chapter obviously raises many questions that readers should follow with curiosity.

What is also clear is the nature of the relationship among traditional African cultures and how each ethnic and culture group serve as sources of influence and cultural enrichment for the other. The cross ethnic interaction between the Yoruba and the Nupe has resulted into the two peoples serving as strong evidence for traditional African sharing and cultural adaptability and sustainability.

9 Traditional Oral Genre in a Muslim Ilorin

Survival Challenges

It is hardly a surprise that when two strong ideas or deeply rooted cultural elements meet, each might the other, and sometimes, one of them might present a dominant impact on the other. Perhaps, the most important fear of globalization in the 21st century, for those who have consistently expressed such a fear, is that of the hegemony of one or a few western cultures (and languages) over all other cultures (and languages) around the world. It is interesting that some dominating tendencies now playing out in the global theater were confronted in smaller scales when the African people played host to new religions and new cultural forms from abroad. Yet, today, what I like to call traditional African social and cultural forms continue to face enormous challenges. Perhaps what is making this more serious for Africa in the global century is the amalgamation of different foreign forces (from the Middle East, to the far East, and to the West) as confronting forces against African traditional forms.

Several African traditional genres today are in a crisis of survival. Like traditional African religions, they are being confronted by the proselytizing religions of Islam and Christianity and are gradually being metamorphosed according to new models. One such genre is *Dadakúàdà*, a traditional form of oral art in Ilorin, which originated from *Egungun*, the Yorùbá masquerade cult. Today, however, *Dadakúàdà* hardly possesses any trace of its origin. The *Dadakúàdà* poets now deny their roots in an effort to conform to orthodox Islamic values, which are dominant in Ilorin. My intention in this chapter, therefore, is to examine the position of *Dadakúàdà* in the context of the modern Islamic city of Ilorin.

ILORIN: A SHORT HISTORY

There are several interesting stories about how Ilorin was founded and about how it became a well-rooted Muslim community today. Ilorin was founded in the early 17th century by Ojo-Isekuse, a Yorùbá hunter (Amao 1983, 2). One account says he came from Oyo-Ile in the former Oyo empire. Another account, however, insists that Ojo was from Gembe-Ilotta, near

Eji (2). Because of the persistent wars in Oyo-Ile, more people migrated from there to Ilorin, making Ilorin their permanent home. Others—Nupe, Hausa, Fulani and Malian migrants—came from the far North to settle in Ilorin later in the century (Na'Allah 1985, 37). During these times, cults of Yorùbá deities were well-established. The first set of Muslim immigrants from the far north and from Mali then introduced Islam to Ilorin (37).[1] There were many Yorùbá converts, and a Yorùbá Muslim leader, Solagberu, was popular around the area of the town called Oke-suna (38).

The next phase in the history of Islam in Ilorin was the establishment of an Islamic emirate system in 1823 by Shehu Alimi (Olaoye 1984, 6–7). According to one account, Alimi came as an army commander of Dan Fodio's jihad movement to conquer Ilorin for Islam. According to another, Alimi had settled in Yorùbá towns around Oyo and was invited by a warrior in Ilorin called Afonja to bring his soldiers to help him bring down the Alafin of Oyo. This was promptly done, and the people of Ilorin were impressed by this singular successful action of Alimi and his Muslim army. Later, however, friction developed what Alimi tried to convert Afonja to Islam. Afonja was then eliminated, and Alimi's first son, Abdul Salam, became Emir in 1823, marking the establishment of an Emirate Council in Ilorin. It was after the emergence of the Emirate that Abdul Salam swore allegiance to and obtained a flag of authority from Abdullahi Dan Fodio, the Emir of Gwandu in the Sokoto Caliphate. According to a third account, it was Afonja himself who invited Alimi to rule. Alimi declined the offer on the grounds that his mission was purely religious and not to ascend the throne. Nevertheless, he sent for his first son, Abdul Salam, who later became the first Emir of Ilorin.

PRE-ISLAMIC POETRY IN ILORIN

African communities have strongly rooted poetry performance traditions before Islam was brought to most of the communities and especially before European colonization and the introduction of western traditions to Africa. A variety of Yorùbá oral poetic forms were practiced in Ilorin, which included the *Egungun* masquerade chants called *Iwi* and the poetry hunters and members of the cult of Ogun, called *Ìjálá*. Others included *Dadakùàdà, Asa, Rara, Oriki, Agbe, Ese Ifá, Iyere Ifá, Owe, Ekun Iyawo, Alo apamo,* and *Ofo or Ogede* (Na'Allah 1990, 2). Some of these forms of poetry are performed in conjunction with religious cults and rituals. *Iwi*, for example, is chanted by the masquerade and its attendants during *Egungun* performances. The songs include praises of the *Egungun* cult as well as praises of and prayers for the people, bringing them tidings of good hope (Olajubu 1984). According to Babalola (1981, 3–17),[2] there are two categories of *Ìjálá*, one chanted by Ologun beggars and the other by trained *Ìjálá* artists. The Ologun beggars perform strictly on command from the

Ifá oracle, while the trained *Ìjálá* artists perform on occasions such as weddings, child naming ceremonies, and house warming. Both *Ese Ifá* and *Iyere Ifá* are purely *Ifá* divinatory chants and are usually performed by *Ifá* cult members. Finally, *Ofo* or *Ogede* are mystical chants meant to activate charms, orders, and commands. Such poetic forms thus constitute what Ruth Finnegan (1967) calls religious poetry.

THE ORIGIN OF DADAKÚÀDÀ[3]

Perhaps Ilorin community is better known to some Yoruba people as the home of *Dadakúàdà*. There is, however, little agreement among *Dadakúàdà* poets on the origin of their art form. During my first interview with Alhaji Jaigbade Alao, a prominent *Dadakúàdà* poet in Ilorin, he told me that *Dadakúàdà* (which took its name from an opening incantations to its performance), originated from *Egungun* poetry.[4] He then claimed that the first *Dadakúàdà* poets were Okulu, Afefelaye, Baba Awe, Akanbi Eri, Awodi, and Abe Numo. Two years later when I returned to interview him, however, Alao denied his first story and insisted that *Dadakúàdà* was never associated with *Egungun*.[5] Instead, he claimed that *Dadakúàdà* poetry arose independently and that Okulu was the first poet. Nevertheless, he could not explain why and how Okulu started the genre. He insisted that Okulu was neither a hunter nor an *Egungun* worshipper. Another *Dadakúàdà* poet, Alhaji Omoeke Amao, claimed that *Dadakúàdà* started from *Rara* chants. He said that the *Rara,* hitherto performed as a one-man, one-drum art and was later developed into *Dadakúàdà* as several poets came together to form a single group. A third *Dadakúàdà* poet, Alhaji Odolaye Aremu, disagreed with the notion that the genre emanated from *Rara*.[6] He said it was God who gave *Dadakúàdà* poetry to Ilorin. He would not comment on the possibility that the genre took root from *Egungun*.

In order to make sense of these competing explanations, it is necessary to understand the current orthodox Islamic sensibilities of Ilorin. From 1823, when Islam was officially institutionalized in Ilorin, until the 21st century, Ilorin has become increasingly Islamic. Over 98% of Ilorin indigenes now profess Islam. All the Yorùbá deities and all non-Islamic religious practices, including those of *Egungun,* have been eliminated. It is difficult in the 21st century to find any faces of Yorùbá deities or orisa in Ilorin no matter where one searches. Even those among Ilorin people who hitherto were acknowledged with elements of Yorùbá deities have changed their names and dropped such features from their identity. Like other Ilorin people today, such people now represent Muslim leadership in Ilorin. For example, it is not uncommon to find Magaji Are, the leader of Afonja descendants, in Ilorin wearing Muslim turban and holding Muslim rosary as a feature of his Islamic devotion. For Ilorin, part of its status as a Muslim city is the fact that consumption and display of alcohol and all other intoxicants have been banned from its traditional parts. There is little wonder then that the poets cited above are eager to dissociate themselves from the *Egungun* origins of *Dadakúàdà* in order to safeguard the continued existence of the genre in modern Muslim Ilorin.

We discovered, however, that the performance techniques adopted in *Dadakúàdà* today are very similar to the techniques of *Iwi* performance. For example, the "Dialogue" and "Call and Response;" techniques identified by Olajubu (1970) in *Iwi: Egungun Chants in Yorùbá Oral Literature* are the same as the "Dialogue" and what I call "Lead and Follow" techniques respectively in *Dadakúàdà*.

Some of Ilorin's Muslim population is aware that *Dadakúàdà* emanated from *Iwi Egungun* and confirm that Okulu, Abe Numo, Akanbi Eri, Laomi, and other past *Dadakúàdà* artists identified by Alhaji Jaigbade Alao were members of the *Egungun* cult. Many of my informants also stated that one of the most famous past *Dadakúàdà* stars, Ajibaye, who lived in the late 19th and early 20th centuries, was himself a masquerade bearer. His *Egungun* was called Janduku. However, Alhaji Jaigbade has insisted that Ajibaye never took his masquerade outfit to *Dadakúàdà* performances and never sang *Dadakúàdà* songs during *Egungun* ritual performances.[7] Although most of my non-artist informants agree that *Dadakúàdà* was never sung during *Egungun* ritual performances, they also said it was the very same *Egungun* bearers and attendants who sang *Dadakúàdà* (mostly singing the same songs as in *Iwi Egungun*) after *Egungun* rituals to entertain people and earn money. If this is true as we believe it is, then the only difference between *Iwi* and *Dadakúàdà* is the name and the context of performance. The same *Iwi* songs were called *Dadakúàdà* whenever they were performed outside *Egungun* shrines. Some of Ajibaye's songs which I was able to gather show that these past poets did not hide their identity even when performing outside the shrines without their *Egungun* costumes. In singing their own praises on stage, they freely referred to themselves as *Egungun* worshippers. Here is an example of such songs:

Ajibaye:	Omomose
Omomose:	Eegun alare
	Se ko si nkan kan?
Ajibaye:	N toda ni n be
Omomose:	N kan be ni ko si nkankan
	Eegun alare Baba Olokooba,
	Janduku Baba Raimi[8]
Ajibaye:	Omomose
Omomose:	Masquerade-poet,
	I hope there is nothing
Ajibaye:	There is a good tiding
Omomose:	Oh, there is nothing but something

Masquerade-poet, father of Olokooba
Janduku, father of Raimi.

Interestingly, according to Saara Odee, despite the fact that it is said that Ajibaye later converted to Islam and went on pilgrimage to Mecca, he never abandoned the *Egungun* cult.[9] The present-day *Dadakúàdà* poets deny this, however, insisting that Ajibaye died a "good Muslim."

ISLAM, ILORIN MUSLIMS, AND ORAL POETRY

The Qur'an provides support for those who condemn oral poetry as "unislamic." Except for performances that are dedicated to the adoration of the Prophet of Islam, Muhammad, other Prophets of Allah, or songs that glorify Allah and teach specific lessons of the religion, orthodox Islam discourages its adherents from patronizing oral poets. Oral poets are described in the Qur'an as liars and exaggerators who must not be accommodated by serious minded people. The Qur'an says:

> And the poets,
> It is those straying in Evil,
> Who follow them:
>
> See you not that they
> Wander distracted in every
>   Valley,
> And that they say
> What they practice not?[10]

In addition, most *Dadakúàdà* poetry, as we have seen, is rooted in traditional ritual performance. Such "paganism" is condemned by most Ilorin Muslims. Another reason why Islam is perceived to be in conflict with African poetry is the characteristic bluntness of traditional Yorùbá poetry. A *Dadakúàdà* poet, for example, sings:

> Oko lo ni e man sepe lemi
> Obo lo ni e man bo m male,
> Kelembe ti o je n gboro
> Maa fi ojue ruuku! (Amao 1979)
>
> It is the penis that says you mustn't curse me
> It is the vagina that insists you mustn't bury me alive
> Any mucus that disturbs my hearing
> I shall make its eyes see the dust!

The Ilorin Muslims typically detest the way *Dadakúàdà* reflects these characteristics of traditional Yorùbá poetry. One informant, Abubakar Ali-Agan,[11] an Ilorin Muslim youth leader, says the *Dadakúàdà* poets who are themselves Muslims are hypocrites. According to Ali-Agan, the usual invocation of and reference to witches, Ogun, Oya, Sango, and other Yorùbá gods in *Dadakúàdà* are evidence of the 'double standards' of the poets. He insists that one cannot claim to be a Muslim and, at the same time, engage in such unislamic practice. Such practices abound in *Dadakúàdà* performances. For example, a *Dadakúàdà* poet, shortly after paying homage to Allah at the beginning of a poetic performance, invokes:

A peran mawa'gun,
Olokiki oru
Iba Iowo yin, atidi muje eyan
Iya min orere ooo! (Aremu 1990)

One-who-kills-a-goat, who-doesn't-go-for-vulture
The famous person of the night!
I pay homage to you, one-who-sucks-a-person's-
Blood-from-his-bottom
Oh, my dearest mother!

In contrast with the Islamic belief that Allah alone deserves worship, adoration, and homage, the *Dadakúàdà* poet here is acknowledging his belief in the power of the witch. He is invoking her spirits to guide him through the oral poetic performance. In another instance, while praising the present Emir of Ilorin, who is officially the custodian of Islam (*Oba Musulumi*) in Ilorin Emirate, Alhaji Odolaye Aremu metaphorically refers to him as the Yorùbá deities Sango and Oya in his songs:

Alabi opo, omo Muhammadu
Ti Larewaju bi n nun,
Omo iyanda opo, omo Muhammadu
Ti Larewaju bi n nun
Ero ti n ba n roke ayun
Kiwon o mabu ango ma,
Baba Larewaju pani o jo'ya lo
Kinihun idi opoto, oya idi ori. (Aremu 1977)

Alabi opo, the offspring of
Muhammad, born by Larewaju
The offspring of Iyanda opo,
The offspring of Muhammad
Who was born by Larewaju

> Whoever is going to Oke-ayun
> Must stop insulting Sango,
> The father of Larewayu kills people
> Faster than Oya,
> The Lion of opoto, the Oya of *ori*!

A former Emir of Ilorin, Alhaji Zulkarnaini Gambari Muhammad, had a Yorùbá praise name: *Alabi opo*. He was the child of Larewaju and has also named one of his children Larewaju. Here, the *Dadakúàdà* poet metaphorically calls him Sango, a deified ancestor associated with thunder and lightning. The poet also refers to him as Oya, another Yorùbá deity associated with strong winds. What is seen as problematic here is not the poet's portrayal of the Emir of Ilorin as ruthless and fearless in order to make his enemies fear him, it is the invocation of the Yorùbá deities in order to accomplish this, which causes offence to Ilorin Muslims. According to Hajia Sher*Ifát* Mustapha,[12] an indigene of Ilorin, such references are blasphemous.

As a result of such attitudes, traditional Yorùbá poetic forms have suffered. Islamic preachers—"Alfas"—arm themselves with various relevant Qur'anic injunctions while publicly condemning the local poets. They discourage Ilorin people from patronizing them. Jaigbade Alao identifies Alfa Aminu, Alfa Agba, and Alfa Alabidun, past Islamic preachers who were notorious for their attacks on poets.

DADAKÚÀDÀ AND ISLAMIC INFLUENCE

According to Jaigbade, the hostility of Islamic preachers towards oral artists has forced the artists to work tirelessly to make their songs interesting so that *'eeyan o lee kati kuro n be maa* (people can no longer boycott us).[13] However, it is not necessarily true to say that *Dadakúàdà* has such a strong hold on the hearts of Ilorin people as Jaigbade suggests.

A survey conducted over ten weeks from September to November of 1990 records the frequency with which *Dadakúàdà* and an Ilorin Islamic oral genre, *waka*, were employed by Ilorin indigenes. For the first six weeks, *Dadakúàdà* was used as only eight out of 24 marriages per week. This figure then fluctuated in the remaining weeks, coming down to between five and six per week. This was unlike *waka*, for which 100% consistent patronage was recorded. Even *Fuji*,[14] a modern Yorùbá genre, was used 15 times per week. In other words, the bride or bridegroom who employed either *Dadakúàdà* or *Fuji*, or even both, also included the *waka* genre, usually on different days of the five-day marriage ceremony.[15]

The amount of patronage that the *Dadakúàdà* artists still enjoy in Ilorin, as small as it may appear, is a result of the adaptability of the artists in, for instance, incorporating Islam into their poetry. Thus, today it is difficult

Traditional Oral Genre in a Muslim Ilorin 143

to trace *Dadakúàdà* to its *Iwi* origin. Besides the above-mentioned performance techniques and the available oral historical evidence, there is no other trace of the *Egungun* cult in today's *Dadakúàdà*. For this reason, it is difficult to link *Dadakúàdà* to *Egungun* poetry from superficial contact. In the present-day performance of *Dadakúàdà*, an *Iba* (homage) is first paid to Allah, usually in the form of a recitation of Qur'anic verses. Interestingly, this is done even though the artists thereafter invoke the spirits of witches and the Yorùbá traditional gods of Ogun, Sango, Obatala, and Oya. The following are the fist Islamic lines chanted at the opening of a *Dadakúàdà* field performance:

Leader:	Bisimillahi al-Rahmani Rahimi
Chorus:	Bisimillahi al-Rahmani Rahimi
Leader:	Makaana aliyya
Chorus:	Makaana aliyya
Leader:	Warafa'a naa u
Chorus:	Makaana aliyya
Leader:	Warafa'a naa u
Chorus:	Makaana aliyya[16]
Leader:	In the name of Allah, the Beneficent, the Merciful
Chorus:	In the name of Allah, the Beneficent, the Merciful
Leader:	In high position
Chorus:	In high position
Leader:	We (Allah) exalted him
Chorus:	In high position
Leader:	We (Allah) exalted him
Chorus:	In high position.

Thus, the poet ushers in the day's performance with verses in Arabic directly picked from the Qur'an. The last lines are prayers to Allah to ensure the artists' exaltation in wealth and position, just as Allah exalted the Qur'anic prophet Idrees.

Other parts of the performance may also be heavily imbued with Islam. The lead poet often tries to promote Islamic values. For example, when, in a performance, a *Dadakúàdà* poet acknowledges the profitable nature of his performances and says that whatever child he has will be a poet, he and a co-poet quickly add:

Omoekee Amao:	Kewu lere oo o
	Kewu lere o
	Eyin omo musulumi!
	Kewu lere.
Boto:	Eman kirun, esi maa kewu! (Amao 1987)

144 *African Discourse in Islam, Oral Traditions, and Performance*

Omoekee Amao: Qur'anic knowledge/recitation is profitable
Qur'anic knowledge/recitation is profitable
Oh you Muslims!
Qur'anic knowledge/recitation is profitable
If ever I have a child he will learn the Qur'an
Qur'anic knowledge/recitation is profitable
Boto: Do always perform *salat*-prayer, and do learn the Qur'an!

In this manner, the *Dadakúàdà* artists are becoming advocates of Islamic values. They acknowledge the advantages of learning the Qur'an, imploring Muslims to learn it and always to perform the *salat* (obligatory prayers). Interestingly, these poets chant the above lines immediately after their acknowledgement of the lucrative nature of their oral art. This can be seen as a way of assuring the Muslim audience that they do not place their poetic preoccupations above Islamic values.

Other Islamic issues often appear in their songs. In another performance, Omoekee Amao, discussing domestic matters, sings:

Omoekee Amao   Yoo salubarika oo
Yoo salubarika oo
Oko tin se yayi fa'yaa
Yo salubarika oo
Aya ni n se yayi fo koo
Yo salubarika oo

Sungbon ko ni salubarika oo
Ko ni salubarika oo
Oko tinse *rena* faya re
Koni salubarika
Aya ni nse rena fokoo
Ko ni salubarika o o. (Amao 1987)

He shall be blessed
He shall be blessed
The husband who honors his wife
He shall be blessed
The wife who honors her husband
She shall be blessed.

But he shall not be blessed
He shall not be blessed
The husband who looks down on his wife
He shall not be blessed
The wife who looks down on her husband
She shall not be blessed.

The above admonition is a direct reflection of the Qur'anic provision which says that the husband is "a garment to the wife"[17] just as the wife is to the husband. They must honor, protect, and defend each other. In the above songs, the poet has even adopted an Arabic word, *al-baraka*, and has changed it morphologically to agree with Yorùbá word structure, *salubarika*. Also, *rena*, which means "to look down upon or disregard," is a Hausa word. In this instance, the *Dadakúàdà* poet has included a word form the language of one of those who introduced Islam to Ilorin. I have noted in another paper (Na'Allah 1990) that many Nigerians, especially Ilorin people, do not essentially make any distinction between Hausa and Islam; they generally view anything Hausa as Islamic. Therefore, Islam is not only apparent in the theme of *Dadakúàdà* song but it is also reflected in the language of the *Dadakúàdà* compositions.

Another aspect of *Dadakúàdà* which has been influenced by Islam is the dances. Whereas the dance accompaniment to *Egungun* is acrobatic, the dance with *Dadakúàdà* today is performed gently and slowly. In addition to this influence on the style of dance, Islam has informed the style of dress of the *Dadakúàdà* artists. Today's *Dadakúàdà* poets dress in *Babanriga* (big gowns) with caps to match, a style which is identified as Muslim. In fact, most of the leading *Dadakúàdà* poets interviewed could not imagine a performance in which they would wear either traditional Yorùbá religious costumes or European shirts or jumpers.

DADAKÚÀDÀ AND THE STRUGGLE FOR SURVIVAL

The rate at which traditional Yorùbá culture is being suppressed in Ilorin is unprecedented throughout Yorùbá-speaking areas of Nigeria. *Egungun* displays and other traditional religious ceremonies have ceased completely in this city. This situation is described in a popular song:

> Ilorin Afonja, enun dun bi'yo
> Ilu tobi to yen
> Ko da won o leegun rara
> Esin leegun ilee won
> Oko loro be.[18]

> Ilorin Afonja, mouth as sweet as salt
> A town as big as that (in Yorùbá land)
> Has no *Egungun* at all!
> Horses are their *Egungun*
> Sword is their *oro* custom.

According to the song, horse-riding and sword customs, which are traditionally identified with the Hausa-Fulani communities, have replaced the *Egungun*, the most common cultic form in the Yorùbá and Nupe areas of Nigeria.

It has only been in the *Dadakúàdà* oral genre, in fact, that indigenous Yorùbá religious forms have survived in Ilorin. However, *Dadakúàdà* must sacrifice much of its "traditional" character in order to survive. In addition to having to include themes relevant to Islam in their songs, many of the *Dadakúàdà* poets embark on pilgrimage to Mecca and take the title of *Al-Hajj*.

Most of the *Dadakúàdà* artists, as confirmed by Alhajis Jaigbade Alao and Omoekee Amao, have Qur'anic *mallams* who teach them the Qur'an and Hadith. Many of them are already very well-versed. Their knowledge of the Qur'an and Hadith is evident in the Qur'anic verses and in the Islamic moral teachings contained in their poetry. In fact, I was informed by Jaigbade that he would soon celebrate his completion of the 114 suras of the Qur'an.[19] Furthermore, the poets generally attempt to conform to the code of the highly Islamized community of which they are a part. For example, they are often careful to omit utterances that are regarded as *al-fasha* "foul speech." Also, alcoholic drinks are not usually allowed on the field of oral performances, especially within Ilorin. This is even more the case now that alcoholic drinks have been officially banned in the traditional areas of Ilorin.[20]

THE STATUS AND STRATEGIES OF DADAKÚÀDÀ ARTISTS

The *Dadakúàdà* artists occupy the lowest social status in the Ilorin community. They are poor because they are poorly patronized. They are seen as *asa*, "people who can say anything," including what society regards as taboo and foul. The *Dadakúàdà* poet is not allowed to come freely to people's homes, except for ceremonies. Even then, he is always told to stay outside. Most of them wear tattered clothes. Most Ilorin people detest eating from the same bowl as them.

There are, however, a few *Dadakúàdà* poets who are quite successful and who could be described as the middle class in terms of their material acquisitions. They are popular and well acknowledge in many circles. Alhajis Jaigbade Alao, Aremu Ose, Odolaye Aremu, Saka Kolobo, and Yakubu Omoekee Amao are among such poets. All these artists have Coaster buses, which convey members of their chorus groups and their equipment to and from performances, and some artists' own quite expensive cars. Despite these poets' successes, however, several Ilorin audiences despise them. They make no distinction between these and other *Dadakúàdà* artists. In fact, although globalization may have changed many attitudes, an Ilorin father can disown his child for taking up *Dadakúàdà* oral performances, regardless of his success. It is still the case that despite the successes of Yorùbá Muslim performers like Ayinde Barister and Kolinton Ayinla, in which they have attained national fame, the local Ilorin person still detest an idea that singing or chanting "traditional" poetry is the way a person follows to achieve success. Yet, Islamic poetic genres occupy an entirely different class of their own and have continued to grow in patronage, respect, and acceptability in Ilorin.

Because of this lack of patronage for "traditional" forms, the *Dadakúàdà* poets also make serious efforts in carrying their poetry to different parts of Nigeria, especially to other poets who also make serious efforts in carrying their poetry to different parts of Nigeria, especially to other Yorùbá communities. Since their home audience does not appreciate and patronize them fully and since what accrues to them materially from Ilorin is relatively small, the poets seek to sell their art to other parts of Nigeria. Some of them choose representatives who lobby on their behalf for patronage in these areas. They ensure that their poetic compositions, especially praise songs, are not concentrated on Ilorin and her people, but are also focused on all the areas from which they enjoy patronage. Some of the poets also make records which are distributed for sale throughout the Nigerian federation. Such strategies, however, may become even more necessary, as there is currently a very strong movement to restrict social parties involving oral performances such as *Dadakúàdà* in the Ilorin metropolis.[21]

CONCLUSION

Our discussion here, perhaps more than anything else, shows that when foreign forms strongly and forcefully come into a society, such as Africa continues to experience in the new global world, traditions that have previously taken roots may actually find new ways to exist and serve its primary or new purposes and not necessarily disappear. We have seen that *Dadakúàdà* poetry, unlike many other examples of Yorùbá religious poetry in Ilorin, still maintains, albeit to a limited extent, its identity. The resilience of *Dadakúàdà* could be explained by D.S. Gilliland's (1971) contention that:

> The way in which the set of movable and fixed rituals are changed in the course of interaction with Islam is related to the aims of the ritual. (149)

> Since *Dadakúàdà* is no longer associated with *Egungun* ritual, the Muslim population in Ilorin may not consider it a serious threat to Islam and, thus, the forces that might have been geared towards eliminating it is tendered. The continued existence of *Dadakúàdà* also testifies, of course, to the adaptability of its poets and to its potential for survival as a poetic form. It may be that oral poetry has a particularly tough and enduring tradition that keep people interested in its performance and, thus, give it an everlasting sustenance.

10 Mamman Shata Katsina and Omoekee Amao Ilorin
Islam, Performance, and Orality

It is very interesting sometimes when people who are exposed to two different cultures found almost exact elements from both cultures, especially when those elements represent core positions in each culture. Perhaps what is even more interesting is if those elements happen to be human elements, meaning human beings, and if they are also poets! Mamman Shata Katsina and Omoeke Amao Ilorin are strikingly stunning, especially in their use of traditional African oral cultural materials and preoccupation with the socio-political realities of their social groups. Their works, created in the local Nigerian languages of Hausa and Yorùbá, respectively, are greatly influenced by Islamic values. Not all Hausa and Yorùbá elements are similar, but Katsina and Ilorin elements are. Yet, Mamman Shata's *Waka* is rooted in Hausa/Fulani tradition while *Dadakúàdà*, the poetry of Ilorin, was thought to have originated in masquerade cultic chants.

I was lucky to have grown up initially living in Ilorin, Sokoto, and Yauri at different times and later going back and forth from one of these places to the other. Yorùbá and Hausa languages became to me the main vehicles for socialization. Even at elementary and high schools, I was probably drawn more to traditional Hausa and Yorùbá songs than I was to mathematics or geography lessons at school. Virtually every time, whether on radio or cassette player or just by friends who were familiar with the songs and could perform the songs, I listened attentively, attended some public performances, and even performed the songs myself. The oral poets became very easily larger than life for me. Poets such as Isiaka Kabaka, Salihu Kuntu, Baba Olobi, Baba Miliki, Jaigbade Alao, Odolaye Aremuu, Aremu Ose, Omoeke Amao, Iyabo Onibaalu, Afusa Onisese, Batimoluwasi Abeke, Haruna Isola, Batuli Alake, Salawa Abeni, Maman Shata, Haruna Na Huge, Sani Dan Daho, and Dan Maraya Jos, and this is a very contracted list indeed! These oral poets from two different Nigerian language groups present good examples of the way in which traditional African oral forms perform the sociopolitical and cultural issues of a modern Africa. It may not be farfetched when I say that all of these poets and others not listed affected me equally when I was growing up as a young person. It is even possible that a poet I have not listed here had more influence on me that the ones I did list. Yet, when I was ready to do this research, the oral poets that readily presented themselves because of their striking similarities were Mamman Shata Katsina and Omoekee Amao Ilorin. This chapter examines the poets' defense of their legitimacy as traditional oral artists in contemporary Islamic settings of Nigeria.

In researching this work, I conducted long interviews with Omoekee Amao. I also derived information from an interview that Dandatti Abdulkadir (a professor of Hausa oral literature) had with Mamman Shata. I spoke with a cross section of fans of the two poets in the Ilorin, Sokoto, Katsina, and Kano communities of Nigeria.

THE ORAL POETS: TRADITIONAL BACKGROUND, STATUS, AND THE NEW ISLAMIC SOCIETY

Both Hausa-Fulani and Ilorin communities were originally inhabited by worshipers of African traditional religions, respectively worshippers of Hausa spirit gods and snakes and Yorùbá deities of Ogun, Sango, and the Egungun ancestry.[1] Ogunjimi and Na'Allah (2005), in their discussion of the nature of the African universe, suggest that the Africans view their world as a pyramidal structure or hierarchy, which enhances both supernatural and natural elements; people worshiping supernatural forces. Some natural forces, like animals, trees, and oceans, may also attain spiritual and metaphysical statuses occasionally.

Quite often, however, natural elements are for rituals and sacrifices that benefit man socio-economically. Man, himself, is at the center of the African universe.

All the elements above man are supernatural forces that he looks up to for sustenance, harmony, peace, and progress. This idea forms the basis for African religion. Man pets, appeases, and worships these supernatural forces so that they can satisfy all his needs.[2] Meanwhile, sacrifices and ritual performances to the supreme God, other gods, spirits, and ancestors were the basic religious practices in traditional Hausa/Fulani and Ilorin communities before Islam was introduced to these areas in the 15th and 18th centuries, respectively. Today, these communities have the largest concentration of Muslims in Nigeria. There, the traditional African religion has now largely given way to the institution of Islamic culture.

Both Shata and Amao, presently in their late 60s, are products of these African-cum-Islamic cultures. They found themselves, as oral poets, projecting these mixed identities in contemporary Africa. Poetic performances, which were at the root of traditional religious ritual in ancient Africa, had become taboo in the new Islamic culture into which both Shat and Amao were born. From the start, they both had problems convincing their parents to allow them to take up traditional oral literary performances. Their parents claimed that Islam was against poetry, and they would not approve of their children's love for the oral arts, insisting that they become traders; farmers; or, better, Islamic scholars.³

However, Shata was already becoming very popular as he had combined his singing talent with his trade of Kolanut selling, using beautiful tunes to advertise his kolanuts. He participated in singing competitions among members of his age and always won. Amao, as well, in the faraway Ilorin community, gained the help of his aunt (who happened to be the mother of Jaigbade Alao, a leading *Dadakúàdà* poet) to plead with his parents to be allowed to take to singing. He joined Jaigbade's group as an apprentice.⁴ Both Shata and Amao are today very successful and popular oral poets in Nigeria. Through oral poetry, they have become property owners in their communities. Their peasant identities as oral poets have given way to petty bourgeois ones.

Shata and Amao now discuss how they came to the arts and their positions as artists in the society. Shata boasts:

> As far as this profession of oral singing is concerned, there is no person on this Earth that could claim he taught me how to sing. . . . I started all by myself and I have never been an apprentice to anybody.
> (Abdulkadir 1975, 271)

While Shata could pride himself on a self-discovered natural talent for poetry, Amao developed his skill during his nine- year apprenticeship with Jaigbade Alao. Amao (1987) declares in a song:

> Songs that teach sensibility,
> Must be what we sing,
> As was the tradition in our training:
> Here I come, the sweet water.

He calls himself "the sweet water" to show that, like water, people are always thirsty for him. Certainly to Shata and Amao, oral literary performance is no mean act. Shata asserts in a song:

> It is like Alhaji Shata.
> Should I own thirty thousand cows,
> And own thirty thousand horses,
> And have thirty thousand cars,
> And on top of them have a moneymaking machine,
> All are valueless without my singing.
> (Abdulkadir 1975, 309)

One might conclude that an inferiority complex makes these poets boast so much about their singing. In the above song, Shata values his singing above all other arts and skills and above wealth. When one realizes, however, that the oral poet has no respectable status in traditional African society, Shata and Amao's "Propaganda" is easy to understand. It is not unlike the "Negritudists," who fought tooth and nail with the pen to counter the early Eurocentric idea that Africa was primitive and without history (Moore 1969, 61). They sing about the beauty of Africa, as if it were unparalleled in the world.

The Ilorin community, especially today, regards the oral artists as shameless and wayward people. The Hausa/Fulani community, which has adopted Islam, places artists at "almost the bottom" of the social and class hierarchy. Second, artists cannot marry the rich, royal, or learned notables of their society, however wealthy they themselves become through their art. Third, the artists are not allowed to move freely among the people, even during ceremonies to which they are invited. Fourth, fathers in Ilorin disown their children whenever they take to professional African oral poetry. Therefore, both Shata and Amao have fought to win respect and recognition for themselves as well as for their fellow oral artists, among their people. Amao sings:

> Poetic art is profitable
> Poetic art is profitable
> If I ever have a child, he will dance (be an artist)
> Poetic art is profitable.
>   (Finnegan 1970, 272)

In other words, his ambition is to institutionalize oral performance as a household profession in his family.

Today, these artists have gone a step further. Shata has taken to partisan politics and has recently been elected as party chairman (of the social Democratic Party) in the Musawa district of Katsina State. The fact that the same people who mocked and despised oral artists voted for him as party leader is evidence that the oral poets are defeating the ways against their trade. And although Amao recently died after a brief illness, he has successfully handed over his art to his younger brother and children who now continue his tradition. They have kept his group and his band name alive, thus fulfilling Amao's proclamation that his children would his singing. This is proof that their father successfully made poetry viable.

SOCIAL COMMITMENT AND AFRICAN CULTURE IN SHATA AND AMAO'S POETRY

Oral potry can easily be described as the radio, television, and newspaper of traditional African society. Poets are the society's journalists. Ruth Finnegan (1970) supports this view when she says that oral poetry takes the position of newspapers among "the illiterate populace." Traditional poetry's function of correcting, educating, and entertaining is not limited, however, to illiterate Africans, but, instead, serves all Africans, literate and illiterate alike. The same poetry that the peasant farmers and petty traders will listen to is also enjoyed by the school teacher, postmaster, and police officer in their African localities, and government workers also patronize the poetry of Shata and Amao. The influence of western and bourgeois taste in modern oral poetic creativity is strong in Africa. The fact remains, however, that both literate and illiterate as well as rich and poor patronize poetry.

Another fact, as Finnegan (1970) agrees, is that a literary work cannot exist in isolation from the realities of its social setting. The traditional oral artist is concerned about the moral, spiritual, political, and educational values of his society. Kofi Anyidoho (1996) describes oral poets as "mythmakers and mythbreakers" in society. According to Anyidoho, the oral poetic creators "make myths that are compatible with their individual existence, or, more often, with the existence of society at large" (5). They create trends, build up myths, and, whenever they so desire, also use their songs to dilute or spoil them. If they so wish, they can easily belittle a man or topic they have made important in the eyes of the people. Pots, however, often use this power of myth making and myth breaking to ensure a politically socially and morally stable community.

Like the Dikan poets of southern Sudan and Somali poets of the Horn of Africa, both Shata and Amao are highly sensitive to the socio-economic and political problems of their society. Shata sings to inject principles of morality into every individual, young and old. On moral matters, Shata, in his "Work hard and pursue Education," says to young listeners:

> Work very hard,
> That is what elders are saying,
> Work very hard,
> That is what elders are saying
> Boys, school children, let us work very hard . . .
> The leaders of the community warn that we should all work hard,
> And eschew useless indolence,
> For that is not our heritage
> Eschew hooliganism, sons of the north, it is not your heritage
> Today there can be no more idle living, pursue knowledge.
>   (Abdulkadir 1975, 32)

Shata is worried about unbecoming indolence among youths, many of whom now take to truancy, thuggery, and theft, which negate societal norms. He is concerned about maintaining the right values among the people and addresses the elders of his people:

> The farmers should work hard
> A butcher should guard his profession

You, petty trader, better pursue your trade . . .
For what the North does not want
Is people wasting away in useless idleness.
   (Abdulkadir 1975, 32)

The "North" is a reference to the Hausa/Fulani communities in Nigeria. In a similar vein, Amao (1984) enjoins the people to conduct themselves well in society and asserts that one's behavior is one's religion.

Good conduct, good conduct is desired, good conduct
If you have money but lack good conduct, the money isn't yours
Good conduct, good conduct is desired, good conduct,
If you sew clothes but do not sew god conduct, the cloth isn't yours,
Good conduct, good conduct is desired, good conduct.
   (Amao 1984)

With good conduct, one will work hard and earn a just living. "The gun and pen robbers" in our society definitely lack good conduct, and, therefore, the money they claim they have is not theirs.

Both Shata and Amao are blunt on political matters. They do not spare anybody and do not care how bitterly the authorities feel about their songs. A renowned African writer, Semebene Ousmane (1970), has depicted how Islamic institutions suppress the genuine protests of the downtrodden in today's Muslim community in Senegal. His *God's Bits of Wood* describes how religion becomes a tool for the enslavement of the people's conscience. It is used to lure the masses into complete obedience, in spite of the authorities' flagrant disregard for their lives. The oral poets in the Hausa/Fulani and Ilorin communities of Nigeria have, however, come out boldly to show that Islam does not debar them from either exposing inept and mischievous leaders or informing the downtrodden of their rights. Shata, for example, criticizes one local chief who, because of his atrocities in office, fell out with his people. Exploring a folktale, he rebukes him strongly:

Hassan, Brother of Usaini, Gizo [the spider] the cunning one,
He does not rely on himself,
His intention is to cheat his neighbor,
One day the doll of wax will expose his deeds,
And his evil deeds will be known.
   (Abdulkadir 1975, 216–217, 326)

Here, Shata has used the Hausa *tatsuniya* (folktale) about a cunning spider who relies on dirty tricks to exploit people in order to depict the wickedness and greediness of the local chief. The folktale narrates how Mr. Spider steals raw food from farms instead of farming himself. The animals, fed up, erect a wax doll onto which Mr. Spider gets stuck magnetically during his next attempt and then gets caught. In fact, Shata is virtually inciting the people to take up arms against the chief and overthrow him.

Amao, on the other hand, is annoyed with the rebel who connived to bring down a government of the people. He believes Nigerians were satisfied with Murtala Muhammed's administration (1975–1976) and describes the 1976 Dimka coup as a coup against the masses. He sings further:

> Even the artists hardly have anything to eat.
> We go about hungry.
> Murtala comes and life becomes easy
> And you become annoyed.
> May God forsake you, never-do-good people!
>   (Amao 1976)

Also, after the Buhari/Idiagbon military coup of December 1983, Amao (1984) warns the military juntas:

> You should get prepared
> For, you too have taken over power now.
> Be warned: we have (just) recounted the woes done before you
> Things that have been perpetuated in Nigeria,
> The common man hardly eats
>   We are in difficulty.

In other words, Amao admonishes the new military leaders to favor the masses.

In another instance, Shata, while praising the newly installed emir of Daura, warns him about his duties as leader:

> This is my only reason
> When I advocate ruthless ruling
> Never ever slacken your duties
> Spend the night thinking of you office
> Spend the day thinking of your office
> And neither underrate the big nor the small ones
> It will make your stay longer in office, son of Musa
>   (Abdulkadir 1975, 300).

The oral poet is prescribing ethics for public administrators. He insists that a person entrusted with a position of authority must not become tyrannical but must instead respect his subjects, young or old, if he, himself, wants to be respected and obeyed and stay long on the throne.

Shata and Amao, to disseminate news about the policies and actions of government and traditional leaders in the community, compose popular songs dealing with the Nigerian government's social and economic programs like the War Against Indiscipline (WAI), Operation Feed the Nation (OFN), Mass Mobilization For Social Justice, Self-Reliance and Economic Recovery (MAMSER), and the creation of states. When WAI was launched in 1985, Amao joined the Nigerian federal government in the campaign. He signs on the ethics of WAI:

> To be late to our working places,
> It's indiscipline; it is not good
> And to say "we must not sweat on government jobs"
> It's indiscipline; it is not good
> And to over profit from our trades
> It's indiscipline; it is not good.
> To "marry" innocent girls before employing them,
> It's indiscipline; it is not good.
> Indiscipline is never good
> All undisciplined people
> Will never be esteemed,
> Let us all understand that![5]

It was, since the military dictatorship of Yakubu Gowon, a fashionable action for the Nigerian military governments to create new states. Yakubu Gowon, during his military derived mandate as head of state of Nigeria, broken the Nigerian four regions to 12 states in 1967. General Murtala Mohammed added seven in 1976, while General Ibrahim Babangida (1985–1993) first raised the number of Nigerian states by two to 21 states in 1987 and later added nine in 1991 to make them total of 30, and Sani Abacha added six to make them thirty six states ("Great Success Achieved in Nigeria: State Leader." Xinhua English Newswire. 1996). Shata enlightens his people about this situation in a song:

> States were created in Nigeria,
> That we may live in peace,
> That we may live in peace,
> That everybody may know his kin . . .
> States were not created to generate animosity,
> States were not created to enflame ethnocentrism.
> A Nigerian who lives in this state,
> Whether a farmer or a businessman,
> If he moves to another state,
> He can farm or trade.
>   (Abdlkadir 1975, 317)

People have not followed Shata's advice concerning the creation of states. Even though Nigerians, regardless of their states of origin, live and work in any part of the country, frequent interethnic and inter-religious clashes illustrate the degree of disunity among the people. Up until today in Nigeria, except for those working for the federal government, civil servants and teachers who work in states other than their own are employed on a contractual basis and are denied several fringe benefits that indigenous people enjoy.

The 1991 creation of new states caused uproar around the country. Controversies arose regarding asset sharing. Old states expelled workers from the newly created states and vice versa. Even teachers in post-primary and post-secondary educational institutions were asked to return to their states of origin. Such developments are clear evidence of Shata's lack of influence over the Nigerian people and the state governments, old or new. Yet several people have memorized the song.

Not only do the poets reflect socio-political developments in their settings but they also promote the rich African cultures. They draw very heavily on various local poetic genres like lineage praise poetry, folktales, proverbs, and traditional adages. First in this exploration is the large percentage of praise poetry in their songs. These songs address an individual person's attributes, tracing him to his ancestors, including the names, physical traits, actions, and social status of the forebears. Whenever a child greets his parents or a younger person greets his elders, the lineage praise poetry of the younger one is recalled in response. Such praise poetry is called *Oriki* among the Yorùbá and *Wakan Yabo* in Hausaland. This type of poetry, whenever chanted for a person or a family, will boost their pride and ego by making them very pleased and happy. Oral artists in traditional Africa easily memorized the praise poetry of individuals, families, and traditional chiefs in their communities. Similar songs also exist for associations, communities, and ethnic groups, linking every group to the history of its ancestors. The attributes of members of such groups and associations are also extolled.

Both Shata and Amao have immense knowledge of the praise songs of the people and ethnic groups of their localities. They sing the praise of royal chiefs, wealthy political leaders, farmers, traders, and the entire proletariat in the society. This praise poetry occupies the majority of their songs, because, at each performance, they strive to reciprocate the generosity of their fans, especially those who offer them material gifts. Amao (1978b) sings as follows for one such fan:

> Do please greet my elder one for me
> Ayinde, the offspring of Aleelo.
> How is Salawu, the offspring of Aleelo?
> You will never be tired, God will not let you lose your credibility,
> Ayinde, the offspring of the elephant in Alo, the offspring of Edidialo,
> The offspring of the black elephant who breathes with royalty.
> He breaks down the mighty tree majestically,
> Alhaji Ayinde, the father of the tall Yakubu
> Your abaja mark is unique, Ayinde,

Alhaji Ayinde, let me see your face,
The father of Tunde, who cuts the face mark for you?
I do not know the Olola-tribal face mark that cuts the face mark for my elder one.
If I do know who cuts it,
I will offer the Olola one bag of money!
Just because of my friend, Ajao, the-mother's-breast-is-sweet.

The repeated use of elements like "offspring of," "father of," "son of," "daughter of," and "child of" is typical of this type of lineage praise poetry by oral artists, with repetition as one of its aesthetic features in Yorùbá. In this praise song, Amao makes references to his patron's tribal mark and describes it as unique. In traditional African society, tribal marks carefully cut on the face in a given pattern represent ethnic and family identification. Some marks also have spiritual, religious, and metaphysical connotations. For example, a mother who gives to her consistently sick and often epileptic child, will mark and apply ritual mixtures on the cuttings and see the child improve and grow healthy and strong. Most of these face marks are beautifying. Those bearing them become highly admired like Amao's patron, Ayinde. Also, in the praise songs, Amao refers to Ayinde as "the father of the tall Yakubu," referring to the physical feature of Yakubu. Maybe either Yakubu's father, his mother, or both of them are tall, and the child, Yakubu, takes after them.

The oral artists' exploration of tales and proverbs is very refreshing. Mamman Shata is very fond of adopting local legends and myths that the Hausas call *Labarun gaske* or true stories. Legendary tales are stories about ancestors who have performed heroic feats on earth. Myths, on the other hand, are about "experiences and actions that link the world of the supernatural and the world of man. . . . the inter-relationships between the cosmic and human forces" (Ogunjimi Na'Allah 2005, 55). These African stories try to explain the various mysteries of life. Such myths include stories about creation, the gods and their power, and the supreme God.

Both legends and myths are regarded as true stories and are told with the expectation that the listener will believe them. The folktales, called *tatsunoyi*—imaginary stories in Hausa and *alo* in Yorùbá—are treated as untrue stories. In traditional African societies, elders tell them to children by the moonlight. The tatsunoyi focus on the natural world and have human and animal characters. They are intended to teach the young ones good morals. Shata frequently explores these African tales to make his messages vivid. For example, in his songs for the Emir of Daura, reproduced by AbdulKadir (1975, 206–7), Shata makes reference to the legend of Abu Yazidu, who, on hearing the plot of his father-in-law, the king of Bornu, to kill him, escaped to Daura where he killed the dreaded snake that disallowed people from getting water from the well called *kusung*, except on Fridays. Shata says to the Emir of Daura:

> The well is yours:
> There is a recorded history in Kusugu well for thematic look.
>   (207)

Shata tries in this song to show that the Kusugu well is a symbolic possession to the Emirship of Daura. Shata's earlier adoption of the tale about the greedy Mr. Spider is an example of a *tatsuniya*. I have already examined how he used it to criticize a local chief.

Amao, in his explorations of folktales, demonstrates Okpewho's (1987) contention that oral prose is dramatic. Unlike Shata, he always performs his tales. There is hardly any disc or public outing in which he does not explore at least one folktale. While condemning greediness, he renders a tale about a greedy, wealthy man who meets his Waterloo. This man has everything but still wants more. He consults an oracle. Unknown to him, a person he has once cheated on is in the oracle house. This person asks him to shave his hair and massage the hair with poison, and before rubbing it on his head, the person sings for him:

> You have twenty slaves, yet you want more, you robber,
> Nothing satisfies you, you robber
> You become the head of a town, yet you want more, you robber
> Nothing satisfies you, you robber
> You want to be Olodumare (God), yet you want more, you robber,
> Nothing satisfies you, you robber
>   (Amao 1984).

As he rubs the poisoned soap on his head, he falls and dies. So the greedy man ends up losing his wealth and life. This song contains an unambiguous message to greedy politicians, businessmen, and traders. It also speaks to Nigerian military leaders. The poet warns the greedy, unfaithful leaders that their elimination by the oppressed masses is imminent.

The adoption of proverbs also adds traditional richness and flavor to oral poetry. J.H. Nketia (1958, 21) was no doubt inspired by traditional oral poetry when he asserted that the adoption of proverbs is a necessity for every oral artist. The proverb is actually at the center of literary and, indeed, poetic creativity in Africa. It is the only element that penetrates all traditional literary genres in Africa. *Dadakúàdà* presents a booming display of proverbs. For instance, Amao (1984) posits in a song that a speech without proverb remains stagnant at the point of utterance:

> Proverb is a horse of speech,
> Speech is a horse of proverb, whenever wisdom is lost,
> Proverb is employed to search (for it).

Both Shata and Amao rely strongly on African proverbs in their poetry. In his songs for the Emir of Daura, Shata says:

> The monkey has neck
> The monkey has neck
> Nonetheless, it is always tied on the waist . . .
>   (Abdulkadir 1975, 299).

This proverb denotes that that monkey, because it is unique among animals, must not be treated as a commoner in obvious reference to the Emir of Daura, who is also special and must be accorded more respect than other Emirs. In another song, Shata sings:

> Whether in the forest or in the city . . .
> A boy will recognize his mother's husband
> The mother's husband is called a father!
>   (Abdulkadir 1975, 310)

This proverb denotes that one person's supremacy over another is not a matter for contention. One's mother's husband, whether or not he is one's father, is definitely one's superior.

Omoekee Amao refers to his folktales as proverbs, just as the Fulani ethnic group regards the *Tindol* (Finnegan 1970, 390–91) as their indigenous folk narrative. While praising Dr. Sola Saraki, the Turaki of Ilorin and senate leader in the Nigerian Second Republic, Amao (1979) also asserts:

> The leopards hunt him about,
> They think he is an animal that can be easily killed.
> The titleholder can't be easily killed
> Though small, he can't be cheated,
> He is the rich that one finds impossible to hate
> Oloye, the father of Bukola,
> A sheep cannot be roasted alive,
> Lest it destroy the father.

The proverb contained in the last two lines of the above song clearly shows the superiority of Saraki over others. It asserts Saraki's power to neutralize all spells.

Apart from the folktales and proverbs considered above, our two oral poets use other powerful metaphors in their songs. For example, Shata is fond of referring to his esteemed patrons as "lions," as I found in two passages from his song for the emir of Daura:

> Long live the lion, Mamman father of
> Galadima, son of Musa
> In the forest there is lion
> In the forest there is lion
> So children should keep away
>   (Abdulkadir 1975, 196)

Also, in his song of Umar Danduna, he sings:
Umar is a red lion and devours other lions
The mighty rock that crushes small rocks,
My master.
In the forest there is leopard
So children should keep away.
   (Abdulkadir 1975, 309–10)

In these songs, Shata uses "lions" to denote the bravery and courage of his characters. The two artists adopt animals as metaphorical expressions in a similar fashion. The leopard here is supposed to be a prey. Ironically, in Omoekee's song, it is not as powerful as the oppressed. Though Omoekee, in Saraki's praise song, is using a weaker animal-the-sheep, for Saraki, he has cleverly raised the sheep above the metaphorical fire. However, we know ourselves that fire can destroy many things, including the leopard that is hunting after Saraki's life.

Oral artists in Africa are the repository of ever fertile traditional literary resources. Dandatti Abdulkadir (1975) summarizes this view:

> An oral singer who is born and reared in the traditional society becomes an integral member of that community and his repertoire therefore represents not only the group sentiments but also the traditions and the social values of his society. (205)

Given the historical background of both Shata and Amao, one is convinced that they have property imbibed the cultures of their respective traditional societies and, therefore, have no difficulty in shaping their creativity in line with the values of their people.

THE INFLUENCE OF ISLAM ON SHATA AND AMAO'S POETRY

The issue of the new Islamic impact on traditional African forms generates much interest. Omibiyi-Obidike (1981, 37–51) has written extensively on the influence of Islamic culture on oral literature in Yorùbáland—an influence that has generated so much controversy regarding which song was Islamic or has Islamic roots and which one is purely traditional. Omibiyi-Obidike cites examples of Nigerian oral genres, *Apala* and *Sakara*, as two Nigerian song forms believed to be essentially of Islamic origin. One reason he gives for this erroneous notion is that these poetic forms are almost always performed by Muslims; another reason is the elements of Islamic culture in this poetry. Omibiyi-Obidike has effectively proven that these poetic forms have no Islamic origins but are instead the creation of pre-Islamic Black African culture.

In the same vein, scholar's categorization of Shata's poetry as outside the Hausa/Fulani tradition is somewhat dangerous, as they are bound to be biased and may classify the *waka* among the Islamic poetic forms, whereas *waka* only means song, any song, in the Hausa language. Also, traditional Hausa culture, before the advent of Islam, revolved around traditional African religion. Today, the poetry of Shata and Amao vividly touches on Islamic culture and, for instance, most of their moral lessons can be traced to different injunctions in the Holy Quran on uprightness, hard work, and selflessness. They also bring various Islamic activities to light in their poetry (For example, in "The Song of Mahde's Journey to Mecca") (AbdulKadir 1975, 318). Mamman Shata, directly or indirectly, reflects the Islamic tradition of festivity when he sings:

> Alhaji Mande son of Abdul-kadir
> When I arrived at Kano the city of Dabo,
> I was caught up by Babbar Sallah, big Islamic festival
> There I performed the Sallah celebration
> Iro Waya accommodated me,
> He offered me the Sallah meat
> But did not give the traditional Sallah gown,
> Because you are absent, son of Abdulkadir.
>   (Abdulkadir 1975, 318)

The culture of generosity inherent in Islam, especially during festivals, is clearly pinpointed here. The prophet Muhammed encouraged this practice in line with Quranic injunctions that every Muslim be made truly happy during Islamic festivals. The rich are expected to give out alms on the eve of or even some days before sallah day so that the have-nots have something to eat and will, therefore, be happy. Also during sallah, resources are shared freely among Muslims. Even one who has never heard of this tradition will know it after going through or hearing the above song. Shata talks about sallah food, thereby identifying the food with sallah. As I have stated in a previous article (Na'Allah 1988b, 26–36), *Dadakùàdà* field performances today always begin with homage to Allah. Here, Amao starts a day's performance:

> Bisimillayi ar Rahmani Rahimi
> Ausu bi llahi mina shaitani Rajimi
> I start today's play,
> The young, the old
> Come and rally round me.
> Support me so that I can perform well
> Oh Allah, let me succeed in this performance.[6]

The poet takes verses in Arabic directly from the Holy Quran; the first two lines translate thus:

> In the name of Allah, the Beneficent, the Merciful
> I seek protection from Allah against Satan, the accursed[7]

The first line starts every chapter of the Holy Quran but one. It is repeated 114 times in the Quran, and this betokens its importance as the very first statement of prayer for Muslims before they start to perform any action. I have stated elsewhere and must reemphasize here that despite the present, heavy Islamic influence on some traditional African oral forms, these forms have not been rendered Islamic. Both Shata's *waka* and Amao's *Dadakúàdà* still retain their identities as true traditional African genres. They portray Islam, because Islam is a reality in their current environment.

CONCLUSION

Perhaps the most important conclusion I can derive from this work is that both Shata and Amao perform their Islam and Africanness through oral poetry. For them, it is not just an art; their poetry is spirituality and it is the platform for society survival struggles. Modern African writers (i.e., novelists, dramatists, and poets) and researchers who are eager to explore traditional oral literary metaphors in their works will find an easy repertoire in contemporary oral singers in Africa. Shata and Amao have demonstrated that neither western civilization nor modern religion can erase traditional African literary culture from the surface of the earth.

Traditional oral poets in Nigeria do not limit their thematic scope to village matters. Shata and Amao have shown that they are interested in national socio-economic issues. They dedicate most of their public performances to rebuking the heartless policies of the government; that is their only legitimacy as oral artists.

Our research has laid to rest any possible misconceived impression that because of the dense Islamic population and culture in Ilorin and, indeed, in the Hausa/Fulani communities in Nigeria, oral poets are to celebrate society leaders or seal their lips on political matters, thus satisfying the often misquoted Quranic injunctions that:

> O ye who believe,
> Obey Allah and obey the Prophet,
> And those in authority among you.[8]

People have misinterpreted this to mean that one should keep totally mute in the face of injustice, intimidation, and oppression from those in positions of authority to be obeyed, only as long as they themselves obey Allah's orders, which command them to maintain justice, equality, and fair play among the people and as long as they see their authority as a trust and do not convert state wealth to their personal use (Abdullahi 1981, 8–40).

Caliph Abubakar, one of the successors to the prophet of Islam, Muhammad, emphasized this before assuming the leadership of the Islamic state (Rahim 1981). The two artists I have concentrated on in this chapter have proved that oral poets in Muslim-populated societies, especially those of northern Nigeria to which the Ilorin and Hausa/Fulani communities of Nigeria belong, do not feel prevented from criticizing misguided political leaders or even inciting the masses to revolt against them.

Appendices

APPENDIX 1

a. The following is my own transcription from *Ajami* to Latin Script of the Hausa story (Abdullahi 1989).

"Makaho Mai Fitila"

> Wani saurayi yana yawo da dare, sai ya hangi wani mutum da fitila. Da suka gamu, yaga ashe makaho ne. Yace, "Kai wannan makaho, kacika rigima! Me ya kaika yawo da fitila? Dare da rana ba duk «aya suke a gareka ba?" Makaho ya ce, "Duk «aya ne mana, Bala dan Jatau, ai har in da dare ne na fi ka ganewa. Fitilannan rika ta ba don kai na ba ne, amma domin irinku ne marasa hankali, dabaku da idon, kada ku hauni."

b. Meaning, from "The Various Uses of cAjami Writing Among Muslims in Nigeria: Hausa and Yorùbá as a Case Study:"

> Once a young man was playing around in the night. He saw someone coming toward him with a lamp, and he was shocked to realize that the lamp man was a blind man. He said to him, "Oh blind man, you must be deceiving yourself. What are you doing with a lamp? What difference is it to you, whether it is night or day?" The blind man said, "Of course, it makes no difference to me, Bala dan Jatau! In fact, in the night I see better than you. This lamp I carry is not because of myself. It is for people like you who have no eyes, so you don't step on me." (81)

APPENDIX 2

a.) My own transcription from Ajami to Latin script of a Yorùbá letter (Abdullahi 1989):

Bismillahi Rahmani Rahim. Wassatu wassalamu ala sayyidina Muhammad bin Abdullahi. Alhamdulillahi ladhi khalaqha nasa min nafsi waahida wa khalaqha minha zaojaha. Min Mallam Abubakar Yusuf ila Mallam Sulaiman. Idunnu ati ayo ni mofi ko wasika min yi siyin. Leyin na omo mi t'ounje Fatimata mofi se saara funyin ki efun omo yin t'inje AbdulRaheem ni tori Oluwa ati ojisêrê Muhammad, salallahu alaihi wassalam. Ki Oluwa fi alubarika si, amin. Asalatu ala nabiyi al-kareem. Alim Abubakar Yusuf. Yaomu al-talata, 13 sahaban, 1465 (6 December 1945).

b.) Meaning of the letter, from "The Various Uses of ᶜAjami Writing Among Muslims in Nigeria: Hausa and Yorùbá as a Case Study:"

In the Name of Allah, the compassionate, the merciful. May the blessing and peace of Allah be upon our Master Muhammad, the son of Abdullahi. Praise be to Allah who has created man from a single soul and then made from it a mate. From Mallam Abubakar Yusuf to Mallam Sulaiman.

With happiness I am writing you this letter. After that, I am hereby giving out my daughter by name Fatimah to you, to give to your son AbdulRahim in marriage, for the sake of Allah and His Messenger, Muhammad (May the peace and blessings of Allah be on him). May Allah bless the offer (Amin).
       Mallam Abubakar Yusuf.
Al-thulathÇ' 13th Shacban 1365. (December 6, 1945) (89)

Notes

NOTES TO CHAPTER 1

1. Important examples would be Abiola Irele (1981, 2001) and Oyekan Owomoyela (1996, 2005), to name only two.
2. See Irele 2001, 10–11, for the discussion about *Ifá* corpus and the Babaláwo.
3. Henry Louis Gates, Jr. is an example of another scholar who previously derived and presented critical methodologies from Yorùbá traditions in his 1987 Signifyin(g) theory. According to Gates, Signifyin(g) was rooted in a pan-African oral narrative of the signifying monkey, "the profane counterpart of Èsù- Èlégbara, the Yorùbá sacred trickster" (Gates 1987, 48). Ropo Sekoni (1994) in Folk Poetics: A Sociosemiotic Study of Yorùbá Trickster Tales. Others are Roland Abiodun (1995) and Adeleke Adeeko (1998) in series of works respectively.
4. This is borrowed from Ato Quayson's Calibrations.
5. This is not intended to mean a socialist detachment, or the type by Bertold Bretch's Epic Theatre, as an opposition to the Formalist's attachment (or illusion of reality), leading to catharsis or purgation. The Èlàlòrò detachment is a "moral ground isolation" from the performer in order to render an unbiased, sincere judgment.
6. I have heard the adage, Òyọ́ a yọ́ ọmọ sílẹ̀, the Òyọ́ person who revels in the art of disarming the (hurting, crying?) child. I also recognize that this saying could be simply a play on the name Òyọ́ (Òyọ́ yọ́) and may not have anything to do with the art of clever disarmament.
7. Ato Quayson's (1995) "Orality—(Theory)—Textuality: Tutuola, Okri, and the Relationship of literary practice to oral traditions" is one such example.
8. Hountondji and other scholars who kick against the "myth of primitive unanimity" can easily quote traditional metaphors and oral traditions to support their cause. It is oral tradition in many performance instances that propounds diversity of thought as a metaphor for life and living.
9. Yorùbá worldview has been described as Humanity based, or as a humanistic worldview, since man (as human being) is at the center of its cosmology. The living are always connected to their ancestors. Human beings attain metaphysical and spiritual essence by becoming deities or gods and goddesses. Òrìsàs—Sàngó, Ọya, Ọbàtálá, etc.,—were all human beings who were deified. A Yorùbá adage says, Ènìyàn ló n bẹ léhìn orò lorò n ké (it is a human being who is behind the sacred masquerade and its spiritual utterances) (quoted from Taye 1996, 148).

168 Notes

10. This principle is discussed in the chapter, "Oral Involvement and Arabic Influence on Yorùbá and Hausa Writing Traditions in Nigeria, and Some Thoughts on Traditional African Aesthetics."
11. My discussion of race here is not in agreement with Kwame Appiah's (2005, 1992) who for example, denies the existence of race because he insists genetic science shows that genes are not race specific. Owomoyela (1996, 171) ably challenges Appiah's view on race. The existence of race, ethnicity, or geographical identity does not mean people should be racist. Racism is caused by racial hatred and myopic cultural tendencies.
12. See Abiola Irele's (2001, 24–38) discussion of this set of scholars and their views, where he cites Jack Goody (1977, 1987) and Walter Ong, (1982) as leading examples.

NOTES TO CHAPTER 2

1. Itamar Even-Zohar (1990) in polysystem theory (Rachel Weissbrod 1998, 7) calls them interlingual and intralingual translation, respectively. Apart from the greater simplicity of the terms intertranslation and intratranslation, they more adequately represent cultures where language or the written text are not the only elements considered as translatable.
2. Each of the words is actually made of two morphemes, *i*, and *tú* and *mò*, respectively, with *i* being a pre-modifier to both of the words.
3. We must be careful not to give another meaning for *tu ú*. For example, it cannot be used for vomit, disgorge, regurgitate, to which *bì* may be appropriate; *ó bì* he/she vomited.
4. It would be interesting to find out whether the Yorùbá have any myths about how Elédùmarè spoke to the Òrìsàs after creation, when he commanded them to go down to the earth. Was there a translator? Was the translator Èsù-Òdara god of the crossroad? If Èsù acted as translator among the gods, how would he have expressed the art of translation?
5. See Chapter 6 for more on *Egúngún*.
6. One can argue actually that this is not an Intratranslation activity in the sense that the *Egúngún* does not seem to really speak Yorùbá or a language intelligible to speakers of any Yorùbá dialect; the *Egúngún* murmurs his speech, and it seems that the translator carries responsibility beyond merely translating the sounds made by his deity.
7. For example, after Soyinka's (1968) translation of D.O. Fagunwa's book *Ògbójú Ọdẹ nínú Igbó Irúnmalẹ̀* into *The Forest of a Thousand Daemons*, a debate ensued about whether or not it was appropriate for the translator to change the actual count represented by *irúnmalẹ̀* in his title into "a thousand." Or, as Soyinka insists, the idea was not the actual number, but the concept of the number. Concepts must not be changed and perhaps for Soyinka, changing the actual number in the target language from the source material reinforced the concept of the source language. It is interesting to note that the Yorùbá use this number for spiritual and metaphysical effects, and *Èlàlòrò* translators must do nothing to compromise this.
8. As far as the Yorùbá people were concerned, it was Christian Missionaries trying to develop Yorùbá orthography and translate the Bible into Yorùbá, and later the British colonialist collaborating with the missionary to produce a primer who began the idea of standard vs. non-standard Yorùbá. The Ife, the Ijebu, the Ijesa, the Oyo, the Ekiti, and others were all equal to each other.

NOTES TO CHAPTER 3

1. Jaigbade Alao is an Ilorin oral singers, and I recollect this Dadakúàdà song from his many songs that I have listened to. He must have composed this particular one around the mid 1980s.
2. See Appendix 1 for this story.
3. Translations from Hausa to English of all the poems cited from *Wakokin Hikima* are mine.
4. In 1993, I was in the Organizing Committee of the ANA annual meeting in Ilorin, was among those who influenced the adoption of the theme on Arabic literature, and was personally responsible for inviting that year's Guest Speaker, Sharia Cout Justice Mutalib Ambali. It is not sure if ANA has done anything since then to encourage Nigerian writers in Arabic to join its fold.
5. Sociolinguists may be interested in examining how politics, religion, and westernization forces continuously affect the status of Arabic writing in Nigeria.
6. I read the statement on Naijanet, a Nigerian discussion group based in the United States, that Soyinka regarded the use of the Arabic script as declaring Islam as a state religion in Nigeria, or giving undue advantage to the Muslims. I was taken aback by the fact that the Nigerian Nobel Laureate does not know that some Nigerians in Borno State are Shuwa Arabs, that many Nigerians write local languages in Arabic script, and that what the Nigerian currency has is an *ajami* writing showing the currency amount to those who cannot read the Roman letters.
7. In August 2000, a Nigerian went to court challenging the use of Arabic script on the Nigerian national currency. He erroneously thought it was Arabic language, which he called a symbol of Islam. [Guardian Newspaper, Saturday August 25, 2000.] Another Nigerian responded on nmn network:
   "Without going into any sentimental innuendoes or any technicalities of law in respect of this application. The application will be defeated on the following bare facts.
   (1) Arabic is the language of the "Shuwa" tribe in Borno State which is part and parcel of Nigeria.
   (2) The Arabic transription on the Naira is not Arabic language. It is Hausa language. Although Arabic alphabets are used, it is the Hausa language, hence the transcriptions read "Naira Daya" e.t.c meaning One Naira e.t.c. For instance, no learned mind will say that "Naira Daya" although transcribed here in English alphabets is English language.
   (3) The transcriptions on the Naira have no religious connotations at all. We are dealing with language and transcription here.
   (4) As a lawyer myself, the "ignorance" of the applicant about the above facts is a bit funny."
8. This issue was featured in a class I had with Professor Awobuluyi at the University of Ilorin in 1989. I believe he has also expressed this view in some of his publications.
9. See Abubakre and Reichmuth 1997, 197–8.
10. See *A Selection of Hausa Stories* xi.
11. I have been using this word in this chapter without its glottal characteristics. I shall now introduce the glottal stop in explaining the phonetic quality of the original Arabic word.
12. Please see the full *Ajami* text in Appendix 1 at the end of this article. Transcription into the Roman Script is also provided.
13. The Hausa word for the Roman Script.

14. I believe this story was in an elementary school Hausa textbook called *Karamin Sani*, and although I cannot remember its author now, I recall the story with ease.
15. See Appendix 2.
16. For interesting discussions on the oral aspects of the written Quran, read W. A. Graham (1987) and several articles in M. Levering (1989).
17. Ramadan-night oral singers were popular in Ilorin and among other Muslim Yorùbá communities as Islamic religious singers. The *Were* singer's main purpose is to wake people up for Sahur, the early morning food, during the Ramadan fast. A Yorùbá genre called *Fuji* has developed from *Were*. Ayinde Barister and Kolington Ayinla have attained national fame as Were/Fuji oral singers.

NOTES TO CHAPTER 4

1. The XVIth Congress of the International Comparative Literature Association (ICLA), Pretoria, South Africa, August 2000.
2. Although *Horses of Memory* was actually copyrighted in 1998, the book was only recently published in 1999, and the *The Word is an Egg* was released in 2000.
3. At several points in the next book, *The Word is an Egg*, Osundare (2000) invokes the number seven: "Before the Word was pierced / By an Arrow from Seven quivers / Bearing seven heads and Seven signs . . . / Seven Rainbows, Seven Winds / Seven Waters breaking before the flow (82, 84).
4. The earth—*ile* is central to Yorùbá's concept of loyalty, service, and selflessness. The saying, *eni to ba da ile yo ba'le lo*, means whoever betrays the land [earth], will grief on the land [or will be swallowed by the earth]. A betrayer (of friend, family, etc) in Yorùbá is called *Odale*, literally meaning one who betrays the land. *Odale Ore* is a betrayer of friendship.
5. This is similar to an earlier poem in this collection, "Scars of Unremembrance," dedicated to another poet, Harry Garuba.
6. Needless to say that what would have been my first review of Osundare's poetry around 1989 did not see the light of the day as I myself failed to pursue its publication and have since lost the manuscript.
7. General Sani Abacha became Nigerian head of state through a military coup that overthrown the Shonekan Interim Administration in 1993. General Abacha got ruthless sending many Nigerians to jail and exile, and silencing several others through incessant execution-style killings. His regime murdered the Nigerian writer, Ken Saro-Wiwa, and eight other Ogoni human rights activist in 1995 (Na'Allah 1998: 3–29).

NOTES TO CHAPTER 6

1. *The Lion and the Jewel* (Soyinka 1963, 44). The translation from Yorùbá into English is mine.
2. The action in question was Soyinka's alleged broadcast on an Ibadan radio station asking Samuel Akintola, former Western Region Premier to "quit the country." His 1967 arrest was prompted by his alleged activities during the Nigerian civil war (Gibbs 1993, 240).
3. Soyinka said in a conference in 1967 that "A tiger doesn't have to proclaim his tigritude" thus challenging Negritude's zeal to counter European primitivist approach that Africa was a savage culture.

4. A fate dictated by the new god of the colonized community, colonial Master Mr. Pilkings, who, as Jane later explains, feels he is doing Olunde some good by sending him to Britain to become a medical doctor.
5. The Yorùbá do not say a king dies; they say *Oba w'aja*, meaning that the king has transited to the ancestral world. *àjà*, actually means "roof," and here it is a metaphor for the ancestral world.
6. Read through all of pages 24–25 and 49 for exchanges between Amusa and the Pilkings about the *egungun* cult.

NOTES TO CHAPTER 7

1. I am grateful to Professor Uri Margolin of the Department of Modern Languages and Comparative Studies, University of Alberta, Canada, for his useful comments on the original draft of this chapter.
2. Even with the newly expanded *The Norton Anthology of World's Masterpeices: Sixth Expanded Edition* (1995), where more African works are included, *The Norton Anthology of World Masterpieces: Fifth Continental Edition* (1987) had included only Wole Soyinka's (1963) *Lion and the Jewel*), Ola Rotimi's *The Gods* (1971), or any os his other works, are missing.
3. I have conducted several research projects on Yorùbá oral traditions and coauthored the *Introduction to African Oral Literature* Vol. 1 (1991), Vol. II (1994). I have never come across a similar folktale/legend of the Oedipus themes.
4. This reviewer strongly suggested a very critical review of the assertions of deep "similarities" between Greek and Yorùbá Gods and between *Oedipus Rex* and *The Gods Are Not to Blame*. The reviewer's view is that *The Gods*, although it followed the plot-line of the Oedipus Rex, is cast within a largely different world view. I am grateful to the anonymous review for his or her useful comments.
5. Perhaps such a narration will help a reader who has no access to Rotimi's (1971) adaptation to have a picture of the Africanized Oedipus story.
6. Of course, there are other changes such as how Jocaster/Ojuola kills herself: in *Oedipus the King* she hangs herself; in *The Gods*, she uses a dagger to kill herself.
7. The translation to English of the Olurombi songs is mine.

NOTES TO CHAPTER 8

1. For more on the concept of nativization in active orality of Africa, read Chapter 5 of my *Cultural Globalization and Plurality: Africa and the New World* (forthcoming).
2. The edict is titled "The Ilorin township prohibition against manufacture, sale, etc., of liquor in certain areas, Edict, 1988." It came into effect January 1, 1989.
3. In the whole of Africa, especially south of the Sahara, a strong obedience is still borne to the African Gods and the tradition beliefs, despite the proclamation of Islam and Christianity by many Africans.
4. Personal interview with Alhaji Muhammad Ndagi Patigi on January 9, 1992. Personal interview with Malam Muhammad Liman Rogun on January 11, 1992. Personal interview with Binta Ibrahim on January 15, 1992.
5. We should note that we earlier encountered one Alapini as the head of the *Egungun* priests. The repeated use of this name here suggests its close asso-

ciation to the myth of *Egungun* in both Nupe and Yorùbá communities. The first Alpini was said to have migrated from Tapa to Yorùbá community (see Johnson, 1973, 160).
6. Sanda is the name of the particular hill Johnson refers to here. *Kusu* or *Kuso* means forest in Nupe.
7. Omoekee Amao, Field Performance, Ile Alhaji Raimi Lyanda, Omonda, Omoda, June 1978.
8. Jaibade Alao, Field Performance, Popoigbona, January 1987.
9. Odolaye Aremu, "Shehu Shagari Geri Ijoba." Ariyo Sound A SSLP 058A, 1979.
10. This was outlawed by the pronouncement of the former Emir (King) of Ilorin, Alhaji Zulkarnaini Gambari Mohammad, in the 1970s. Olajubu, who brought in Egungun during his inaugural lecture at the University of Ilorin on December 10, 1987, referred to this and said his action was not a defiance to the Emir and Ilorin people's order but was purely "an exercise of academic freedom."
11. There were a number of uproars after the death of Chief Obafemi Awolowo as to who was to take over for him as the political leader of Yorùbá. Lateef Jakande, for example, who many, including Dr. Tai Solarin and some Yorùbá social and cultural groups, suggested should succeed Awolowo, was publicly and privately accused of being from a Nupe ancestry. A popular Yorùbá Ewi poet, Lanrewaju Adepoju, boldly addresses this issue in his record "Iku Awolowo" LALPS 136, sides A&B, 1987. Jakande later embarked on a historical journey to Omuaran, a Yorùbá town, where, according to him, his household lineage praise poetry and indicates that it is his true home. See *Sunday Concord*, May 17, 1987, 1, 20; *Sunday Herald*, May 17, 1987, 1, 9; *The Herald*, May 23, 1988, 1, 3, etc.

NOTES TO CHAPTER 9

1. See also H.O. Danmole, 1980 *The Frontier Emirate: A History of Islam in Ilorin*, Ph.D. thesis, University of Birmingham,. 15–121.
2. Ologun beggars are mostly female Ogun worshippers who perform *Ìjálá* on the instruction of the *Ifá* oracle. They beg from door to door, performing *Ìjálá* chants.
3. This is only a short introduction to how *Dadakúàdà* poetry started in Ilorin. Detailed discussion of *Dadakúàdà* and its development can be found in a different book, *Dadakúàdà: Poetry, Performance and Ilorin Art History* (forthcoming).
4. This interview, conducted in October 1985, informed my first article on *Dadakúàdà*, "Dadakúàdà: the Music of Ilorin," *The Herald*, November 5, 1985, 8.
5. Personal interview with Alhaji Jaigbade Alao, August 9, 1987.
6. Both Alhajis Omoekee Amao and Odolaye Aremu were interviewed on August 8, 1987.
7. Personal Interview with Alhaji Jaigbade Alao, August 9, 1987.
8. Interview with Saara Odee, 70, September 2, 1987.
9. Ibid.
10. Qur'an, Sura 26, verses 224–226.
11. Personal interview with Abubakar Ali-Agan, November 10, 1990.
12. Personal interview with Hajia Sher*Ifá*t Mustapha, November 22, 1990.
13. Personal interview with Alhaji Jaigbade Alao, August 9, 1987.

14. Fuji is not an Ilorin indigenous genre; it is, however, popular in contemporary Nigeria, especially among the Yorùbá.
15. Marriage ceremonies in Ilorin usually take five days from Tuesday to Saturday. There are customary activities for each day.
16. Jaigbade Alao, Field Performance, August 15, 1987.
17. Qur'an, Sura 2, verse 187.
18. This is a popular praise song for Ilorin among the contemporary Yorùbá. See A. Na'Allah, "Ilorin Afonja," *Sunday Concord*, August 16, 1987, 8.
19. Interview with Alhaji Jaigbade Alao, December 8, 1990.
20. Kwara State Government edict in effect from January 1, 1989.
21. A recent letter from one Yusuf A. Jimoh to some Ilorin Islamic associations, complaining bitterly about the havoc caused by night parties in Ilorin and requesting immediate action to restrict night parties, further galvanised the Muslim leaders of Ilorin to make more effort to curtail such parties in the town. Already, the Emir of Ilorin, in mid-January 1991, advised that parties involving oral performances in Ilorin be limited to functioning between 6 a.m. and 6 p.m. See *Ilorin Watch* January 16, 1991, 1.

NOTES TO CHAPTER 10

1. Egungun ancestor worshippers are masquerade worshippers. This existed in Ilorin before the advent of Islam.
2. For more intensive discussions of African religion, see Awolalu and Dopamu 1979, Idowu 1963, Kunene 1980, Mbiti 1969, and Ogunjimi and Na'Allah 2005.
3. Personal interview with Jaigbade Alao, November 20, 1988. Also, the interview with Shata is reproduced in Abdulkadir (1978, 246).
4. Personal interview with Omoekee Amao, August 7, 1987.
5. This is my translatation from the jingles that Amao made for Radio Kwara in 1984 during the peak of the War Against Indiscipline (WAI) campaign of the Nigerian Federal Government.
6. Omoekee Amao, Field Performance, Ode Alausa, Ilorin, June 25, 1988.
7. This is a well-known English translation of these lines, often the lines at the beginning of Quranic chapters.
8. Holy Qur'an, Chapter 4, Verse 59.

Bibliography

Abdullahi, A. 1989. The various uses of Ajami writing among Muslims in Nigeria: Hausa and Yorùbá as a case study. B.A. thesis, University of Ilorin, Nigeria.
Abdullahi, S. U. 1981. *On the search for a viable political culture: Reflections on the political thought of Shaikh Abdullahi Dan-Fodio*. Kaduna: New Nigeria Publications Bureau.
Abimbola, W. 1977. *Ifá divination poetry*. New York: Nok Publishers Ltd.
———. 1971. *Ifá* divination poetry and the coming of Islam into Yorùbáland. *Pan-Africana Journal* 4 (4): 440–54.
AbdulKadir, D. 1975. The role of an oral singer in Hausa-Fulani society: a case study of Mamman Shatta. Ph.D. thesis, University of Indiana.
Abubakre, Razaq D., and S. Reichmuth. 1997. Arabic writing between global and local culture: scholars and poets in Yorùbáland (southwestern Nigeria)". *Research in African Literatures* 28(3): 183–209.
Abu-Haidar, F. 1997. Introduction: Arabic writing in Africa. *Research in African Literatures* 28.(3): 1–4.
Abiodun, R. 1995. *"What follows six is more than seven": Understanding African art*. London: British Museum Department of Ethnography.
Achebe, C. 1989. *Hopes and Impediments: Selected Essays*. New York: Doubleday.
Adakawa, R. S. N. 1986. Wakar Kishi. In *Wakokin Hikima*, ed. I. Y. Yahaya, 60–4. Ibadan: University Press Limited.
Adeeko, A. 1998. *Proverbs, textuality, and nativism in African literature*. Gainsville: University Press of Florida.
Ahmed, A. R. 1986. Sutura ita ce mutum. In *Wakokin hikima*, ed. I. Y. Yahaya, 38–43. Ibdan: University Press Limited.
Alao, Jaigbade. 1987, August 9. Personal interview. Ilorin, Nigeria.
Amao, E. O. 1983. Baalu chants and songs in Ilorin, Kwara State. M.A. thesis, University of Ibadan.
Amao, O. 1987. *Orin Lere*. OLPS 0225 I, Omo-Aje Sound Studio.
———. 1984. *Owe Lesin Oro*. ORCLP 1521.
———. 1979. *Mogberede*. OLP5 0232A. Omo Aje Sound Studio.
———. 1978a. *Mo Gberede*. Omo-Aje Sound Studio. OLPS 02251.
———. 1978b. *Eku Alele Raimi Iyanda*. LPS 0225 II.
———. 1976. *Ologbe General Murtala Ramat Mohammad*. Omo-Aje Sound Studio, OLPS 0080 A.
Amuta, C. 1989. *The theory of African literature*. London: Zed Books Ltd.
Anyidoho, K. 1986. Mythmaker and mythbraker: The oral poet as earwitness. In *African literature in its social and political dimensions*, eds E. Julien, M. Mortimer, and C. Schade. Washington, D. C.: African Literature Association and Three Continents Press, Inc.
Appiah, K. A. 2005. *The ethics of identity*. Princeton, N.J.: Princeton University Press.

———. 1992. *In my father's house: Africa in the philosophy of culture.* New York: Oxford University Press.
Apter, E. 2001, Winter. On translation in a global market. *Public Culture* 13(1):
Aremu, O. 1977. *Iku Akintola.* ORCLP 21A, Olatunbosun Records.
———. 1979. *Shehu Shagari Geri Ijoba.* Ariyo Sound A SSLP 058A.
———. 1990. *Olowe Mowe.* NEMI, 0654A.
Aristotle. 1982. The poetics. In *Oedipus Rex: A mirror for Greek drama*, ed. A. Cook, 55–82. Prospect Heights, IL: Waveland Press, Inc.
Arnold, S. 1996. A peopled persona: Autobiography, post-modernism and the poetry of Niyi Osundare. In *Autobiographical genre in Africa*, eds. J. Reisz and U. Schild, 142-165. Berlin: Dietrich Reimer Verlag.
Awolalu, J. O.. 1975. The African traditional view of man. *Orita* 2: 8–35.
———. 1979. *Yorùbá beliefs and sacrificial rites.* London: Longman.
Awolalu, J. O., and P. Dopamu. 1979. *West African traditional religions.* Ibadan: Onibonoje Publishers.
Babalola, A. 1981. Ìjálá poetry among the Oyo-Yorùbá. In *Oral Poetry in Nigeria*, 3–17. Lagos: Nigerian Magazine.
Badejo, P. 1970. Premier production: the gods are not to blame. *African Notes* 3(2): 64–5.
Banham, M., E. Hill, and G. Woodyard. 1994. *The Cambridge guide to African and Caribbean theatre.* New York: Cambridge University Press.
Booth, J. 1993. Self-sacrifice and human sacrifice in Soyinka's *Death and the king's horseman.* In *Research on Wole Soyinka*, ed. J. Gibbs and B. Lindfors, 127–47. Trenton: Africa World Press.
Brathwaite, K. 1993. *Middle passages.* New York: New Directions.
———. 1976. *Black + Blues.* El Vedado, La Habana, Cuba: Casa de las Américas.
———. 1973. *The Arrivants: a new world trilogy.* London, New York, Oxford University Press.
Calder, A. 1992 Niyi Osundare's *waiting laughters. Cencratus* 44: 27–9.
Camara, S. 1997. A'jami literature in Senegal: The example of Sëriñ Muusaa Ka, poet and biographer. *Research in African Literatures* 28(3): 163–82.
Conrad, J. 1994. *Heart of darkness.* Harmondsworth, Middlesex, England; New York, N.Y., USA: Penguin Books.
Cook, A. 1982. *Oedipus Rex: A mirror for Greek drama.* Prospect Heights, IL: Waveland Press, Inc.
Culler, J. D. 1982. *On deconstruction: theory and criticism after structuralism.* Ithaca, N.Y.: Cornell University Press.
———. 1979. Jacques Derrida. In *Structuralism and since*, ed. J. Sturrock, 154–80. Oxford and New York: Oxford University Press.
Dance Thearter of Harlem. 1997, April 29. Chereography. Arthur Mitchell, et. al. Classical, Color, NTSC. Studio: Kultur Video. VHS Release,117 minutes.
Danmole, H. O. 1980. *The frontier emirate: A history of Islam in Ilorin.* PhD thesis, University of Birmingham.
Dasylva, A. O. 1997, April. Osundare, The tribune-poet at 50. In *Honors*, 33–35.
Denby, D. 1995, November 6. Jungle fever. In *The New Yorker*, 118–130.
Derrida, J. 1998. *Of grammatology*, trans. Gayatri Chakravorty Spivak. Baltimore: Johns Hopkins University Press.
———. 1962. Traduction et introd. *L'origine de la Géométrie* by Husserl, Edmund, 1859–1938. Paris, Presses Universitaires de France.
Diawara, M.. 2004. *We won't budge: An African exile in the world.* New York, NY: Basic Books.
Dimic, Milan V. 1996. CLit 527 Course Notes, University of Alberta, Edmonton, Canada.
Dimic, M. V. and M. K. Garstin 1988. The polysystem theory: A brief introduction, with bibliography. In *Problems of Literary Reception*, ed. E. D. Blodgett

and A. G. Purdue, 177–196. Edmonton, Albeta: University of Alberta. http://tau.ac.il/itamarez/ps/dimic_ps.html.
Eliot, T. S. 1999. *On poetry and poets. Catalan* (Sobre poetes I poesia). Manresa: Faig.
Even-Zoha, I. 1990. *Poetics today.* 11(1): 45–51.
Finnegan, R. 1970. *Oral literature in Africa.* Oxford, Oxford University Press.
Gates, H. L. 1988. *The signifying monkey: A theory of Afro-American literary criticism.* New York: Oxford University Press.
———. 1987. *Figures in black: Words, signs, and the "racial" self.* New York: Oxford University Press.
Gbadegesin, S. 1991. *African philosophy: Traditional Yorùbá philosophy and contemporary African realities.* New York: Peter Lang.
Gérard, A. 1990. *Contexts of African Literature.* Amsterdam: Rodopi.
Gibbs, J. 1993. Tear the painted masks, Join the poison stains: A preliminary study of Wole Soyinka's writings for the Nigerian press. In *Research on Wole Soyinka,* ed. J. Gibbs and B. Lindfors, 225–61. Trenton: Africa World Press.
———. 1990. Ola Rotimi and Ken Saro-Wiwa: Nigerian popular playwrights. In *Sings Signals: Popular culture in Africa,* ed. R. Granqvist, 121–35. Umea: Acta Universitatis Umensis.
Gilliland, D. S. 1971. African traditional religion in transition: The influence of Islam on African traditional religion in North Nigeria, PhD thesis, Thettarford Seminary Foundation.
Gleason, J. Il. 1971. *Orisha: The gods of Yorubaland.* New York: Atheneum.
Goody, J. 1987. *The interface between the written and the oral.* New York: Cambridge University Press.
———. 1977. *The domestication of the savage mind.* New York: Cambridge University Press.
Gordimer, N. 1994. Soyinka the Tiger. In *Wole Soyinka: An appraisal,* ed. A. Maja-Pearce, 36–42. Portsmouth, NH: Heinemann Education Publishers.
Graham, W. A. 1987. *Beyond the written word: Oral aspects of scripture in the history of religion.* Cambridge: Cambridge University Press.
Great success achieved in Nigeria: State leader. 1996. Xinhua English Newswire. HighBeam Research. Retrieved March 5, 2009, from, http://www.highbeam.com/doc/1P2-18018638.html
Homer. 1950. *The Iliad,* trans. E. V. Rieu. Harmondsworth, Middlesex, Eng.: Penguin Books.
Hunwick, J. 1997. The Arabic literary tradition of Nigeria. *Research in African Literatures.* 28(3): 210–223.
Husserl, E.1962. *L'Origine de la* Géométrie. Traduction et introd. par Jacques Derrida. Paris: Presses universitaires de France.
Idowu, B. 1963. *Olodumare: God in Yorùbá belief.* London: Frederick A. Praeger, Inc. *Ilorin Watch.* 1991, January 16. Ilorin, Nigeria.
Irele, A. 2001. *The African imagination: Literature in Africa and the black diaspora.* Oxford, UK: Oxford University Press.
———. 1981. *The African experience in literature and ideology.* London: Heinemann.
Jencks, C. 1989. *What is Post-Modernism?* (3rd ed.). London: Academy Editions; New York: St. Martin's Press.
Johnson, S. 1973. *The history of the Yorùbás.* London: Routledge & Kegan Paul Ltd.
Johnston, H. A. S. 1966. comp. and trans. *A Selection of Hausa Stories.* Oxford: Clarendon Press.
Karenga, M. 1993. *Introduction to Black Studies.* (2nd ed.). Los Angeles: The University of Sankore Press.

Killam, D. and R. Rowe, eds. 2000. *The companion to African literatures.* Bloomington: Indiana University Press.
Kunene, M. 1980. The relevance of African cosmological systems to African literature today. *African literature today* (11): 190–205.
Leopardi, G. 1992. The Bloom. In *The norton anthology of world's masterpieces*, (Vol. 2, 6th ed), ed. M. Mac, 646–654. New York: W.W. Norton & Company.
Levering, M. (ed.) 1989. *Rethinking scripture: Essays from a comparative perspective.* New York: State of New York University Press.
Lindfors, B. 1993. Wole Soyinka and the horses of speech. In *Research on Wole Soyinka.* eds. J. Gibbs and B. Lindfors, 25–33. Trenton: Africa World Press.
Lord, A. B. 1960. *The Singer of Tales.* Cambridge: Harvard University Press.
Mack, M. 1987. A note on translation. In *The norton anthology of world masterpieces.* (5th Continental ed.), gen. ed. M. Mack, 2651-7. New Yrok and London: W. W. Norton & Company.
Makkai, A. 1996. 'Idiomatic-Adaptive' vs. 'Literal-Traditional Translation.' *The Hungarian Quarterly*, XXXVII (141). Retrieved February 10, 2009, from www.hungarianquarterly.com/no141/p109.shtml.
Matatu. 1994. *Journal of African culture and society* (12): 203–16.
Mbiti, J. S. 1969. *African religions and philosophy.* London: Heinemann.
Miller, C. 1993. *Theories of Africans: Francophone literature and anthropology in Africa.* Chicago: University of Chicago Press.
Moore, G. 1969. The politics of negritude. In *Protest and conflict in African Literature*, eds. C. Pieterse and D. Munro, 26–42. London: Heinemann.
Na'Allah, A-R. 1985. Arabic and Islamic education in Ilorin. *Unilorin Pedagogue*, 2(1): 37–50.
———. 1987, February 7. The Africanness of African Poetry. *The Punch*, 10.
———. 1987, August 16. Ilorin Afonja. *Sunday Concord*, 8.
———. 1988a. Dadakúàdà: *Trends in the Development of Ilorin Traditional Oral Poetry.* B.A. (Ed.) thesis, Department of Modern European Languages, University of Ilorin, Nigeria.
———. 1988b. Dadakúàdà: Origin, Artist and Performance Techniques of Ilorin Oral Art. *Nigeria Magazine* 56 (I and 2): 26–36.
———. 1990, December 9–12. Waka: The dialectical essence of an Ilorin Islamic oral genre'. Paper presented at the 3rd National Conference on Literature in Northern Nigeria, Bayero University, Kano.
Na'Allah, A-R. 1998. "Introduction" in *Ogoni's agonies*, ed. Abdul-Rasheed Na'Allah. Trenton: Africa World Press, 3–29.
———. 1999. Yoruba folktales: Cultural plurality and oral narratives. PhD. Dissertation, University of Alberta, Edmonton, Canada.
———. and M. Rice-Maximin. 1999. Thresholds: Anglophone African literatures Conference. *ALA Bulletin: A Publication of the African Literature Association.* 25(3): 61–73.
Na'Allah, A-R. 2000, August. Èlàlòrò: An indigenous African theory for critical discourse. Paper given at the ICLA congress, Pretoria, South Africa.
———. ed. 2003. *The people's poet: Emerging perspectives on Niyi Osundare.* Trenton, NJ: African World Press.
Nadel, S. F. 1942. *A black byzantium: The kingdom of Nupe in Nigeria.* Oxford University Press, Oxford.
———. 1954. *Nupe Religion.* London: Routledge & Kegan Paul Ltd.
Ngugi wa T. and M. Mugo. 1976. *The trial of Dedan Kimathi.* London: Heinemann.
Njoku, T. U. 1984. Influence of Sophocles' *Oedepus Rex* on Rotimi's *The gods are not to blame. Nigeria Magazine CLI*, 88-92.
Nketia, J. H. 1958. Folklore of Ghana. *The Ghanian I*: 21.

Obafemi, O. 1987. *Suicide syndrome*. Benin: Arena Press.
———. 1986. *Night of a mystical beast*. Benin: Adena Publishers.
Ogunjimi, B. and A-R. Na'Allah. 205. *Introduction to African oral literature* and performance (Rev. ed.). Trenton: African World Press.
Ojaide, T. 1996. *Poetic imagination in black Africa*. Durham, NC: Carolina Academic Press.
———. 1998a. *Great Boys: An African Childhood*. Trenton, NJ: Africa World Press.
———. 1998b. *Delta Blues and Home Songs*. Ibadan, Nigeria: Kraft Books.
———. 2003. *I want to dance and other poems*. Lagos, Nigeria: African Heritage Press.
———. 2005. *A creative writing handbook for African writers*. Lagos: Malthouse Press Ltd.
Okediji, M. 1990. *Metaphors dwell in the eyes: The lyrical syntax of contemporary Yorùbá images*. Ile-Ife: Ona Artists, Exhibition of Contemporary Yorùbá Art.
Okigbo, C. 1986. *Collected poems*. with a preface by Paul Theroux and an introduction by Adewale Maja-Pearce. London: Heinemann.
Okpewho, I. 1979. *The Epic in Africa: Toward A Poetics of the Oral Performance*. New York: Columbia University Press.
———. 1987. Towards a faithful record: On transcribing and translating the oral narrative performance. In *The oral performance in Africa*, ed. I. Okpewho, 111–35. Ibadan: Spectrum Books.
Okri, B. 1991. *The Famished Road*. New York: Doubleday.
Olajubu, O. 1970. Iwi: *Egungun chants in Yorùbá oral literature*. M.A. thesis, University of Lagos, Nigeria.
———. 1984. The Yorùbá Egungun Masquerade Cult and its Role in Society. In *The Masquerade in Nigerian History and Culture*. ed. N. Nzewunwa, University of Port Harcourt.
———. 1987, December. *The voice of the artist: The Voice of the People. Twenty-eight in the series of Inaugural lecture*, University of Ilorin, December.
Olaniyan, T. 1988. Rotimi, Soyinka and Achebe as interpreters of history: From gemeinschaft and gesellschaft. *Odu*. (33): 201–218.
Olaoye, R. A. 1984. The Ilorin emirate and the British ascendancy 1897–1918: An overview of the early phase of Ilorin provincial administration. M. A. thesis, University of Ilorin.
Olayiwola, A. 1999, January 4. Garlands for the lyrical poet. *The guardian,* 38.
Olokun, O. I. n.d. *Imole Aye*. Ilesa, Nigeria.
Omibiyi-Obidike, M. A. 1981. Islamic Influence on Yorùbá Music. *Africa Notes* 8(2):
Ong, W. J. 1982. *Orality and Literacy: The Technologizing of the Word*. London; New York: Methuen,.
Osofisan, F. 1982. *Morountodun and other plays*. Lagos: Longman.
Osundare, Niyi. 1988. *Moonsongs*. Ibadan, Nigeria: Spectrum Books.
———. 1994. Niyi Osundare, "How Post-Colonial is African Literature?" *Matatu: Journal of African Culture and Society*. (12): 203–16.
———. 1998. *Horses of Memory*. Ibadan: Heinemann Educational Books (Nigeria) Plc.
———. 2000. *The word is an egg*. Ibadan: Kraft Book Limited.
Ousmane, S. 1970. *God's bits of wood*. London: Heinemann.
Owusu, M. 1998. Analysis and interpretation of Ola Rotimi's *The gods are not to blame*. Accra: Afrique Publications.
Owomoyela, O. 1996. *The African Difference: Discourses on Africanity and the Relativity of Cultures*. Witswatersrand: Witswaterand University Press.
———. 2005. *Yorùbá Proverbs*. Lincoln, NB: University of Nebraska Press.

Palmer, Richard E. *Hermeneutics*. Evanston: Northwestern University Press, 1969.
Parry, M. 1928. *Les formules et la métrique d'Homère*. Paris, Société d'éditions "Les belles lettres"
Personal Discussion with Onokome Okome. 2006, February 10.
Personal Interview with Tanure Ojaide,
Quayson, A. 2003. *Calibrations:Reading for the social*. Minneapolis: University of Minnesota Press.
———. 1995. Orality (theory) textuality: Tutuola, Okri, and the relationship of literary practice to oral traditions. In *The Pressures of the text: orality, texts and the telling of tales,* ed. S. Brown. (Birmingham University African Studies Series No. 4): 96–117.
Rahim, A. 1981. *Islamic history*. Lagos: Islamic Publications Bureau.
Rotimi, O. 1971. *The Gods Are not to blame*. London: Oxford University Press.
Rotimi, O. and C. Maduka. 1984. Understanding The gods are not to blame: A detailed interview with Ola Rotimi on his award-winning tragedy, The gods are not to blame. Benin: Kurumi Adventures.
Sekoni, R. 1994. *Folk poetics: A sociosemiotic study of Yoruba trickster tales*. Westport, Conn.: Greenwood Press.
Sophocles.———. 1926. Antigone *(Aintioghoiné)*. Pádraig de Brún d'aistrigh ó'n nGréigis. Baile-Átha-Cliath: Ponsoinbi agus Gibbs.
———. 1982. *Oedipus Rex*, ed. R.D. Dawe. Cambridge; New York: Cambridge University Press.
———. 1982. *The Trachiniae*. ed. P.E. Easterling. New York: Cambridge University Press.
———. 1999. *Ajax. Aias (Ajax)*: translated by Herbert Golder and Richard Pevear. New York: Oxford University Press.
———. 2001. *King Oedipus; and, Oedipus at Kolonos*. Trans. and intro. Kenneth McLeish. London: Nick Hern.
Soyinka, W. 1963. *The Lion and the Jewel*. Oxford: Oxford University Press.
———. 1968. *The forest of a thousand daemons: a hunter's saga; being a translation of 'Ogboju ode ninu igbo irunmale' by D. O. Fagunwa*. London: Nelson.
———. 1975. *Death and the King's Horseman*. New York: Hill and Wang.
———. 1976. *Myth, Literature and African World*. London: Cambridge University Press.
———. 2000. *The burden of memory, the muse of forgiveness*. Oxford: Oxford University Press.
Standiford, R. E. 2000, April 2. The People's Poet: An Interview with Nigerian Writer Niyi Osundare. In *Sunshine*, 4–5.
Sturrock, J. (ed.) 1979. *Structuralism and Since: From Levi Strauss to Derida*. New York and Oxford: Oxford University Press.
Tayo, T. 1996. A Philosophical Critic on Aesthetics of Yorùbás: A study of Oral Traditions and the Implications for Artistic Criticism. *School of Vocational Education: Book of Readings*. Kano: Federal College of Education. 1(1): 144–150.
The Norton Anthology of World Masterpieces. 1995. (vol. 2, 6th *Expanded ed.*). New York: W. W. Norton & Company.
The Norton Anthology of World Masterpeices. 1987. (5th *Continental ed.*). New York: W. W. Norton & Company.
Weissbrod, R. 1998. Translation Research in the Framework of the Tel Aviv School of Poetics and Semiotics. *Meta*, LIII(1): 1–15.
Yahaya, I. Y. (ed.) 1986. *Wakokin Hikima*. Ibadan: University Press Limited.

Index

A
Abimbola, 3 40, 41, 42, 175
Abiola Irele, 1, 15, 167, 168
Adakawa, 34, 35, 36, 175
Adam Abdullahi, 46, 47
Adebayo Alayande, 2
Ademola Dasylva, 72, 176
African languages, 2
African revival, 84, 86, 87
Ajami, 34, 38, 39, 45, 48, 49, 50, 51, 165, 166, 169, 175
Albert Gérard, 38, 177
Arnold, 11, 56, 176
Arnold Toynbee, 11
Augus Calder, 72, 176
Awolalu, 129, 131, 134, 173, 176

B
Banham, 99, 100, 117, 176
Ben Okri, 7, 8, 9
Bilingualism, 125
boka, 39

C
Chief Imam, 52, 53
Chinua Achebe, 13, 15, 72, 85, 122, 125, 127, 175, 179
Christopher Okigbo, 72, 75, 179
community rhetoric, 1
concept of translatability, 21
cosmopoli, 22
cultural interpretation, 1
cultural paradigms, 1
cultural pluralism, 10, 11, 71

D
Dadakúàdà poetry, 4, 133, 138, 140, 147, 172
Dandatti Abdulkadir, 149, 160

Derida, 29, 30, 31, 180
Dikan poets, 152
discourse analysis and interpretation, 1
discursive modes, 2
Dopamu, 129, 134, 173, 176
dual framework, 29

E
Edward Kamau Brathwaite, 76, 77, 176
Eldred Durosimi Jones, 93
Emily Apter, 25, 176
ersatz, 10
European formalist paradigm, 26
Even-Zohar, 17, 25, 26, 101, 168
Extertranslation, 18

F
Forlon Nichols, 56, 64

G
Gbadegesin, 85, 86, 177
Giacomo Leopardi, 72, 178
global village, 11, 24, 71
Global Village metaphor, 24
Gordimer, 85, 86, 177

H
Hausa cultural theory, 29

I
Ifá, 3, 4, 40, 41, 42, 52, 107, 108, 109, 110, 117, 123, 131, 137, 138, 167, 172, 175
Igunnu cults, 135
Ìjálá poets, 4
Ilorin indigenes, 133, 138, 142
Intertranslation, 18, 21, 168
Intratranslation, 18, 19, 20, 21, 24, 168
Isa Hashim, 36

Index

Islamic Emirate, 44, 137
Islamic values, 136, 143, 144, 148

J
Jaigbade, 12, 13, 30, 138, 139, 142, 146, 148, 150, 169, 172, 173, 175
Jencks, 10, 11, 177
John Hunwick, 42, 43, 45, 177
Johnson, 17, 128, 129, 130, 131, 133, 144, 172, 177
Jonathan Culler, 29, 176
Joseph Conrad, 5, 6, 13, 14, 15, 176
Judith Gleason, 3, 177

K
Kofi Anyidoho, 56, 152, 175
Kusugu well, 158

M
Makaho, 31, 165
Marguerite Garstin, 25, 26, 27, 176
Maulana Kurenga, 37
Maynard Mack, 17, 100, 101, 178
medicinal people, 39
Micere Mugo, 117, 118
Milan Dimic, 17, 25, 26, 27, 176
Moore, 151, 178
Muahammadu Zayyanu, 36
Murtala Muhammed, 154
Muslim turban, 138

N
native wisdom, 1
Ngugi, 115, 117, 127, 178
Niyi Osundare, 5, 13, 14, 55, 56, 57, 58, 60, 64, 176, 178, 179, 180
Nupeland, 128

O
Oedipus Rex, 21, 98, 99, 100, 101, 103, 104, 105, 107, 109, 111, 113, 115, 116, 117, 119, 121, 123, 125, 126, 127, 171, 176, 180
Oedipus-character, 104
Ogun, the god of metal, 75
Okediji, 16, 179
Okpewho, 158, 179
Ola Rotimi, 21, 98, 115, 171, 177, 179, 180
Olajubu, 128, 131, 133, 134, 137, 139, 172, 179
Olayiwola, 72, 179
Olokun, 3, 40, 41, 99, 179
Omibiyi-Obidike, 160, 179
Òsanyìn, 19, 22
Ovonramwen Nogbaisi, 99
Owomoyela, 16, 167, 168, 179

P
Pablo Neruda, 72
poetics of "Bari" and "Oho", 29, 30, 31, 33
Polysystem, 17, 25, 26, 27, 168, 176

Q
Quayson, 8, 9, 167, 180

R
Rabiíu Ahmed, 31, 32, 33, 34, 36, 37, 175
racial connivance, 6, 14, 15
Radio Kwara, 2, 3, 173
Radio Nigeria, 2
Radio O-Y-O, 2
Razaq D. Abubakre, 44, 46, 47, 51, 169, 175
rhetorical tool, 1, 2
Richard Palmer, 101, 180
Rima Radio, 2
Ruth Finnegan, 138, 151, 152, 159, 177

S
S. F. Nadel, 128, 129, 131, 133, 134, 178
Samuel Johnson, 17, 128, 129, 130, 131, 133, 134, 172, 177
Sana Camara, 48, 49, 51, 176
Saraki, 159, 160
Sembene Ousmane, 153, 179
Shuwa Arab, 45, 169
Sokoto Caliphate, 43, 48, 137
Soyinka, 8, 45, 47, 56, 72, 75, 84, 85, 86, 87, 88, 89, 90, 91, 93, 95, 96, 97, 98, 101, 102, 103, 115, 117, 121, 125, 127, 168, 169, 170, 171, 176, 177, 178, 179, 180
Standiford, 72, 180
Stefan Reichmuth, 44, 46, 47, 51, 169, 175

T
Tanure Ojaide, 56, 61, 73, 74, 75, 76, 77, 78, 79, 80, 81, 82, 179, 180
Taye, 16, 167
Theory of translatability, 20

U
udje music, 83
Urhobo god, Aridon, 74, 75, 77, 78, 79

W
Wakokin Hikima, 28, 31, 36, 37, 169, 175, 180
Walter Ong, 42, 168, 179
Weissbrod, 25, 26, 168, 180

Y
Yakubu Gowon, 155
Yemi Zubair, 2, 3
Yorùbá discourse, 1, 3
Yorùbá semantic poetics, 3
Yorùbá semantics, 18

Z
Zulkarnaini Gambari Muhammad, 142

For Product Safety Concerns and Information please contact our EU
representative GPSR@taylorandfrancis.com
Taylor & Francis Verlag GmbH, Kaufingerstraße 24, 80331 München, Germany

www.ingramcontent.com/pod-product-compliance
Lightning Source LLC
Chambersburg PA
CBHW070612300426
44113CB00010B/1499